BALANC

BALLE

Conversations

Balanchine and Suzanne Farrell rehearsing Davidsbündlertänze, *1980.*

H I N E ' S
R I N A S

with the Muses

By Robert Tracy
with Sharon DeLano

Portraits by Shonna Valeska
Designed by Bob Ciano

Linden Press/Simon & Schuster
New York 1983

Published by Linden Press/Simon & Schuster
A Division of Simon & Schuster, Inc.
Simon & Schuster Building
Rockefeller Center
1230 Avenue of the Americas
New York, New York 10020
LINDEN PRESS/SIMON & SCHUSTER and colophon are trademarks
of Simon & Schuster, Inc.

Manufactured in the United States of America
Production directed by Jeanne Palmer
10 9 8 7 6 5 4 3 2 1

Library of Congress Cataloging in Publication Data

Balanchine's ballerinas.

   Bibliography: p.
   1. Balanchine, George.   2. Choreographers—United States—Biography.
3. Ballerinas—Interviews.   I. Tracy, Robert.   II. DeLano, Sharon.
GV1785.B32B34   1983   792.8′2′0924 [B]   83-13544
ISBN 0-671-46146-X

ACKNOWLEDGMENTS

Helen F. Carroll, Judith D. Peabody, and Berry Delahanty Richardson have been particularly gracious and supportive of this project. We are grateful also for the help of Robert Bridge; Alan Brody; Donald H. Coleman; Robert Cornfield; The Dance Collection of the Library and Museum of the Performing Arts at Lincoln Center, Genevieve Oswald, curator; The Dance Collection of the Victoria and Albert Museum in London; David Daniel; Helen Rice Dolan; Freddie and Isabel Eberstadt; James Elliott; Tamara Glenny; Nigel and Maude Gosling; Susan Hendl; Lorenzo Homar; Melanie Jackson; Leslie Katz; Mary Ellen Kristen; Lisa Laidlaw; Lillian Libman; Russell Lynes; John and Sylvia Mazzola; New York City Ballet; Carlos Noceda; Rudolf Nureyev; Jacqueline Onassis; Samuel Peabody; Bernard Perlin; Joseph Reed Petticrew; Claudia Roth Pierpont; Luigi Pignotti; Susan Sarandon; School of American Ballet; Eva Siu; Nikole Tracy; Francis Xavier; and Cynthia Cannell and Joni Evans at The Linden Press. Henry Wisneski provided unparalleled assistance in locating photographs.

For their help with the portrait photographs, we thank Richard Avedon, Jon Falzone, Thomas King Flagg, Jesse Gerstein, Alec Hanna, David Kinigson, Scott Osman, William Stevens, Ernest Swain, and Maia Wechsler; and thanks to makeup artist Peter Brown for his counsel and generosity.

The idea for this book came to me while I was attending the classes and lectures conducted from 1973 to 1976 by Melissa Hayden at Skidmore College. The actual conversations began in Chicago in 1978. Maria Tallchief was then directing the Chicago Lyric Opera Ballet's spring season, and I was dancing with her company. The following year, when I became a student at the School of American Ballet in New York, I continued taping conversations with Balanchine's dancers, starting with Felia Doubrovska and Alexandra Danilova. The final interview was conducted in 1982 with Suzanne Farrell after Balanchine had created his last work, *Variations for Orchestra*, a solo made for Farrell on the occasion of the Stravinsky Centennial Celebration. Mr. Balanchine died as the manuscript was being prepared for the press.

R.T.

CONTRIBUTING PHOTOGRAPHERS

Martha Swope
George Platt Lynes
Steven Caras
Costas
Carolyn George

PHOTO CREDITS

Courtesy of the Dance Collection, Library and Museum of the Performing Arts, Lincoln Center, New York: pages 1, 15, 22, 32, 38, 58, 59 (bottom), 60, 62 (top), 63 (bottom), 69, 78, 79 (bottom), 91, 95 (left), 96, 97, 112, 131 (bottom).

Steven Caras: pages 3, 145 (top and bottom right), 157, 164, 165 (left), 172 (bottom), 179, 181.

Courtesy of Tamara Geva: pages 14, 33.

George Platt Lynes, courtesy of the Dance Collection, Library and Museum of the Performing Arts, Lincoln Center, New York: pages 16, 52 (top), 67, 72, 75, 79 (top), 80, 81, 82, 87, 89, 95 (top), 105, 106, 107, 108.

Courtesy of the New York City Ballet: pages 17 (left), 98 (top), 99, 140.

Courtesy of the Victoria and Albert Museum, London: pages 16 (bottom), 17 (right), 20, 21, 23, 26, 31, 39.

Courtesy of Alexandra Danilova: page 24.

Courtesy of Felia Doubrovska: pages 40, 41, 42, 43.

Courtesy of Tamara Toumanova: pages 49, 50, 51, 52 (bottom).

Courtesy of Lew Christensen: pages 59 (top), 61.

Courtesy of Elise Reiman: pages 62 (left), 73.

Courtesy of Vera Zorina: page 63 (left).

Courtesy of Suzanne Farrell: page 98 (bottom).

Martha Swope: pages 100, 113, 115, 117, 118, 121, 122, 124, 126, 131 (top), 132, 133, 136, 139 (top right and left), 145 (top left), 152, 153 (top), 156, 162, 171, 172 (center).

New York Post staff photo by Lenore Davis: page 101 (top).

Costas: pages 101 (bottom), 145 (center), 146, 153 (bottom), 155, 172 (top), 186 (bottom).

Courtesy of Violette Verdy: page 139 (bottom).

Carolyn George: pages 144, 165 (right), 186 (top).

Susan Kuklin: page 175.

Contessa Giovanna Agusta: page 187.

Shonna Valeska: pages 18, 28–29, 34–35, 36–37, 44–45, 46–47, 54–55, 64, 71, 76, 84–85, 103, 110, 128–129, 135, 142–143, 148–149, 158, 160–161, 166–167, 168–169, 176–177, 182–183, 184–185.

For Giovanna

CONTENTS

INTRODUCTION

Put sixteen girls on a stage and it's everybody —the world. Put sixteen boys and it's nobody.

—BALANCHINE

George Balanchine loved women. They were the inspiration for his ballets, his companions, the instruments of his work. When he was still in his early twenties he was taken on as choreographer for the Ballets Russes but did not become part of Diaghilev's coterie, partly, one assumes, because of what Diaghilev referred to as his "morbid interest in women." After Diaghilev died, and Lincoln Kirstein was trying to persuade Balanchine to come to America, Kirstein wrote in his diary that the prospective architect of his new ballet was "a Georgian, half Moslem, half orthodox, essentially oriental. He has TB in one lung, will die in three years, and adores girls; this is important since The Dance is Woman—Terpsichore, *La Danse*. . . . His is an angelic vision; dancers are sent for his purpose." Later, when Kirstein was struggling to keep the School of American Ballet going, he had to contend with the director's complaint that Balanchine was "interested only in pianos, automobiles, and girls," and wasn't being serious.

Balanchine's collaboration with his ballerinas produced the most important work in twentieth-century dance and gave rise to the figure known as the "Balanchine dancer," the model for the contemporary ballerina. Those who, like R. P. Blackmur, didn't like what they saw thought that such creatures made up a "ballet of pinheads" with "echoless technique." Others, like Arlene Croce, perceived "mortal goddesses, yet reachable," dancers with distinct qualities that helped shape the ballets Balanchine made for them: "Kent's feyness, Hayden's swagger, Verdy's rhetorical drive, Adams's dignity, Farrell's creaturely impact, . . . McBride's purity of conscience as a classical dancer." The ballerinas themselves, in the following interviews, testify to their individuality and describe how Balanchine integrated their idiosyncrasies into his ballets, drawing from them what was natural, spontaneous. Balanchine nurtured his dancers and trained them in his technique, but finally it was the special quality of an individual dancer that inspired him to make a ballet. When he was asked in the early sixties what kind of dancer he would mold if, like Pygmalion, he could create the ideal woman, he declined to speculate. Such a woman could for him be only a "nobody." A great dancer brings something special, sublime, unteachable to her work. "Sometimes you see a body and you say it's not beautiful. But then she moves, and the mechanics of her moving produce an impression of beauty. . . . So what you look for in a dancer is what she can give you."

Balanchine spent his life with dancers. He was married to four of them and enamored of numerous others. Not all of his work was based on personal relationships, of course, but when he was emotionally involved with a dancer he tended to find inspiration in her for the creation of new ballets. A pattern of great spurts of artistic energy that parallel emotional alliances can be traced. Since there is no narrative line to most of Balanchine's work one can't really say that the personal life is reflected in the ballets, although there are recurrent figures that indicate certain preoccupations, most notably the poet who yearns for beauty he may not possess, as in *La Sonnambula,* and, concomitantly, the figure of the aloof, unreachable woman—the girl in the "Unanswered Question" section of *Ivesiana,* and the Farrell figure in the last section of *Vienna Waltzes*—but much of his work is indeed pure movement, patterns that evoke unspecified emotions or refer to concepts too broad to be simply autobiographical.

The man behind the work remains enigmatic. Dancers invariably describe him as quiet, mild-mannered, never angry or abrasive, sometimes demanding but always accommodating of an individual's limitations, calm in the midst of chaos, a fast worker. He was playful, witty, charming. And always, of course, enchanted by young girls. The joy he took in a beautiful young woman's company is perhaps most touchingly visible in the snapshots of him playing with Tamara Toumanova in a swimming pool in Monte Carlo in the summer of 1932. The same playfulness is evident in Ruthanna Boris's reminiscence of Balanchine making Christmas ornaments in a Houston hotel room during a Ballet Russe tour a decade later, hiding out in the dancers' room and telling stories.

The playfulness remained in later life but was leavened into a sort of wry wit. He was by no means consistently easygoing, and could, and often did, reduce a dancer to tears with a terse comment delivered with his habitual rabbitlike sniff and a preliminary "Well, dear. . . ." He was unpredictable, some would say perverse, and was accused of running his company in the style of Stalin, demanding loyalty and refusing to forgive those who he thought had failed him. He once said that as the Pope represented Christ he represented Terpsichore, the goddess of dance, and he expected from his dancers the kind of commitment that is proper to such a mission. A mystical link with tradition and history was implied, and when Balanchine said that he had just spoken to Tchaikovsky or that Stravinsky had called him on the phone (some time after the composer's death), he wasn't being merely whimsical.

Like many emigrés from Soviet Russia, Balanchine was politically conservative and enamored of the American scene. He wore cowboy shirts with pearl snaps, Western-cut suits, string ties, and turquoise bracelets. He was unashamedly patriotic, as when at the end of the 1982 spring season, which closed on July 4, he came on stage to announce that he had just received a new composition from Stravinsky, and the orchestra played "The Star-Spangled Banner." Or when he revised the company's schedule on the day the American hostages in Iran were released, and put on a performance of *Stars and Stripes* in which each of the dancers wore yellow ribbons.

Balanchine, the greatest choreographer of our age, perhaps of any age, repeatedly referred to his work as a craft, saying that he was like a gardener, or a tailor, or a cook. "What I do is to assemble ingredients—it is like opening an icebox door and you look inside to see what you have stored away—and then I select, combine, and hope that the results will be appetizing." The ingredients were his dancers, selected and prepared to his specifications, yet each with her own special qualities of talent and personality and breeding. He was endlessly fascinated by them, and they rewarded his attention by helping to create an astonishing number of masterpieces.

Balanchine and Tamara Toumanova, Monte Carlo, 1932.

1. 1904-1933

The Years
in Russia
and
Europe

G eorgi Melitonovich Balanchivadze, the son of a Georgian composer who had settled in St. Petersburg, was accepted as a ballet student at the Imperial Theater School in 1914, when he was ten, and was trained as a dancer during the convulsive years of war and revolution that followed. Children enrolled in the school were formally members of the Tsar's household. They were instructed in the courtly details and technique of the classical ballet tradition, given lessons in academic subjects, and assigned small parts in evening performances of operas and ballets at the Maryinsky Theater. They inhabited a remote, insular world that was devoted to dancing and that remained to a surprising degree intact after the October Revolution, except for a brief hiatus during which the students had to fend for themselves. When school resumed, student performances were given at noisy Party meetings or in unheated theaters before hungry audiences, but classes were conducted much as they had been when the Tsar was the Theater School's patron.

Artistic experiments were permitted in the early 1920s, and Balanchivadze began to put together dances. When he was sixteen he made a pas de deux to music by Anton Rubinstein. It was considered too erotic by some of the school's staff and wonderfully lyrical and innovative by others. In any case, Balanchivadze continued to experiment. He graduated in 1921 and became a member of the corps de ballet at the State Theater of Opera and Ballet and also enrolled in the Petrograd Conservatory of Music. The next year he and several friends, some of them pupils of the theater director Vsevelod Meyerhold, formed a group they called the Young Ballet. One of their programs, held in the hall of the Duma, where Mayakovsky, Essenin, and Blok had read their poems, was called "The Evolution of Ballet: From Petipa Through Fokine to Balanchivadze."

Balanchivadze's early work was influenced by the ideas of Kasian Goleizovsky, a choreographer at the Bolshoi Theater in Moscow who had his own school and a small company. Goleizovsky's dances were presented with simple costumes and decor and featured sculptural poses and sensuous, sometimes acrobatic movements to contemporary music. The Young Ballet, like Goleizovsky's group, had a popular following and was troubling to theater officials. In one of their programs there was no music at all. A chorus chanted Blok's poem "The Twelve" while the dancers mimed movements plotted out by Balanchivadze. Finally the Maryinsky authorities threatened to fire anyone who danced with the Young Ballet.

Balanchivadze's partner in these performances was often Alexandra Danilova or Lydia Ivanova, who were also at the Maryinsky, or Tamara Gevergeva, a sixteen-year-old singer and a student in the evening classes at the ballet school. Balanchivadze and Gevergeva also performed in nightclubs to pick up extra money. They were married in 1922, and two years later Balanchivadze, Danilova, Gevergeva, Nicholas Efimov, and several other Maryinsky performers left Russia with a group they called the Soviet State Dancers. The trip was organized by Vladimir Dimitriev, a former opera singer who convinced the authorities that the West should be exposed to

Balanchine and Tamara Geva, 1923.

Alicia Markova in Le Chant du Rossignol, *1925.*

Soviet art. The singers in the troupe soon went back home, but the four dancers and Dimitriev toured summer resorts along the Rhine and then were booked into the Empire Theatre in London, where they performed for two weeks.

The little band left for France when their work permits expired, and were in Paris running out of money when a telegram arrived asking them to go to Misia Sert's for an audition with Serge Diaghilev. Diaghilev, whose access to well-trained Russian dancers had been limited by the revolution, soon hired them, and Georgi Balanchivadze became Georges Balanchine, choreographer and dancer for Diaghilev's Ballets Russes. He was given the central creative place in the company soon afterward, when Bronislava Nijinska, who had been the Ballets Russes' chief choreographer for three years, broke with Diaghilev over what she viewed as a usurpation of her position. Balanchine was a useful replacement because he worked quickly, he could adapt to various styles, and finally, of course, because within five years he had produced two great ballets—*Apollon Musagète* and *Prodigal Son.*

At first Diaghilev asked Balanchine to rework some opera ballets. (The company supported itself in the winter by dancing with the Monte Carlo opera.) Then he was asked to restage Stravinsky's *Le Chant du Rossignol.* In Balanchine's production the Nightingale was danced by a fourteen-year-old English girl, Alicia Markova, who made her official debut when Balanchine's choreography was seen for the first time in Paris. The production was a success, and from then on Balanchine regularly provided the Ballets Russes with dances that were popular and that worked in the various bouillabaisses of librettist, composer, and designer that Diaghilev handed him. His facility was remarkable. Lydia Sokolova, an English ballerina, recalled that when *The Triumph of Neptune* was about to premiere in London she was upset because she didn't have a part in what was a very English ballet —with music by Lord Berners, a libretto by Sacheverell Sitwell, and a set inspired by Victorian popular prints. She mentioned her annoyance at the final orchestra rehearsal, and Balanchine, who "had the quickest invention of any choreographer I ever knew," put together a part for her in an hour.

La Chatte, produced the following season in Monte Carlo, was in a completely different style from the rather daffy English work of the previous year. *La Chatte* had a plastic Constructivist set by the Russian sculptor Naum Gabo and his brother Anton Pevsner. Olga Spessivtseva, as the favorite cat who becomes a woman and then regresses to chasing mice, wore a mica headdress and a mica cone over her white tutu and tights. Serge Lifar, in mica armor, performed a series of corkscrew turns at the end and fell dead in grief on the black oilcloth covering the stage. Danilova says that in *La Chatte* Balanchine created the style that made Lifar, Diaghilev's favorite, a ballet deity—his own neoclassic pose.

By the summer of 1927, Alexandra Danilova had replaced Tamara Gevergeva as Balanchine's romantic attachment. Gevergeva (now Geva) joined the Chauve-Souris company and went to America, while Danilova became the leading ballerina of the Ballets Russes. Balanchine had badly injured his knee during a rehearsal of *The Triumph of Neptune,* and his career as a dancer was more or less over, but as a choreographer he was about to create one of his greatest works, *Apollon Musagète.*

Stravinsky had finished the score in January 1928, and it was performed the following April in Washington, D.C., with choreography by Adolph Bolm. The European rights were reserved for Diaghilev, however, and *Apol-*

Irina Baronova in the early forties.

Balanchine and Vera Nemtchinova in Aurora's Wedding, *1925.*

Tatiana Riabouchinska in the early forties.

lon was rehearsed in Monte Carlo that spring and premiered in Paris in June. Years later Stravinsky wrote to Balanchine, "My memories of our staging of *Apollo* for Diaghilev are among the most satisfying in my artistic life." For Balanchine too the collaboration was important:

> Stravinsky's work altogether satisfies me. . . . When I listen to a work by him I am moved—I don't like the word "inspired"—to try to make visible not only the rhythm, melody and harmony, but even the timbres of the instruments. . . . I myself think of *Apollo* as white music, in places as white-on-white. . . . For me the whiteness is something positive (it has in itself an essence) and at the same time abstract. Such a quality exerts great power over me when I am creating a dance; it is the music's final communication and fixes the pitch that determines my own invention. . . .

Apollo (as it has been called since the mid-fifties) is still in the repertory of Balanchine's company, along with *Prodigal Son,* the last ballet he created for Diaghilev, which once again demonstrated Balanchine's versatility. In *Apollon* the dancers were asked to deport themselves austerely; in *Prodigal Son* the choreography was emotionally expressive, even passionate. And Balanchine was at his most inventive. Richard Buckle in his life of Diaghilev mentions the choreographer's resourcefulness:

> Balanchine complained that in Kochno's librettos there always occurred the word "promenade." In *Le Fils Prodigue* this came after the Prodigal passed out, drunk, and it gave rise to some of Balanchine's most fantastic inventions—the dividing of the spoils; the insect-like pattering around of the exultant robbers, back to back, arms interlocked, knees bent; and the upturning of the long table, which became a boat, with the men's arms for oars, the Siren as figure-head and her long crimson cloak for a sail.

Prodigal Son, with Felia Doubrovska in the role of the Siren, premiered in Paris on May 21, 1929, and the company then went to London. On July 24 there was a gala for King Fuad of Egypt, who had asked especially to see *Prodigal.* That evening Diaghilev saw his company dance for the last time. He died in Venice on August 19. Balanchine was in London with Lydia Lopokova and Anton Dolin waiting to complete a dance sequence for the film *Dark Red Roses.* He had lost his artistic guide, the mentor who had introduced him to European culture, given him ballets to make, brought him together with Stravinsky. "It is because of Diaghilev that I am whatever I am today," he said many years later.

The Ballets Russes collapsed immediately with Diaghilev's death. Balanchine was asked to stage Beethoven's two-act *Les Créatures de Prométhee* by the director of the Paris Opéra, and to become the Opéra's *maître de ballet,* but he had just started work when he fell ill with pneumonia, then tuberculosis, and was told he would probably die. He recovered, slowly, and in the meantime gave the Beethoven commission to Serge Lifar, helping him with the choreography and giving Lifar the credit while he took the fee to pay his medical bills. He was sequestered in a sanitorium for months, during which time Lifar finessed the Opéra appointment for himself.

In 1930 Balanchine staged a few pieces for the Cochran Revue, a chic show at the Pavillion Theatre in London which used ballet dancers like Nikitina and Lifar and painters like Derain and Bérard. Later that year he went to Copenhagen as guest ballet master for the Royal Danish Ballet, but in a few months he was back in England, putting on ballets for a variety show. In 1932 he became *maître de ballet* of the Ballets Russes de Monte-Carlo company managed by René Blum and Colonel Wassily de Basil. For that season he engaged three "baby ballerinas," children of Russian emigrés in Paris: Irina Baronova, Tamara Toumanova, and Tatiana Riabouchinska, all young teenagers.

Balanchine.

The "babies" provided a *frisson* of girlish innocence and the technically dazzling manner of sophisticated ballerinas. Balanchine's ballets for them played with this ambiguity, and *Cotillon,* for Toumanova, was thought by some English balletomanes to be his greatest work. Balanchine had an unpleasant relationship with Colonel de Basil, however, and was replaced during the spring season. Boris Kochno, Diaghilev's closest aide and then de Basil's artistic director, left with Balanchine to form a new company, Les Ballets 1933. At first they were supported financially by Coco Chanel, but a real season was made possible when Kochno turned up a rich Englishman named Edward James. James wanted to please his estranged wife, the Viennese dancer Tilly Losch, who had performed for Balanchine once in a Cochran revue, and he more or less bought her a ballet company. He spent over a million francs hiring dancers, buying costumes, and renting the Théâtre des Champs-Élysées. All to no avail. Losch divorced him, and Les Ballets 1933 disbanded after six weeks of performances in Paris and London. For Balanchine, though, the season had a happy consequence. The company was seen by Lincoln Kirstein, a wealthy Bostonian who offered Balanchine the chance for a career in America. Kirstein had chosen him as the creator of an American ballet.

Balanchine, 1929.

Alexandra Danilova

When Balanchine made *Apollon Musagète* for the Ballets Russes in 1928, the ballet he calls "the turning point in my life," he chose Alexandra Danilova to take the part of Terpsichore, muse of the dance. (She in fact shared the role with Alice Nikitina, the "favorite" of Lord Rothermere, who was one of Diaghilev's principal backers.) Danilova was then the leading ballerina of the Ballets Russes, and Balanchine's lover. She had studied at the Imperial School of Ballet in St. Petersburg, danced as a soloist at the Maryinsky Theater, and was to be for nearly two decades the prima ballerina of the Ballet Russe de Monte Carlo, the company that brought ballet to provincial America in the forties and fifties.

Danilova was eight and a half years old when she entered the Imperial School as a boarding student. "Choura," unlike most of the students at the school, was from a wealthy, privileged family, but she was also an orphan and had become accustomed to displacements and unusual arrangements. After the October Revolution her family's circumstances were altered considerably, but Danilova's training was only temporarily disrupted. She was taken into the Russian State Bal-

> Maybe I lasted longer because my dedication went deeper. My dedication, like Balanchine's, goes very, very deep.

Danilova (far right) in Barabau, *1925, the first work commissioned especially for Balanchine by Diaghilev.*

let Company after graduation and made a soloist in 1922. In addition to the ballets in the Maryinsky repertory she danced in "experimental" pieces by Fyodor Lopokov, the artistic director of the theater, and in Balanchine's work for the Young Ballet. In 1924 she left with the Soviet State Dancers for the tour of German spas that ended with Diaghilev absorbing the little company into his Ballets Russes.

During the Diaghilev years Danilova danced in ballets by Fokine, Massine, and Nijinska, as well as in *Swan Lake* and *Aurora's Wedding* and in Balanchine's work. In July 1929, at the end of the London sea-

son, Diaghilev went backstage to say goodbye to his company, kissed Choura, and left for Paris. He died a month later, and the Ballets Russes de Serge Diaghilev disbanded.

Danilova and Balanchine separated. She danced in Monte Carlo with the opera for a season and then went to London to dance in Sir Oswald Stoll's musical *Waltzes from Vienna.* There she married an Italian engineer who designed air-conditioning for South African gold mines. According to Danilova, "This being married didn't work at all." In any case, she was soon back in Monte Carlo with the Ballets Russes organized by Colonel de Basil, for

which Massine was the ballet master. There followed a long association with the de Basil company and then, after 1938, with Sergei Denham's Ballet Russe de Monte Carlo, which was based in Monte Carlo until the war in Europe began and the dancers fled to the United States.

Danilova was enormously popular, with perhaps the most famous legs in ballet. Massine said that she was like "champagne on the stage." One of her most acclaimed parts was that of the Glove-Seller in his *Gaîté Parisienne,* and her entrance in that role traditionally met with a standing ovation.

In 1944 Balanchine came to the

Danilova with Serge Lifar in Apollon Musagète, *1928.*

Ballet Russe as resident choreographer, an arrangement that lasted only two years but that gave Danilova new Balanchine ballets to star in. The first was *Danses Concertantes,* to music by Stravinsky. Edwin Denby thought the ballet was "like a conversation in Henry James, as surprising, as sensitive, as forbearing, as full of slyness and fancy. The joyousness of it is the pleasure of being civilized." The work was later revived in the New York City Ballet's 1972 Stravinsky Festival in a quite different, and less successful, version. *Night Shadow* (later *La Sonnambula*) premiered in February 1946. Danilova, in a white night-gown, carrying a lighted candle, elicited gasps from the audience when she folded the poet (Nicholas Magallanes) into her arms and stepped backward into the wings. That season Balanchine and Danilova also collaborated in a new production of *Raymonda,* the three-act ballet originally choreographed by Petipa in 1898.

Danilova gave her last performance as a regular member of the Ballet Russe in Houston on December 30, 1951. The curtain fell on *Gaîté Parisienne* before a tearful, cheering audience. She made guest appearances with various companies during the next two years and in 1954 formed her own touring company, Great Moments of Ballet. She danced as a guest with the Ballet Russe at the Metropolitan Opera in 1957, stopping the show for several minutes with her opening-night entrance, as usual. Later that season she gave her farewell performance.

Since her retirement as a dancer Danilova has staged productions for several companies, including *Chopiniana* and *Coppélia* (in collaboration with Balanchine) for the New York City Ballet. Since 1963 she has taught advanced classes at the School of American Ballet, where she brings to her students a quality Denby observed in her dancing:

Danilova in Le Bal, *1929.*

Among ballet stars, Danilova has a special gift. At the height of a classical variation, while she is observing all the restrictions of the grand style, she seems suddenly to be happy to be dancing, with a pleasure like a little girl's. It gives her a sort of natural grace that is unique.

One of the first works Balanchine made for you was a duet to the music of Zdeněk Fibich—*Poème*. That was in 1921, and he choreographed several more pieces in those years before you left Russia. What were they like?

There were many evenings of experiment then. We danced when poetry was spoken. And there was sometimes singing. Balanchine's dances were, how do you say, the opposite of round . . . square movements. Sharp and angular. In *Poème* he lifted me over his head and then put me down on pointe. But he did that before, when he was sixteen, for Olga Mungalova and himself, in his first choreography, *La Nuit* of Rubinstein. He put her up and carried her to the wings. And he repeated that movement for me when he made *Triumph of Neptune*, when Lifar carried me in arabesque. That was very daring then. We did a ballet in leotards in the Young Ballet too. Very modern.

But both of you had been rigorously trained in the classical tradition.

Yes. We received good classical training. There was Balanchine, Lydia Ivanova, and myself, and we had been counted the most promising pupils. But I think the monotony of classical dances was not what Balanchine wanted. He was influenced by Kasian Goleizovsky, but Goleizovsky was more narrower. Balanchine's point of view on art is much broader. Goleizovsky was a

step between. Like Agnes de Mille would have never did *Rodeo* if she didn't seen *Billy the Kid*. Eugene Loring was step between that opened the eyes more. Goleizovsky show us that we can be different style of dancing than just position and *développe à la seconde*. Balanchine would do everything. You know, if you think that classic is all on the toes, and then we go bourréeing on flat feet. . . . Not just parallel, which Fokine did in *Carnaval*. Here we get off the toes. It was a different way of dancing.

You were going to school and then dancing at the Maryinsky during a very tumultuous period. Was it hard for you to keep working?

We were afraid, and we went through hunger. For a year we thought that the school would be closed, and everybody left town. I went to the Cossack country. The last days of the revolution, you know, it was a war with the Germans. And then Lunacharsky persuaded Lenin they should improve the ballet. The Bolsheviks were all different. Some were educated and they wanted a lot of education, and theater. So I come back and school was open.

When I finished the school I received solo parts right away at the Maryinsky. Because Fyodor Lopokov, the artistic director, loved me very much. He gave me two ballets to dance. His *Firebird*, which was very, very modern. A lot of angular movement. Then he gave me Fokine's *Nuit d'Égypte*.

Did Lopokov like Balanchine too?

No. He was jealous and astounded. It was kind of shock when new talents appeared.

But your own career at the Maryinsky was very promising.

Danilova in The Gods Go A-Begging, *1928.*

Danilova as the Black Dancer in Jack in the Box, *1926.*

Did you know you were leaving Russia for good when you went to Germany in the summer of 1924 with Dimitriev and Balanchine and the others?

We didn't know we would never come back. We really went to see the world. It took two years to pull the strings from all over so we could go. And then Ivanova canceled because she was at a party where a woman was telling the future and told her to beware of water. I was furious. And I say, "How can you think about such a thing?" And then she goes with her admirers on the motorboat to Kronstadt and she drowns.

Some say she was killed by the security police.

That is a mystery. She was going with the elite officers, and they had the boat and everybody was saved except her. She was much more womanly than I was. You know, going out. And I was doing my *grands battements* or reading. She was a year younger but much more ahead of me. I always say I am retarded, and I think as a woman I developed later than the other girls. In my family I was more sheltered. But then I began to develop during Diaghilev. Maybe, being women, the others left the art earlier, and I lasted longer because my dedication went deeper. My dedication, like Balanchine's, goes very, very deep.

When you were dancing with Diaghilev's company and were in love with Balanchine and he was making ballets for you it must have been a tremendously happy time.

Of course at the time you don't think about it. You don't know if you are happy or what you are doing. It's later that you understand that that was your happy days. I didn't expect that Balanchine and I would be together. I didn't know. We were always good friends. You know how it is. When you finish the school you stick together. But then he said if I wouldn't be with him he would go to America. He would leave Diaghilev. I thought maybe I should go back to Russia. I know he was very unhappy when he separated from Tamara Geva. This was big boom when they separated. He had done *La Pastorale* for Doubrovska, and Tamara was the Fiancée in it. So I had to dance for Tamara because she decided if they wouldn't be together then she go to Paris and join Balieff. Tamara did a small part very nice. But then she went to Balieff, and then to Ziegfeld and did marvelously. She became a star.

Balanchine and I got along very well. We were both very dedicated. But, you know, we talk very little. About his ballets he always talked with Boris Kochno. And I was so busy. To learn the choreography you had to work by yourself. Especially *Le Bal* and *Apollon.* It was difficult.

Barabau was the first Balanchine ballet I did for Diaghilev. It was done on the Italian song. It was funny. We all been padded with bosoms and derrières. The choir stood behind the wooden fence. Maybe twelve, sixteen people in funny hats. And they be singing and we be dancing. Diaghilev did it, I think, as a little bit of a tribute to Monte Carlo. It was gay and Italian, with eating and drinking.

Later I did *Gods Go A-Begging* with Léon Woizikowsky, who was not a particularly good partner. When I first joined the company I had to dance a Russian dance with Woizikowsky, and he refused to dance with me. He said, "Who is she? Nobody knows her. I am the star." And I start to cry, and Diaghilev was told, and so he come and say that I am dancing solos in Maryinsky Theater and all this is nonsense. If he think I am good, I am good. And later Diaghilev said to me, in front of everybody, that nobody danced as beautifully as I did this Russian dance.

My official really big ballet was *Triumph of Neptune.* Lord Berners wrote the music. It was about a journalist who went from one place to the other. Diaghilev had been inspired for it by all sorts of Victorian prints.

In *Le Bal* Balanchine made for me and Anton Dolin a beautiful adagio. This was the first time we danced off balance. Like Maria Tallchief did later in *Firebird.* I was off balance and Dolin promenaded me all the way around. It was very difficult. More angular than *Apollon.*

To be with Diaghilev was very important for Balanchine. He pushed him. Diaghilev explain and George understand how the choreography was done. Very, very important for a young choreographer. Then Diaghi-

lev died and there was no company. Balanchine went to England and was with the Cochran Revue, which I was supposed to do but didn't.

You didn't work with Balanchine again for a long time—fifteen years. Was the separation from him bitter? I've read that when he was *maître de ballet* with the Ballets Russes in 1932 he told you that you were "too old" to be in the company.
At that time he was unbelievably mad. He told me that to hurt me, because of the emotional separation. But finally we understand each other. He has an attraction to me because he feel artist in me the same that he is. And he needs different women. Like a painter has a favorite model, he change the model, and eventually he sleeps with the model. And for each one he is a different choreographer. Because you see each one moves differently. And they awake in him something different. For Suzanne Farrell he does this very feminine, mystic thing. Or Brigitta [Vera Zorina] was on the Broadway and he did all kind of intricate revue. For me he did in the beginning really the beginning of neoclassical ballet. And later, when we worked together during the war, he made *Danses Concertantes* for me, with very witty steps. I think sincerely that he could mold from me anything he wanted. With some of the other women they had a will and not a capacity for strictly dance.

When you got together again professionally, in the forties with the Ballet Russe, you collaborated for the first time on a production—recreating *Raymonda.* How did you help one another?
You don't help Balanchine. The choreography just pours out of him. But we sort of fulfilled each other. He did the first act, and I did my own

variation, and the end. It was very natural, although I think the kids from the company were nervous at first how I will do. But it comes so naturally for us that nobody was disturbed.

You've taught advanced classes at the School of American Ballet for many years. Do you have the same approach to teaching that your teachers in St. Petersburg had?
Yes. It's like in every art. Classic is the basic. In painting the same. Or voice. Balanchine and I grew up in the same style, and I'm very proud to work in his school. He always tell me he give me absolutely carte blanche. I can do whatever I want because he trust me. And I know how to make dancers. The school has improved. In the beginning it didn't have that much money. Now Balanchine can choose and get capable people.

Does it surprise you that Balanchine has achieved so much? Did you think there would be something as large as the institution you're now involved in?
I never thought, no. But now I feel very privileged. It only happened because of his dedication. Diaghilev died. Kochno disappeared. Lifar was put by Balanchine in the Paris Opéra. But Balanchine is sincere to the art. And it is a new art introduced to America, a new way for a lot of young dancers to express themselves. I am only worried because I don't think they are cultured enough. I wish they would go to the museum. I try to bring them things, but they are so surprised if I do. I wish they would be more intellectual. Some of them I am pleased to see at concerts. I think they would perform better if they had more knowledge.

Danilova in The Triumph of Neptune, *1926.*

**Ballets in Which Balanchine Created
Roles for Alexandra Danilova**

POÈME

music: Zdeněk Fibich
costumes: George Balanchine
role: Lead with Balanchine
premiere: Concert at Petrograd Theater
Ballet School, sometime prior to
Balanchine's graduation on April 4, 1921

WALTZ

music: ?
role: Lead with Balanchine
premiere: August 15, 1922, resort at
Sestroretsk, near Petrograd

ADAGIO

music: Camille Saint-Saëns
role: Lead with Balanchine
premiere: June 1, 1923, Alexandrinsky
Hall, Duma, Petrograd
Young Ballet

MARCHE FUNÈBRE

music: Frédéric Chopin
decor: Boris Erbshtein
costumes: Vladimir Dimitriev
role: LYRIC
premiere: June 1, 1923, Alexandrinsky
Hall, Duma, Petrograd
Young Ballet

INVITATION TO THE DANCE

music: Carl Maria von Weber
role: Lead
premiere: Spring 1924, Pavlovsk

L'ENFANT ET LES SORTILÈGES

music: Maurice Ravel
libretto: Colette
decor: Alphonse Visconti
costumes: Georgette Vialet
roles: Shepherdess; Butterfly
premiere: March 21, 1925, Opéra de
Monte-Carlo
Ballets Russes de Serge Diaghilev

BARABAU

music and book: Vittorio Rieti
decor: Maurice Utrillo
role: Servant of Barabau
premiere: December 11, 1925, Coliseum
Theatre, London
Ballets Russes de Serge Diaghilev

ROMEO AND JULIET ENTR'ACTE

music: Constant Lambert
painting: Max Ernst and Joan Miró
role: PAS DE TROIS
premiere: May 4, 1926, Opéra de Monte-
Carlo
Ballets Russes de Serge Diaghilev

JACK IN THE BOX

music: Erik Satie
decor and costumes: André Derain
role: Black Dancer
premiere: June 8, 1926, Théâtre Sarah-
Bernhardt, Paris
Ballets Russes de Serge Diaghilev

THE TRIUMPH OF NEPTUNE

music: Lord Berners
decor: Prince A. Schervashidze
costumes: Pedro Pruna
role: Fairy Queen; Neptune's Daughter
premiere: December 3, 1926, Lyceum
Theatre, London
Ballets Russes de Serge Diaghilev

APOLLON MUSAGÈTE

music and book: Igor Stravinsky
decor and costumes: André Bauchant;
new costumes by Coco Chanel in 1929
role: Terpsichore (alternate with Alice
Nikitina)
premiere: June 12, 1928, Théâtre Sarah-
Bernhardt, Paris
Ballets Russes de Serge Diaghilev

THE GODS GO A-BEGGING

music: George Frederick Handel,
arranged by Sir Thomas Beecham
libretto: Sobeka (Boris Kochno)
decor: Léon Bakst
costumes: Juan Gris
role: Serving Maid/Goddess
premiere: July 16, 1928, His Majesty's
Theatre, London
Ballets Russes de Serge Diaghilev

LE BAL

music: Vittorio Rieti
libretto: Boris Kochno
decor: Giorgio de Chirico
role: The Lady
premiere: May 7, 1929, Opéra de Monte-
Carlo
Ballets Russes de Serge Diaghilev

SONG OF NORWAY (operetta)

music: Robert Wright and George Forrest
adaptation of music of Edvard Grieg
lyrics: Robert Wright and George Forrest
book: Milton Lazarus, from a play by
Homer Curran based on the life of Grieg.
roles: ANITRA'S DANCE; THE SONG OF NORWAY
premiere: June 12, 1944, Philharmonic
Auditorium, Los Angeles
Los Angeles and San Francisco Civic
Light Operas

DANSES CONCERTANTES

music: Igor Stravinsky
decor and costumes: Eugene Berman
role: Ballerina
premiere: September 10, 1944, New York
City Center
Ballet Russe de Monte Carlo

PAS DE DEUX (from entr'acte of
The Sleeping Beauty)

music: Peter Ilyich Tchaikovsky
decor and costumes: Eugene Berman
premiere: March 14, 1945, New York City
Center
Ballet Russe de Monte Carlo

NIGHT SHADOW

music: Vittorio Rieti's arrangement of
Vincenzo Bellini
decor and costumes: Dorothea Tanning
role: Sleepwalker
premiere: February 27, 1946, New York
City Center
Ballet Russe de Monte Carlo

RAYMONDA (choreographed with Danilova)

music: Alexander Glazunov
decor and costumes: Alexandre Benois
role: Raymonda
premiere: March 12, 1946, New York City
Center
Ballet Russe de Monte Carlo

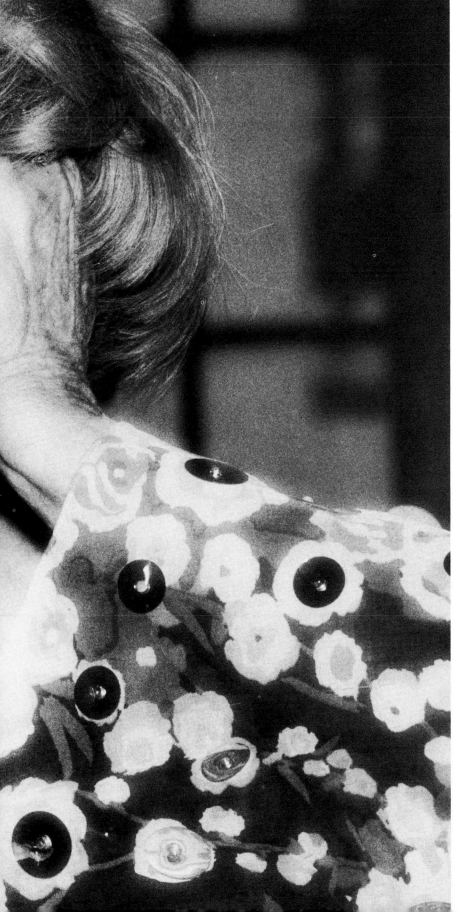

Tamara Geva

Tamara Gevergeva and Georgi Balanchivadze were married in 1922, when she was a fifteen-year-old ballet student. He was eighteen and a member of the corps de ballet at the old Maryinsky Theater. Gevergeva's parents were wealthy before the revolution, and she had been taken to the theater, given French and German lessons, educated. Her father was a Tatar, a Moslem who had converted to Christianity and who inherited a lucrative business dealing in religious artifacts and regalia for the clergy. He was an art collector and a bibliophile, a patron of avant-garde artists such as Vsevelod Meyerhold and Mayakovsky. Her mother was Swedish, had been a singer in a music hall, and didn't marry Tamara's father until the child was six.

Gevergeva began taking private ballet lessons after the revolution, and was admitted to the evening classes at the Theater School when they were opened to private pupils in a move to eliminate "elitism" from the arts. To earn a little money or some flour or potatoes she danced at private performances and in variety shows. Balanchivadze asked her to dance with him in his Evenings of the Young Ballet, and they married shortly after they met, living at first with her parents and then in a bare apartment they could afford only because they got jobs in nightclubs, where Gevergeva sang German torch songs and Balanchivadze played the piano. In 1924 Vladimir Dimitriev asked them to join the troupe of singers and ballet dancers he was taking to Germany for the summer, and Gevergeva left Russia for the last time. She spent two years in the Diaghilev company with her husband, dancing in the corps and in a few solo parts, but they soon separated and she joined the Chauve-Souris company as a guest star on a tour of America, billed as Tamara Geva.

In December 1927, at the end of the Chauve-Souris season, John Martin, dance critic for *The New York Times*, wrote that he was glad Geva had decided to stay in America, even though her dancing "gives one the feeling that he is eating rusty nails along with his ice cream." He admired her stage presence:

Her sense of the comedy value of line simply for itself is phenomenal and her instinct for timing is faultless. . . . It is a matter of no doubt that she would be a delight to watch in

Les Sylphides or the *Lac des Cygnes*. That she has gone ahead and done something different means simply that she has increased her range.

Geva danced for Florenz Ziegfeld in *Whoopee*, which starred Eddie Cantor and Ruby Keeler, and had her first speaking part in *Three's a Crowd*. In 1936 she and Ray Bolger were the stars of *On Your Toes*, the musical in which Balanchine collaborated with George Abbott, Richard Rodgers, and Lorenz Hart. The Princesse Zenobia Ballet in Act I and the "Slaughter on Tenth Avenue" section provided Geva with her most famous role.

Tamara Geva had a long career in musical and dramatic plays and films in England and America. In 1972 she published her autobiography, *Split Seconds*. In 1980 she directed *Diaghilev: A Portrait* for the BBC. She lives in New York, where she writes and paints.

You and Balanchine were married when you were very young, and you danced in his early ballets. Did he have a big influence on you?
He picked me out of the Theater School to be his partner because he thought I was talented, and of course he influenced me, but later on I did it all myself. Our worlds forked in different directions, and most of my development took place away from him. But in the beginning we were sharing dreams, testing new things together. We got married because my father thought that two people who were constantly thrown together in their work and who showed more than an affection for one another were in a somewhat dangerous position, according to the propriety of the time. We listened to his proposition and said, "OK."

In Petrograd in the 1920s many artists were experimenting, doing outrageous things. What sorts of ballets did Balanchine make for you?
One of the first was a pas de deux to music by Rubinstein called *Romance*. I held one leg high up in arabesque and supported myself by a kiss on his lips. It was considered rather erotic and made people talk. I think my favorite, though, was an Egyptian number. I had flexible arms, and Balanchine wanted to use my arms and hands in an Egyptian manner. He had me bend like a weeping-willow tree, exploring the movement of my torso and limbs, and I did little patting bourées with my feet, which gave a flowing quality to a friezelike pose.

I also danced *Valse Triste*. I was meant to be blind, and I danced to the edge of the proscenium and just before the orchestra pit I would turn sharply around. The movement was completely unexpected and made the audience gasp, because they thought I would fall.

Then there was *Enigma*, which we danced together, and many more.

What were the *khalturas* that you and Balanchine performed in?
Khalturas were professional appearances that were illegal, but they were overlooked because of hard times. We not only danced but sometimes Balanchine would compose and play the piano and I would sing. I had a good voice, and Balanchine played beautifully. Of course, we performed actually for our bread and salt. We had to earn a living.

Balanchine was also making ballets for Lydia Ivanova and Alexandra Danilova, and partnering them. They had been formally trained in the Theater School and then joined the

Geva and Serge Lifar in La Pastorale, *1926.*

Maryinsky. What did you think of them?

Of course they were both very talented, but in some ways I was more flexible, less stiffened by tradition, therefore more adaptable for experimentation. Danilova was a brilliant technician, and deserves her reputation. But Ivanova was the most incredible dancer I have ever seen. She was like a gift from God. She was the only woman I've seen who jumped like a man—just soared into the air. Her death right before we were all supposed to leave Russia was very mysterious. She had always been very well taken care of. I remember that she had clothes and a hat with a veil, which at that time was like having jewelry. How she got them in those hard times we never knew and never asked. When we

were about to leave on tour her friends took her for a picnic and a motorboat ride, and then there was that dark accident and she drowned.

Did you think of the trip with the Soviet State Dancers as an escape from Russia?

No. We were going along without any preconceived ideas. It was arranged and we followed. There were so many mysteries, and much of that time seems like a cloudy maze. I had faith in some intangible force that I believed was on my side. I just did my job and was blank to the consequences. I liked being in the troupe. There was no seniority, and we weren't concerned with how many turns someone could make. In Germany we danced in some real holes. And in London at the Empire

Theatre we got sacked pretty quickly. Our costumes were put together with hooks and snaps, and it took us a long time to change. The orchestra and the management got tired of waiting between numbers, so we got fired. It was Anton Dolin who saw us there and brought us to the attention of Diaghilev.

You stayed with the Diaghilev company over two years, but according to your memoirs you stopped living with Balanchine before you left. Was that a big break for you?

We just went in different directions. None of the parts Balanchine made for me during the Diaghilev period were of any special consequence. Anton Dolin had me do *Le Train Bleu* with him, but he soon left the company, and the ballet was dropped. Diaghilev cast me as the Polovetsian Girl in *Prince Igor,* and I danced several classical variations, but I was restless. My interests were expanding.

Then someone told Nikita Balieff, the producer of the Chauve-Souris, that I wanted to get out and explore. His company was aging and old-fashioned and he was looking for young blood. I said I would join him if I got top billing and could do my own dances—not any of the Chauve-Souris repertoire. When Diaghilev heard I was departing he told me I was crazy, because Lydia Sokolova was leaving the company and he said I would inherit her roles. But my contract to go to America with Balieff was already signed.

And you asked Balanchine to help you with the pieces you would dance in New York.

Yes. Even that early I knew there was a talent to reckon with. The fact that he is a genius is no surprise to me. He had a fantastic imagination. I asked him to help, and he agreed instantly. He choreographed a takeoff

Geva and Demetrios Vilan in the Princesse Zenobia Ballet section of On Your Toes, *1936.*

on a bullfight, *Grotesque Espagnol*, to Isaac Albéniz' music. It had a tragic quality, and an unexpected development of movements. Then he choreographed *Sarcasm*, to a Prokofiev score, which was very outrageous in 1927. But the audience always screamed for more because the piece was so mesmerizing. The third thing I danced was to Glazunov's music, *Romanesque*. I choreographed it myself and it was very elegant. I danced on pointe between two wooden borzois.

The program was a big success. Balieff knew he had something good, but I didn't want to go back to Europe with the company when the season was over, so I stayed and was signed by Ziegfeld. In the first musical I did, *Whoopee,* I stopped the show, doing a strut on pointe, dressed in a top hat, tails, and black tights. In *Three's a Crowd* I did my solo, "Talkative Toes," and danced "Body and Soul" with Clifton Webb, and in *Flying Colors* I sang and danced "I Can't Help Being a Two-Faced Woman." Half of my costume was white and the other half was brown. I had six white girls on one side and six black girls on the other. Eventually they merged, which was an innovation in those strict racial times. In Boston they made me change it a bit, but I reconstructed it for the New York opening.

When did you work with Balanchine again?
In 1935 Balanchine needed some star guest artists for the premiere of the American Ballet, so I did *Errante*, which he had created for Tilly Losch in Les Ballets 1933. I danced with a ten-foot train, and got seventeen curtain calls. The following year we did *On Your Toes*, by Rodgers and Hart. Balanchine completed his transition to America with that show. He incorporated many new things into it and really changed the conception of a

musical. It was the first time dancing was integral to the action and not just a number that interrupted the play.

"Slaughter on Tenth Avenue," the gangster ballet which Balanchine made for the finale of *On Your Toes,* was a great success for you.
Yes. For me and Ray Bolger, who was splendid. Balanchine reconstructed it years later for Suzanne Farrell, but that version had no relationship to the first choreography. At the end of our "Slaughter" the audience was on its feet, and people would return to see it over and over again.

Why didn't you do the film version of *On Your Toes?*
Why didn't Angela Lansbury do the film version of *Mame* instead of Lucille Ball? Soon after I decided to stop dancing, I turned down a film contract offered to me after I did *Manhattan Merry-go-round* so that I could do the Lynn Fontanne part in *Idiot's Delight* in London. That was the beginning of what turned out to be a career in straight plays, including *Trojan Women, Dark Eyes, Misalliance,* etc. Then I did a lot of work on the Coast. In the sixties I dropped everything and went into the horse business.

You were a part of what has been a very long and illustrious life for Balanchine.
When I left we were still so young. But we kept up a deep friendship through the years. He is inspired by many women, by certain of their qualities. I was his first Galatea, but after there were many others. And of course he does what he does better than anyone else. Artistically every woman gets something out of him. They say, "Make something of me," and usually he obliges.

Geva with Ray Bolger in On Your Toes.

Ballets in Which Balanchine Created Roles for Tamara Geva

MARCHE FUNÈBRE
music: Frédéric Chopin
role: TRAGIC
premiere: June 1, 1923, Alexandrinsky
Hall, Duma, Petrograd
Young Ballet

ÉTUDE
music: Alexander Scriabin
role: Lead with Balanchine
premiere: 1923–24
Young Ballet

ORIENTAL DANCE
music: Modest Moussorgsky
role: Lead with Balanchine
premiere: 1923–24
Young Ballet

ELEGY
music: Sergei Rachmaninoff
role: Lead with Balanchine and Nicholas
Efimov
premiere: 1924
Young Ballet

L'ENFANT ET LES SORTILÈGES
music: Maurice Ravel
libretto: Colette
scenery: Alphonse Visconti
costumes: Georgette Violet
role: Moth
premiere: March 21, 1925, Opéra de
Monte-Carlo
Ballets Russes de Serge Diaghilev

BARABAU
music and libretto: Vittorio Rieti
decor: Maurice Utrillo
role: Servant of Barabau
premiere: December 11, 1925, Coliseum
Theatre, London
Ballets Russes de Serge Diaghilev

ROMEO AND JULIET ENTR'ACTE
music: Constant Lambert
painting: Max Ernst and Joan Miró
role: PAS DE TROIS
premiere: May 4, 1926, Opéra de Monte-
Carlo
Ballets Russes de Serge Diaghilev

LA PASTORALE
music: Georges Auric
libretto: Boris Kochno
decor and costumes: Pedro Pruna
role: Fiancée/A Young Lady
premiere: May 29, 1926, Théâtre Sarah-
Bernhardt, Paris
Ballets Russes de Serge Diaghilev

GROTESQUE ESPAGNOL
music: Isaac Albéniz
role: Solo
premiere: October 10, 1927,
Cosmopolitan Theater, New York
Balieff's Chauve-Souris

SARCASM
music: Sergei Prokofiev
role: Solo
premiere: October 10, 1927,
Cosmopolitan Theater, New York
Balieff's Chauve-Souris

ERRANTE (originally presented by Les
Ballets 1933, Paris)
music: Franz Schubert
costumes: Pavel Tchelitchev
role: Lead
premiere: March 1, 1935, Adelphi Theatre,
New York
American Ballet

ON YOUR TOES (musical)
music: Richard Rodgers
lyrics: Lorenz Hart
book: Richard Rodgers, Lorenz Hart, and
George Abbott
roles: Vera Barnova; Princesse Zenobia;
Strip Tease Girl
premiere: April 11, 1936, Imperial
Theatre, New York

Sometimes when you are young you don't appreciate things. I took for granted that around me there was Picasso and Cocteau and Auric and Prokofiev— everybody.

Felia Doubrovska

When Balanchine joined the Diaghilev company in 1925 one of the dancers he picked out for leading parts in his new ballets was Felia Doubrovska, who Diaghilev had thought was perhaps too tall (five feet six inches) to be a ballerina. She was in fact almost a prototype of what would later be called "a Balanchine dancer": tall, thin, elegant, with long legs.

Doubrovska was born in St. Petersburg in 1896 and entered the Imperial School of Ballet when she was ten. She and Olga Spessivtseva graduated with honors in 1913 and became members of the corps de ballet at the Maryinsky Theater. Doubrovska was promoted to soloist but wasn't given leading roles, apparently because of her height. She recalls that she was quite happy dancing at the Maryinsky. Her mother was in despair over the grim living conditions in Russia, however, and in 1920 they escaped across the border to Finland with several other people, including Pierre Vladimiroff, premier danseur at the Maryinsky. Through a Russian friend of her mother's in Paris, a concert was arranged for Doubrovska and Vladimiroff at the Théâtre des Champs-Élysées. They got good reviews, and were asked to join Diaghilev, with whom Vladimiroff had danced in the summers of 1912 and 1914.

Vladimiroff was the Prince in the financially disastrous full-length production of *The Sleeping Princess* staged by the Ballets Russes in London in 1921. Doubrovska was the Fairy of the Pine Woods. The following year they were married, and both of them danced with the Ballets

Doubrovska and Balanchine in Le Bal, *1929.*

Doubrovska, right, with Léon Woizikowsky and Lubov Tchernicheva in The Gods Go A-Begging, *1928.*

Russes until 1925, when Vladimiroff went on a tour with Tamara Karsavina. He later toured with Anna Pavlova until her death in 1931. Doubrovska stayed with Diaghilev and was the Bride in Nijinska's production of Stravinsky's *Les Noces* in 1923. She took over Nijinska's role of the Hostess in *Les Biches.*

Balanchine created the part of Polyhymnia, muse of mime, for Doubrovska in *Apollon Musagète.* In *Prodigal Son,* the last ballet Balanchine made for Diaghilev, she danced the Siren, her most famous role. Agnes de Mille, who saw the original production in 1929, said that the pas de deux between Serge Lifar and Doubrovska was "one of the most important seductions to be found on any modern stage." Doubrovska wrapped herself around Lifar like a belt, her hands clutching her ankles, and slowly slid down his body to the floor. At the end of the

scene she stood on the shoulders of her bald, grotesque attendants, towering over the Prodigal. "No actress by voice or presence could dominate the situation more completely."

When the Diaghilev company disbanded, Doubrovska joined her husband for the last season of the Pavlova company. Then for two years she danced with a company formed by Serge Lifar, and in 1936 came to America, where Vladimiroff was teaching in Balanchine's School of American Ballet. She danced the leading role in Balanchine's *Serenata,* presented by the American Ballet in Hartford, Connecticut, and appeared with Colonel de Basil's Ballets Russes. She was a guest ballerina with the Metropolitan Opera Ballet during the 1938–39 season and then retired. Doubrovska, her mother, and Vladimiroff lived in Lakewood, New Jersey, until her mother's death in 1947. From 1948

until 1979 Doubrovska taught at the School of American Ballet. She died in New York on September 18, 1981.

You were in Diaghilev's company when Bronislava Nijinska was the chief choreographer, before Balanchine came. What was it like for you then?

Sometimes when you are young you don't appreciate things. I took for granted that around me there was Picasso and Cocteau and Auric and Prokofiev—everybody. Every day something new and different. One time Diaghilev invite me to a party at Coco Chanel's house and Stravinsky is playing the piano, very difficult music. When Diaghilev passed by where I was sitting he hit me on the shoulder and said, "Doubrovska, eat later. Now listen and try to learn something." And it was *Les Noces.* Later I was cast as the Bride. She

LEFT—Orphée aux Enfers, *1932; CENTER*—Apollon Musagète, *1928; RIGHT*—Apollon Musagète *(with new costume by Coco Chanel), 1929.*

didn't see the groom until the marriage ceremony, which of course is the way of the Russian peasants. Nijinska choreographed the ballet half in the modern style and half in the classical style, but she was not so new and inventive as Balanchine.

Do you remember Balanchine from before? When you were both in Russia?

I remember hearing about this talented Georgian boy. And I saw him in rehearsals at the Maryinsky, where everybody is in the same room—principals, soloists, *coryphées*, children. He stared at people's feet. But I don't remember him as a student choreographer. My husband said he did very well.

So you didn't really meet him until he came to the Ballets Russes.

Yes. Diaghilev hired Balanchine because he heard he was so musical, and he asked him, "Do you like Stravinsky?" Balanchine of course said yes. And Diaghilev said he had a

Stravinsky ballet in the cellar. That was *Le Chant du Rossignol.* All the costumes and scenery by Matisse was in the cellar, because it was tried before but was not very successful. So Balanchine tried it and Diaghilev liked what he did.

My role was the killer of the Nightingale. Matisse fixed my face so well that I myself truly looked dead. It was one of the first ballets where I wore just tights. No tutu. I asked Matisse, "What about my hair?" and just then flowers were coming into the theater from a fan who had seen me the night before in the classical ballets. So Matisse grabs a red-and-yellow chrysanthemum and sticks it above the forehead.

I liked dancing the Balanchine ballets. It was very exciting to dance *Apollon* because Balanchine was so crazy about Stravinsky. He said to me about Stravinsky, "I think the same way." You really had to know how to dance for *Apollon.* It was pure classical form. But different from Maryinsky because there the ballerina could express something

of her own and show what she feels. I got into trouble one time at the end of my variation as the muse of mime. I was so happy that I had accomplished my pirouettes with my finger over my mouth that I ran forward and let out a little sigh. Afterward Boris Kochno come up and tell me to go to Diaghilev. And he say, "Doubrovska, I am not pleased with you." And I say, "But did you see my three pirouettes?" And he say, "But what about all that emotion at the end? This is a serious theater, not a music hall." I think Balanchine learned from Diaghilev that being modern is being cool. No feeling.

You danced with Danilova in *Apollon* and in several other ballets when you were with Diaghilev, and then years later you both taught in Balanchine's school. What do you remember about her from the early years?

Balanchine was in love with her, and she was young and ambitious and always trying to be the most attractive around men. But later Balanchine told me he remember not a thing about his relationship with Danilova.

At a rehearsal for *Prodigal Son* when Choura was watching in the audience and Balanchine was making me do these strange, uncomfortable acrobatic feats, I saw that she had her scarf out and is hiding her face because of laughter. I remember, too, one time when Balanchine and I dance *Le Bal* and Danilova has to come on stage after we make an exit, and she forgets the choreography. While we was dancing she was criticizing us. I always use it as a story for young dancers. One must always concentrate before entering the stage.

Prodigal Son must have been strange for you to learn. The role of the Siren is very far from the classical parts you were trained for.

Yes, it was difficult. But Diaghilev and Balanchine tell me to go home and think about my part. About the pas de deux with Lifar. And I think about a snake, which is not human, but which hypnotizes and bewitches. I used my eyes, and the movement comes from my stomach. I had to perform without any feeling. I approach it like a snake, without any added chi-chi.

Serge Lifar was Diaghilev's principal dancer when you were with the company, and he partnered you frequently. What did Balanchine make of Lifar?

Balanchine was hired to create for Lifar. Diaghilev think man is ballet. So Balanchine present Lifar on a gold plate. He could create for both

Prodigal Son, *1929.*

men and women. I think Balanchine liked to use Lifar as my partner because of our contrasts—I am so tall and Lifar was not very big. In *La Pastorale* Lifar comes in on a bicycle, falls in love with me, the star of a movie, and then goes back to his fiancée. The adagio for Lifar and me was new and very difficult. Lifar turns me by the knee while I am standing on one foot with my other leg in very high arabesque. It is the same movement that you see now in *Serenade,* only more difficult because now there is a long tutu, and in *La Pastorale* I have a very short dress so the audience sees the whole movement.

After the Ballets Russes disbanded you didn't work with Balanchine very much. Except for the operetta he made in Paris in 1931.
I was the lead in that, *Orphée aux Enfers.* Balanchine made a very nice pas de deux and variation for Anatole Vilzak and me, and then one day we are warming our bodies up backstage and Balanchine sees this young girl, Irina Baronova, doing fouettés. Balanchine comes up to me and says he is cutting some of my music to give this girl, only twelve years old, a chance to show off her technique. Irina leaves her place in the corps, comes to the center and does her turns, and goes back to the corps. But people think she was the star of the show.

Then Balanchine says he is going to do a new season with the Baby Ballerinas. Danilova and I are finished. We have to sit in the audience and watch these children, and we don't want them to dance very well, but they do.

I didn't join Balanchine's first company in America, because I am not invited. I don't know that he didn't want me, but I know he liked very young dancers. Danilova, I think, would have liked to dance

with Balanchine in America. When she come later she worked the hardest of anyone I know, really honestly.

People in America don't know me, because I never dance here. After one year with the Metropolitan Opera I retire very quietly. There is no salutation for me when I stop, like for Melissa Hayden.

What did you do when you retired?
For seven years I enjoy. Social events, life, concerts, nightclubs. When you dance you only think about dance. When I retire I relax. Then before my mother died she say, "Felia, I think you should do something with your life." And later I met Balanchine and Maria Tallchief on the street. Balanchine said, "I'm sorry about your mother. I need a teacher in the school and I ask you for last time today." Balanchine wants teachers in his school to teach the way we were taught in Russia. That is why he ask both Pierre and me to teach for him.

You've taught at the school for thirty years, so almost all of Balanchine's present dancers have been your students. Which ones come to mind as being special?
Allegra Kent was a most wonderful student. But she spoil her career. Balanchine like her very much, and so do I. I remember on Christmas she give me a present. I say, "Allegra, there is rule, no presents for teachers." But she run away, saying, "There are no rules for me." Balanchine always ask me to speak with Allegra, because I think he is afraid of her. After her second performance of *Swan Lake* he say, "Felia, go upstairs and tell Allegra it was even better than first time. She doesn't trust me."

When the company went to Russia, Allegra was the biggest success,

Doubrovska in class with Suzanne Farrell, 1961.

even bigger than Maria Tallchief. Allegra pleases audiences. I asked her why she had such fantastic performances in Russia and why she is always off and on in New York. She said, "In Russia I only think about ballet. In New York my heart and mind are at home with my children."

Once Balanchine asked me to teach a special class for Suzanne Farrell and a few gifted girls. He chose one boy from the school, Paul Mejia, to dance with Suzanne. Later, of course, they get married and leave the company.

Gelsey Kirkland was a difficult student, and she hate me because I ask her to leave class if she doesn't listen. She stops in the middle of a step and refuse to continue. But I admire her now.

Balanchine once asked me to watch Merrill Ashley at a rehearsal. He say, "I ask her to do the step faster and faster. She does what nobody else does. I don't know how she goes so fast."

After your husband died in 1970 it must have been very comforting to have your students and to be able to go to the school where you both had taught.
When Pierre died I thought I could not continue alone. And then I think it is for the best, because he could not live without me as his wife. The wife is what is important. I know he flutter around when he is young, but how could I expect a talented man, full of life, to be pure like a kitten? Women are much stronger and can survive more difficulties than men. I once say to Balanchine that I want to retire to finish my days in Monte Carlo. I was lonely. But Mr. B. say, "Everyone in their heart is alone."

You've known Balanchine for a long time. Are you very close?
I think no one really know Mr. Balanchine. He is a mystery. I am com-

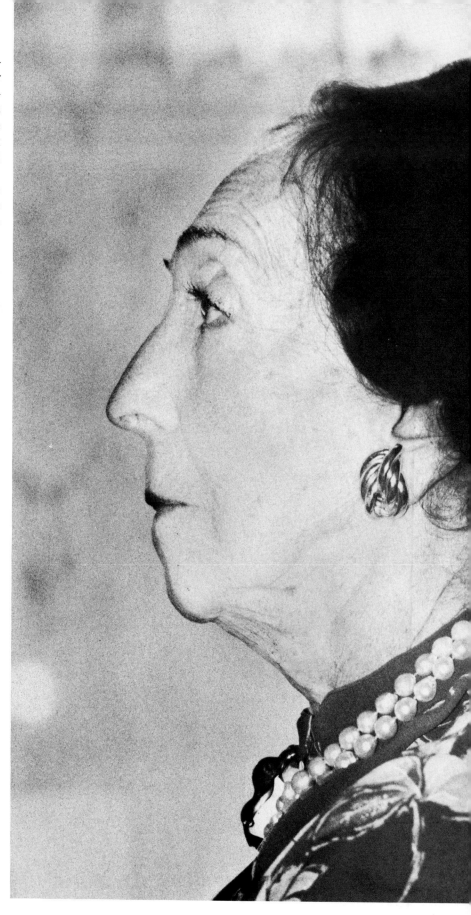

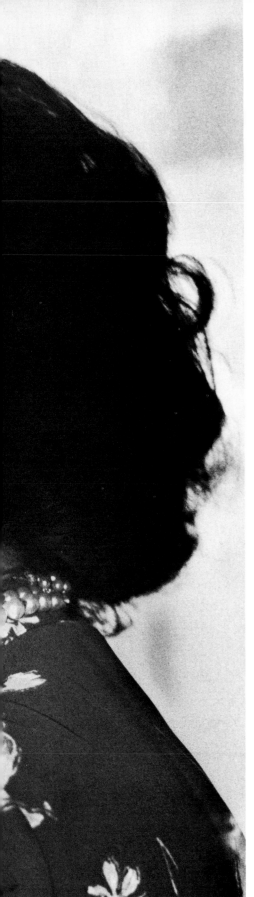

fortable with Balanchine because I never did something wrong to him. He has an elephant's memory if you do something wrong to him. We always spend Easter together, when everybody was supposed to be praying.

Balanchine feels very comfortable with the girls in his company, and they like his conversation. He once say to me, "Our relationship is so nice, the way we can look each other in the eyes. My girlfriends and wives I try to forget." I said I was a little sad that I am never a girlfriend or wife, because maybe then I would be famous.

Ballets in Which Balanchine Created Roles for Felia Doubrovska

ROMEO AND JULIET ENTR'ACTE
music: Constant Lambert
painting: Max Ernst and Joan Miró
role: PAS DE TROIS
premiere: May 4, 1926, Opéra de Monte-Carlo
Ballets Russes de Serge Diaghilev

LA PASTORALE
music: Georges Auric
libretto: Boris Kochno
decor and costumes: Pedro Pruna
role: Film Star
premiere: May 29, 1926, Théâtre Sarah-Bernhardt, Paris
Ballets Russes de Serge Diaghilev

JACK IN THE BOX
music: Erik Satie
decor and costumes: André Derain
role: Dancer (one of two)
premiere: June 8, 1926, Théâtre Sarah-Bernhardt, Paris
Ballets Russes de Serge Diaghilev

APOLLON MUSAGÈTE
music: Igor Stravinsky
decor and costumes: André Bauchant
role: Polyhymnia
premiere: June 12, 1928, Théâtre Sarah-Bernhardt, Paris
Ballets Russes de Serge Diaghilev

THE GODS GO A-BEGGING
music: George Frederick Handel, arranged by Sir Thomas Beecham
libretto: Sobeka (Boris Kochno)
decor: Léon Bakst
role: one of two ladies, with Lubov Tchernicheva
premiere: July 16, 1928, His Majesty's Theatre, London
Ballets Russes de Serge Diaghilev

LE BAL
music: Vittorio Rieti
libretto: Boris Kochno
decor: Giorgio de Chirico
role: SPANISH ENTRANCE
premiere: May 7, 1929, Opéra de Monte-Carlo
Ballets Russes de Serge Diaghilev

PRODIGAL SON
music: Sergei Prokofiev
libretto: Boris Kochno
decor and costumes: Georges Rouault
role: Siren
premiere: May 21, 1929, Théâtre Sarah-Bernhardt, Paris
Ballets Russes de Serge Diaghilev

ORPHÉE AUX ENFERS (operetta)
music: Jacques Offenbach
libretto: Hector Crémieux and Ludovic Halévy
roles: Première Danseuse; Aurora
premiere: December 24, 1931, Théâtre Mogador, Paris
Ballets Russes de Georges Balanchine

DANS L'ÉLYSÉE
music: Jacques Offenbach
role: Solo
premiere: July 3, 1933, Savoy Theatre, London
Ballets Serge Lifar

SERENATA: "MAGIC"
music: Wolfgang Amadeus Mozart
decor and costumes: Pavel Tchelitchev
role: Lady
premiere: February 14, 1936, Avery Memorial Theater, Hartford, Connecticut
American Ballet

I think God at that
moment sent the right
angel when Balanchine
said, "I will take you with
me, and I will do the best
possible."

Tamara
Toumanova

Balanchine saw Tamara Toumanova for the first time in 1931 at the Paris studio of Olga Preobrajenska, the former prima ballerina of the Imperial Ballet who had been one of the judges on the panel that accepted him into the school in Petrograd, when he was ten. Balanchine was now looking for dancers for the first season of the Ballets Russes de Monte-Carlo, and Preobrajenska showed him one of her most promising students—the young Toumanova, a beautiful girl with luminous dark eyes and long black hair. Her parents were impoverished Russian emigrés who had managed to send their precociously talented daughter to ballet classes, and Toumanova had already danced with Pavlova's company at the Trocadéro and as a guest ballerina at the Paris Opéra in *L'Éventail de Jeanne,* a ballet written for the Opéra "rats" by several French composers, including Poulenc, Ravel, Auric, and Milhaud.

Balanchine hired Toumanova immediately. He soon added two other very young girls to the company, Irina Baronova and Tatiana Riabouchinska, and the three of them were promoted by Colonel de Basil as the Baby Ballerinas, a sobriquet under which they became famous in Europe and then in the United States. Toumanova was known as the "Black Pearl of Russian Ballet," daughter of a Georgian princess, born in a boxcar in Siberia during a harrowing flight from the Bolsheviks.

Balanchine made three new ballets for Toumanova that first season: *Le Bourgeois Gentilhomme, La Concurrence,* and *Cotillon.* In all of them she played a vivacious *jeune fille* and astonished audiences with dazzling technical feats, such as the seemingly endless series of fouettés —whipping turns around one stationary, pointed leg—that she produced with no apparent effort. After the company's Paris performances the French critic André Levinson wrote that Toumanova reminded him of the famous Russian ballerina Tamara Karsavina. She had "a certain Oriental languor and that very rare poetic gift which imbues each movement with a flowing elegiac lyricism. But the languid air and sorrowful expression . . . and those great eyes filled with melancholy astonishment, hide a mechanism, a vigor, and a perfection that not one of the 'Imperial' Sylphides of 1909 possessed." Massine used her as the spinning Top in the surrealist nursery created by Joan Miró for *Jeux d'Enfants.*

Toumanova stayed with Balanchine when he broke with de Basil, and she was the de facto star of Les Ballets 1933, the company that represented "youth and new ideas and elegance," as Virgil Thomson noted in his review of the season in which the Balanchine company appeared at the Théâtre des Champs-Élysées while de Basil's Ballets Russes were at the Châtelet with Massine and Danilova and most of the other Russian dancers whom Balanchine had worked with before. Les Ballets 1933 disbanded after a short London season, and Toumanova went back to de Basil. For the next ten years or so she danced with the various Ballet Russe companies in new ballets and in classical roles.

During the 1944–45 season Toumanova was a guest ballerina with Ballet Theatre at the Metropolitan Opera, where Bronislava Nijinska choreographed *Harvest Time* for her. In 1947 Balanchine was invited to be guest ballet master at the Paris Opéra after Lifar was dismissed on charges of collaboration with the Nazis, and he asked Toumanova to dance in the Adagio section of his spectacular production of *Le Palais de Cristal* to Bizet's Symphony in C. Three years later, when Lifar had been reinstated, Toumanova danced the title role in the Lifar-Cocteau production of *Phèdre.*

Toumanova has appeared in several films: *Days of Glory* (1943) with Gregory Peck; *Deep in My Heart* (1953), with José Ferrer and Merle Oberon; *Tonight We Sing* (1953), in which she played Pavlova; *Invitation to the Dance* (1956) with Gene Kelly; Hitchcock's *Torn Curtain* (1966); and Billy Wilder's *The Private Life of Sherlock Holmes* (1970). For ten years in the late forties and early fifties she was married to Casey Robinson, a movie writer and producer. The following interview took place in Toumanova's home in Beverly Hills, where she lives with Madame Eugenia Toumanova, perhaps the most famous ballet mother in dance history.

You were living in Paris in the late twenties. Had you seen Diaghilev's company, and did you know of Balanchine?

TAMARA: In their last season, just a few months before Diaghilev died, they danced at the Théâtre Sarah-Bernhardt. I was invited because my name was very well known in Paris already with *L'Éventail de Jeanne.*
MAMA: She received the headline in fourteen newspapers.
TAMARA: After the performance Tatiana Chamié and another dancer invited me and Mama to come backstage and drink lemonade, and I saw Balanchine, Lifar, Diaghilev, and Tchelitchev. I was so absolutely amazed. There was some sort of incredible power there. I remember how Balanchine stood looking very casual. I knew that he was important, that he was not a person to come and go. I had the feeling then with Diaghilev's company that this will never be the same again. With Pavlova too. When I saw Pavlova's last performance before she went on tour, Mama and I went backstage and I could feel that I would never see her again, and I didn't.

But you did see Balanchine again, two years later when he

arrived in Preobrajenska's class.

TAMARA: When Balanchine came I could feel his electrifying greatness. Preobrajenska asked me to do the most difficult technical movements, and I did everything, and then of course there was my personality. She told Balanchine, who was always the same, quiet and gentle, to ask me about Mozart and then said I should play the piano. So Balanchine asked me, "Do you like the music of Mozart?" I said yes, very much, and so he said, "Could you play it for me?" and I went to sit down to play Mozart for him. He took me right away.

How were you able to afford ballet and music classes? You must not have been able to take much out of Russia when you fled after the revolution.

MAMA: When Tamara went to school I told her she must be the best and outshine everybody else because that way I wouldn't have to pay so much money. It was a very expensive school. Tamara said, "I will try, but this is all new to me."
TAMARA: The dean of my *lycée* absolutely started to adore me because I was such a good girl and a good student. All my books and everything were given to me. I was the chosen one.

Irina Baronova was also at Preobrajenska?

TAMARA: She came after me, but when she did come she already knew the basic positions. Balanchine didn't take her to the Ballets Russes at first, he took her to the Mogador in Paris, where he was staging *Orphée aux Enfers* with Felia Doubrovska.

And then you met Tatiana Riabouchinska in Monte Carlo?

TAMARA: Tania arrived from America. She arrived from the Chauve-Souris with a fur coat, and I said to Mama, "My God, how rich can you be?"

Toumanova with Balanchine at the Paris Opéra, 1947.

Were you friends?

TAMARA: I was friends with those who wanted to be friends.

But you were presented as a sort of team. The Baby Ballerinas.

TAMARA: This Baby Ballerina thing became like a toothache. Basil invented all of that. Of course we were publicized.

Did you get along with the rest of the company? People say that the first season of the de Basil/Blum company was a mess of intrigue.

TAMARA: I remember that one time when Balanchine was away from Monte Carlo the regisseur, Grigoriev, was rehearsing me in *Concurrence* and made me do fouettés until I collapsed.

MAMA: Grigoriev said, "Once more, once more, once more, once more."

TAMARA: And then I just went and lost consciousness.

MAMA: I didn't complain. Balanchine came and I didn't tell him. He said, "Madame Toumanova, how did the rehearsal go?" I said all right. He said, "Did something happen to Tamara?" I said I didn't know.

TAMARA: Mama didn't say anything because she didn't want to overuse Balanchine's powers.

MAMA: So Balanchine said, "She lost consciousness?" He was so angry with Grigoriev.

What were the ballets like that Balanchine created for you?

TAMARA: First Balanchine did *Cotillon* for my dramatic personality. It was a challenge for me because I

Toumanova rehearsing for La Concurrence, *1932.*

loved drama and I loved technical things but I didn't like to think about those things on stage. I don't think technique is good if you are showing how difficult it is. Technique is the greatest mastery when you do it . . .

MAMA: Like nothing.

TAMARA: *Cotillon* was about a girl's first coming-out ball. It was a symbolic thing for me.

MAMA: Balanchine is a genius.

TAMARA: Whenever Balanchine showed me a movement I picked it up so fast. I had very good coordination, and I could easily catch the subtleties of Balanchine. I think this fascinated him. In *La Concurrence* I was in a long blue Derain dress, and Balanchine had me do something very simple—descending off my pointes to sleep—and it was a sensation. I went to sleep in my own dream.

Le Bourgeois Gentilhomme had a very beautiful pas de deux, and it was very sad to Strauss's music. I entered with my long hair down, and I was crying because I was getting married to the Moor. Benois did the scenery and costumes, which they said were burned, but there were many intrigues.

I was only thinking to get ahead to do my ballets. I didn't even know if there was an audience or not. As far as I was concerned even if there was one mouse in the theater that was important. Complete devotion and forgetting about everything else—this is what is lacking today.

But you had Balanchine to protect you then, and help you.

TAMARA: Yes. After the Paris season Balanchine arranged for Mama, Papa, and me to go to Monte Carlo for our holiday. We went to the beach, and the club, and the swimming pool, and Balanchine gave me classes every day.

MAMA: Private classes.

TAMARA: Balanchine rented a large

Toumanova (center) in Balustrade *with the Original Ballet Russe, New York, 1941.*

space where they stored things from the opera, took it over, did the floor, brought the piano, and every day I had a class and he played the piano. MAMA: And I was writing down everything Balanchine said, every position. I believed Balanchine one hundred percent.

TAMARA: My bag with many of my very precious things was stolen just before the war in London. One of my most beloved presents was Balanchine's watch which he gave me when I became twelve years old.

What happened when Massine was called in to replace Balanchine?

TAMARA: I went with Balanchine. Whatever happens in life, sometimes you miss a bus, you miss your car, your limousine, your train and

the whole fate of your life changes in that moment. I think God at that moment sent the right angel when Balanchine said, "I will take you with me, and I will do the best possible."

When he formed Les Ballets 1933 it came at the right time. It was the sophistication of Paris: the elegance of the best elite of *la société française, l'elégance du théâtre, du grand monde.* It suddenly erupted like a volcano of art. Derain, Bérard, Milhaud, Tchelitchev, Kochno, Weill, Lotte Lenya. It was not to be believed. It was musically, theatrically, the most superb production. Who's who in Paris was at the Théâtre des Champs-Élysées. And I was so involved with my work that I didn't realize what was going on. Of course, if I had seen the same audience later

I probably would have been very interested in who's who. At the time it didn't matter.

That was when he made *Mozartiana* for you.

TAMARA: *Mozartiana* was breathtaking. Bérard did fabulous costumes. Balanchine also made *Les Songes,* which ended up being a lot of technical things. The story was about a young girl who was in a dream which was becoming a nightmare. I preferred *Mozartiana* because it was more pure for me.

Tilly Losch was supposed to be the star of Les Ballets 1933. What was she like?

TAMARA: She was so kind to me. She was not from our school of ballet. She was an actress, mime—more

Toumanova in the early forties.
*BELOW—With Balanchine in Monte
Carlo, 1932.*

plastic in movements. Of course, Balanchine did wonders with her. The way Balanchine worked on her and Lotte Lenya in *Seven Deadly Sins* was incredible. I never saw a remake of that ballet, but our production was beautiful.

Balanchine made *Errante* for Losch then, and later Tamara Geva and Vera Zorina danced in it. Were they like her?

TAMARA: Tilly Losch had warmth and softness as an artist. Zorina had a figure and looked so extraordinary when she entered in *I Married an Angel,* but I didn't see either her or Geva in *Errante.*

In 1933 Lincoln Kirstein wrote in his diary: "Balanchine's in love with Tamara Toumanova; her mother thinks she is too young to marry; besides, Balanchine will not live long."

TAMARA: That's Lincoln Kirstein's nonsense. I worshiped Balanchine like I do now. I never called him George, never up to today. I called him Georgi Melitonovich. He was a musician, a poet. Balanchine is to me and Mama the closest person we have.

MAMA: I believe every word he tells.

TAMARA: I remember in 1944 when I got married in a Russian Orthodox church, with the crowns and veils and with our candles walking around the altar, that after the ceremony suddenly Balanchine appeared. I said to him, "I can't tell you how happy I am that you came." He answered, "How can I not be at the wedding of my child? I flew in especially to be at your wedding." It is my most beautiful memory.

What caused the split between you and Balanchine when he went off to work in America in

1934? You didn't work with Balanchine for almost eight years.

TAMARA: Basil. He caught me off guard.

MAMA: He lied.

TAMARA: He lied to me. Basil had a contract to take the Ballets Russes to America, but Hurok insisted that he would not take the company unless I was in it. I was with my parents in Paris when Basil called and said to us that he had "good news," that Balanchine had signed a contract with him and that I should do the same and go to London, where Balanchine would be. So I went to London, and when I arrived I found that Balanchine was not coming. Basil was so clever. He split us up.

But you worked with Balanchine again, in New York and Paris.

TAMARA: Balanchine made *Balustrade* for me in 1941, with the Original Ballet Russe. This was a sensation.

MAMA: Breathtaking.

TAMARA: Whenever I did a movement the audience went, "Ah," "Oh," "Ah." It was very shocking, especially when Balanchine had a man slide between me and my partner to break us up. It was so modern. Then I was invited to dance at the Paris Opéra in 1947 as a guest star, and Balanchine did those magnificent ballets for me, *Le Palais de Cristal* and a recreation of *Le Baiser de la Fée.* To me it was Paris, April, and *Baiser de la Fée.* Balanchine changed the ending for me. When the boy was taken away from me the curtain came down like a net, and in front of the curtain I saw an ocean which was swallowing me. I could hear sounds, and I would think I saw him and I would go on balance, and a wave would take me away.

MAMA: *Palais de Cristal* was full of mystique.

TAMARA: I danced the Adagio. Sometimes, when you close your eyes and you think you are in another world, where you can hear the music of Chopin from far away, you imagine yourself to be on a cloud. This was *Palais de Cristal.* The movements Balanchine made and the slow renversé at the end used to cause a silence and then suddenly a burst of applause and screams. It was the last time I worked with Balanchine.

Do you see him very often now?

TAMARA: We live very far apart, Hollywood and New York. When his company comes to Los Angeles of course we see each other and go backstage. One time he called to someone and said, "You know, this is the mother of Miss Toumanova. She's the one who used to wear Tamara's new ballet shoes to break them in." I had forgotten all about that.

I'm sorry I can't be with him more, because every moment with Balanchine is a gift. He's the most dignified person I've ever worked with. He never screams, never argues, but he always gets what he wants. Because he's right. And he is an admirer of many great things. He never wanted me to dance just his works but also to do *Giselle, Petrouchka, Swan Lake, Les Sylphides.* There was no feeling that he would crush me to him. Once I remember I did a ballet by Bronislava Nijinska with Ballet Theatre—*Harvest Time.* Very difficult. And when Balanchine came backstage afterward he said, "Tamara, you are like Heifetz on the violin with your feet." And it wasn't even his ballet!

MAMA: Thank God we met Balanchine.

TAMARA: He is my good luck.

Ballets in Which Balanchine Created Roles for Tamara Toumanova

COTILLON
music: Emmanuel Chabrier
libretto: Boris Kochno
decor and costumes: Christian Bérard
role: Young Girl
premiere: April 12, 1932, Opéra de Monte-Carlo
Ballets Russes de Monte-Carlo

LA CONCURRENCE
music: Georges Auric
libretto and book: André Derain
curtain, decor, costumes: André Derain
role: The Girl
premiere: April 12, 1932, Opéra de Monte-Carlo
Ballets Russes de Monte-Carlo

LE BOURGEOIS GENTILHOMME
music: Richard Strauss
decor and costumes: Alexandre Benois
role: Lucille
premiere: May 3, 1932, Opéra de Monte-Carlo
Ballets Russes de Monte-Carlo

SUITES DE DANSE
music: Mikhail Glinka
role: VALSE
premiere: May 5, 1932, Opéra de Monte-Carlo
Ballets Russes de Monte-Carlo

MOZARTIANA
music: Peter Ilyich Tchaikovsky
decor and costumes: Christian Bérard
role: Ballerina
premiere: June 7, 1933, Théâtre des Champs-Élysées, Paris
Les Ballets 1933

LES SONGES
music: Darius Milhaud
libretto: André Derain
decor and costumes: André Derain
role: Ballerina
premiere: June 7, 1933, Théâtre des Champs-Élysées, Paris
Les Ballets 1933

FASTES
music: Henri Sauget
book: André Derain
decor and costumes: André Derain
role: Young Girl
premiere: June 10, 1933, Théâtre des Champs-Élysées, Paris
Les Ballets 1933

BALUSTRADE
music: Igor Stravinsky
decor and costumes: Pavel Tchelitchev
role: THIRD AND FOURTH MOVEMENTS
premiere: January 22, 1941, Fifty-first Street Theatre, New York
Original Ballet Russe

LE PALAIS DE CRISTAL
music: Georges Bizet
decor and costumes: Léonor Fini
role: ADAGIO
premiere: July 28, 1947, Paris Opéra
Ballet de l'Opéra

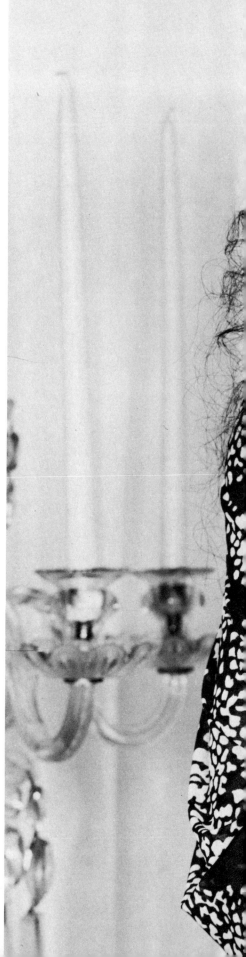

2. 1934-1948

America—
A School,
a Company

Balanchine and Edward M. M. Warburg, patron of the American Ballet, in the thirties.

Balanchine arrived in America in the fall of 1933 with Vladimir Dimitriev, who had organized the trip out of the Soviet Union in 1924 and who was now Balanchine's manager. They came with a promise from Lincoln Kirstein that they would be given a school and a company, or passage back to Paris if things fell through. Kirstein was obsessed with transplanting ballet to America and had fixed on Balanchine as the architect of his project. He had the financial backing of his friend Edward M. M. Warburg. Another friend, A. Everett Austin, had promised the use of a theater and classroom space in the new wing of the museum of which he was director, the Morgan Memorial in Hartford, Connecticut.

Kirstein's elaborate plans were nearly smashed when Balanchine and Dimitriev refused to settle in provincial Hartford. But they didn't want to go back to Europe either, and the initial crisis passed when Kirstein found space in a loft building on Fifty-ninth Street and Madison Avenue in New York, where Isadora Duncan had once had her studio. The School of American Ballet opened there on January 2, 1934. During the following years of fluctuating fortunes for both Balanchine and Kirstein, while ballet companies were formed and disbanded, projects taken on and abandoned for lack of funds, SAB continued to train dancers and provide material for the American ballet Kirstein had envisioned. Dimitriev was the director of the school until 1940, when Kirstein bought him out and assumed the title. Balanchine was on the faculty, along with Pierre Vladimiroff, who had been premier danseur at the Maryinsky Theater and then Pavlova's partner, and who was married to Felia Doubrovska. Many of the first students came from Catherine Littlefield's ballet school in Philadelphia, and Littlefield's sister Dorothy became Balanchine's assistant.

Within a few months of the opening of the school Balanchine began making a ballet, using whatever students happened to be in class. The result was *Serenade,* to Tchaikovsky's Serenade in C for strings, which, fifty years after it was first performed at a "demonstration" on the Warburg estate, is still in the repertory of the New York City Ballet. A year later a professional company was established, the American Ballet, which gave a two-week New York season at the Adelphi Theatre. There were twenty-seven dancers in the company, all of whom were students at SAB, and two guest stars for the Adelphi performances—Tamara Geva and Paul Haakon, a young protégé of Mikhail Fokine.

The opening-night audience in New York was sophisticated, knowing, enthusiastic. Subsequent audiences, and the press, were less appreciative. They were accustomed to the theatricality of the Russian ballet and didn't know what to make of Balanchine. John Martin of *The New York Times* thought most of his ballets were "evidence of the decadence of the classic tradition as it is found in certain European environments, examples of what someone has aptly called 'Riviera aesthetics.' While every region is entitled to whatever decadences it pleases, there is nothing to be gained from our importing them." Until the early fifties this was to be the attitude of the most influential dance critic in America.

In the fall of 1935 the new manager of the Metropolitan Opera, Edward Johnson, invited the American Ballet to become the opera's resident company. Balanchine would provide opera ballets, and his company could also present its own repertory. At first this seemed like a wonderful arrangement. Balanchine turned out opera ballets easily (they had been his first assignments from Diaghilev in Monte Carlo), and the dancers would have steady work. John Martin, of course, regretted that "once again American artists have been passed by for a high artistic post," and suggested in print that Kirstein use the occasion to jettison Balanchine and concentrate on the ballet school.

In fact Balanchine's association with the Metropolitan Opera was never a happy one. Although the general audiences seemed to like Balanchine's work, music critics and the management did not. Most of what he did was for the standard opera repertory—the Bacchanal in *Tannhäuser,* the Divertissement in *Carmen,* the Market Scene in *Faust*—with a few nights scheduled for ballet alone. In the spring of 1936 Balanchine was permitted his own staging of Gluck's *Orpheus and Eurydice,* with sets and costumes by Pavel Tchelitchev. The singers were in the orchestra pit, and on stage dancers in gray body paint and chiffon moved sensuously through a set made of chicken wire and dead branches. The Hell of Act II was a concentration camp; Heaven was a planetarium. The production was not well received and was given only twice.

The following year the American Ballet produced a Stravinsky Festival at the Metropolitan, although the opera company was not a sponsor. Edward Warburg was the principal backer. A new piece was commissioned from Stravinsky, *Card Party,* and the company also performed *Apollon Musagète* and *Le Baiser de la Fée,* with new choreography by Balanchine. Stravinsky conducted. The festival attracted a ballet audience rather than an opera audience and was well liked, even by the press, but this success did not induce the Metropolitan to give dance a larger role in its operations. Early in 1938 Balanchine had a final, public falling out with the management. "The tradition of the ballet at the Metropolitan is bad ballet," he told the newspapers. "My dances the critics and dowagers did not like. They were too good. So I think. What shall I do? I will try something worse, maybe they will like it." The American Ballet disbanded.

For some time Balanchine had not had to rely on the ballet company for work, since he had a very busy career as a musical-comedy choreographer. In 1936 he had been asked to do the dances for *On Your Toes,* which had music and lyrics by Richard Rodgers and Lorenz Hart and starred Ray Bolger and Tamara Geva. Balanchine's work transformed American musicals. The dances he made were integral to the plot rather than simply interpolated numbers, and his corps could really dance, not just do high kicks. "Slaughter on Tenth Avenue," in the last act of *On Your Toes,* became a classic, and Balanchine was much in demand to work in other shows. Soon after the 1938 Stravinsky Festival he left for Hollywood to do the choreography for *The Goldwyn Follies,* taking several American Ballet dancers with him. For the ballerina part Goldwyn hired Vera Zorina, who had been dancing the Geva role in the London production of *On Your Toes,* and Balanchine made for her the now famous water-nymph ballet, in which she enters from the center of a pool, completely dry. The following spring Zorina starred on Broadway in *I Married an Angel,* with choreography by Balanchine. That Christmas they were married. The marriage was by nearly all accounts an unhappy one for Balanchine. They were frequently separated, and Balan-

The Stravinsky Festival at the Metropolitan Opera, April 1937. TOP *—Gisella Caccialanza and William Dollar taking a curtain call with Stravinsky, who has just conducted* Le Baiser de la Fée. BOTTOM*— Balanchine and Lincoln Kirstein.*

chine spent several years in an apparent agony of unrequited love. His professional life was more successful, at least for a time.

When *I Married an Angel* opened, John Martin had written, "George Balanchine has clinched his right to the title of the first choreographer of Broadway." He implied that Balanchine should stick to musicals and not fall into the trap of those "superb comedians who want to play Hamlet." But Broadway shows and films were not Balanchine's primary interest. They simply supported him, handsomely at times, when he had no opportunities to stage ballets. And during the late thirties he had no other invitations. When Lucia Chase formed Ballet Theatre in 1939 Balanchine was practically the only choreographer in America not asked to contribute work.

Kirstein meanwhile had been occupying himself with Ballet Caravan, a small "chamber" ballet company that toured outside New York—appearing mainly in gymnasiums and movie houses. The company presented ballets on American subjects—*Billy the Kid, Filling Station, Pocahontas.* In the summer of 1940 it appeared at the Ford Pavilion of the New York World's Fair in *A Thousand Times Neigh!*—a ballet about horses and automobiles, choreographed by William Dollar, which went on twelve times a day, on the hour. Ballet Caravan more or less dissolved after this engagement, but the following year some of the group's dancers were teamed with others from the defunct American Ballet for an ambitious South American tour led by Kirstein, with Balanchine as the artistic director.

American Ballet Caravan was the offspring of Nelson Rockefeller, another friend of Kirstein's, who had been appointed by President Roosevelt to head a State Department agency devoted to fostering goodwill between North and South America. He promised Kirstein that the State Department would underwrite the company's deficits, which turned out to be rather large, since American Ballet Caravan was more successful with the critics than at the box office. The summer before the Ballet Russe de Monte Carlo had mounted a very glamorous, star-studded South American tour, and American Ballet Caravan seemed by contrast too avant-garde and not entertaining enough. South American intellectuals attended, but the company didn't incite popular support. Balanchine made two new ballets for the tour: *Ballet Imperial,* to Tchaikovsky's Second Piano Concerto, and *Concerto Barocco,* to Bach's Double Violin Concerto. They were his first "pure dance" ballets, with no suggestion of a story. Marie-Jeanne, the first important ballerina to emerge from the School of American Ballet, starred in both of them.

At the end of the South American tour the American Ballet repertory was offered to Ballet Theatre, and was refused. Balanchine's works in the repertory at that time included *Ballet Imperial, Concerto Barocco, Le Baiser de la Fée, Card Party, Apollon Musagète, Errante, Mozartiana,* and *Serenade.* Most of them were subsequently taken over by the Ballet Russe de Monte Carlo, which then included many young dancers trained by Balanchine. Balanchine became the Ballet Russe's resident choreographer for several seasons. He had gone to California in the summer of 1944 to stage the operetta *Song of Norway,* for which the entire Ballet Russe, including Alexandra Danilova and Frederic Franklin, was engaged. The show was a hit, with a long run on Broadway, where a second cast took over when the Ballet Russe dancers had to start their regular season, and Balanchine was asked to stay with the company and make new ballets as well as restage old ones.

Balanchine's association with the Ballet Russe de Monte Carlo brought new life to a company that had deteriorated badly in the two years since the

Vera Zorina and Charles Laskey in I Married an Angel, *1938.*

departure of Léonide Massine for Ballet Theatre. His first season opened on September 10, 1944, with a new work, *Danses Concertantes,* which Edwin Denby called "as beautiful and elusive as the play of bright birds in a garden," although other critics found Stravinsky's score too difficult. Balanchine also revived *Le Bourgeois Gentilhomme,* originally done for Tamara Toumanova in 1932, and *Ballet Imperial,* danced now by Mary Ellen Moylan, who became permanently associated with the part. The following spring Balanchine restaged *Mozartiana,* also originally done for Toumanova, and created a pas de deux to the *Sleeping Beauty* entr'acte for Danilova and Franklin. In the fall the company performed *Concerto Barocco* for the first time, with Marie-Jeanne returning to the role she originated in South America. Eugene Berman had withdrawn his decor for the ballet, so it was performed in black tunics against a plain backcloth, which even the usually enthusiastic Denby found disconcerting.

In the spring of 1946 *Le Baiser de la Fée* was revived, with Stravinsky conducting the opening night and Maria Tallchief dancing the role of the Fairy. *Le Baiser de la Fée* is a sinister tale that ends with the Bridegroom being drawn to a cold fate by the relentless Fairy. A few days after it was

Balanchine rehearsing with Gisella Caccialanza and Daphne Vane in the late thirties.

The Goldwyn Follies *corps girls, 1938.*

first performed by the Ballet Russe, Balanchine premiered another ballet also in the neo-Romantic vein, *Night Shadow* (now *La Sonnambula*), in which a poet falls under the spell of a mysterious, beautiful sleepwalker, is killed by her jealous husband, and then is carried off by the sleepwalker herself. It reminded Denby of Edgar Allen Poe, and, as he pointed out, was completely different in form and sentiment from the other premiere of the season, the reconstruction by Balanchine and Danilova of Petipa's three-act *Raymonda*, which was the longest, grandest ballet most New Yorkers had ever seen.

Balanchine and Maria Tallchief were married in the fall of 1946 (he and Zorina had finally gotten a divorce earlier in the year), and Balanchine left the Ballet Russe to join Lincoln Kirstein's new project, Ballet Society, an organization with a private subscription audience. Subscribers were promised theater pieces, dance performances, operas, dance books and articles, dance films, record albums, and the chance to sponsor young dancers and choreographers. According to Kirstein, the eight hundred people who subscribed the first year got everything except the record albums. Mostly they got ballet, including *The Seasons*, Merce Cunningham's first work, but also Gian Carlo Menotti's opera *The Medium*, and some Javanese dancing. Balanchine produced two new works, first performed on November 20, 1946, in the auditorium of the Central High School of Needle Trades on West Twenty-fourth Street: Ravel's *L'Enfant et les Sortilèges* and *The Four Temperaments*. *The Four Temperaments*, which has turned out to be, arguably, Balanchine's greatest ballet, was set to music by Hindemith that Balanchine had commissioned in the late thirties with money saved from his Broadway and Hollywood projects. It was presented at first with costumes by Kurt Seligmann. They have been described most succinctly by Kirstein as "cerements, bandages, tubes, wraps, and tourniquets" and were discarded after a few seasons.

Stravinsky in rehearsal with Elise Reiman, Balanchine, and Lincoln Kirstein, 1937.

Late in February the following year Balanchine sailed for Paris, where he had been asked to stage several works for the Opéra. Serge Lifar, director of the Opéra since 1929, was temporarily suspended on charges of collaboration with the Nazis, and the company needed a choreographer. Balanchine revived *Serenade, Le Baiser de la Fée,* and *Apollon Musagète,* and created a new ballet to music by a French composer—Georges Bizet's Symphony in C Major. Balanchine called the piece *Le Palais de Cristal* and made of it everything that he couldn't make in the cramped and drab auditoriums he was forced to work in at home. He used fifty dancers, with a set full of balconies, a staircase, and hanging crystal. Each of the four movements was designed in a different color, so that the costumes in the finale produced a rainbow effect. Tamara Toumanova, the glamorous "Black Pearl of Russian Ballet," danced the Second Movement Adagio, one of Balanchine's most romantic creations.

In August, Balanchine and Tallchief, who had danced Terpsichore in *Apollon* and the Fairy in *Le Baiser de la Fée,* returned to America. Balanchine began work with Stravinsky on *Orpheus,* which had been commissioned by Ballet Society and which premiered the following April, with Tallchief as Eurydice and Tanaquil Le Clercq as the Leader of the Bacchantes. On the same program was another Balanchine ballet made that season, *Symphonie Concertante,* to Mozart, in which Tallchief danced to the viola solo and Le Clercq to the violin. A scaled-down version of the Bizet work for the Opéra, now called *Symphony in C,* with Tallchief in the First Movement and Le Clercq in the Adagio, had been given a few weeks before. These three ballets made a big impression on many people, including Morton Baum, the chairman of the finance committee of New York City Center, from which Ballet Society had rented the old Mecca Temple on West Fifty-fifth Street for four performances. City Center sponsored a theater group and the New York City Opera, and Baum decided he also wanted Ballet Society as a resident company. Kirstein and Balanchine were offered a permanent home, and the company took a new name: the New York City Ballet. It was a company that in only five years would be called by Edwin Denby "both in style and repertory, more sound, more original, more beautiful than any you can see anywhere in the Western world."

Balanchine rehearsing Vera Zorina.

Zorina in the Water Nymph Ballet in Goldwyn Follies.

> I think I'm the only
> woman who has
> choreographed for his
> company.

Ruthanna Boris

Ruthanna Boris was one of the twenty-five girls admitted to the School of American Ballet when it opened in 1934. She was in class the day Balanchine started to choreograph *Serenade,* the first ballet he made in America, and she performed in most of Balanchine's early pieces.

Boris was born in Brooklyn and grew up in Oceanside, Queens. Before she came to Balanchine she had been trained at the Metropolitan Opera ballet school. She was a principal in the American Ballet when it was the Metropolitan's resident company, and after Balanchine had a falling out with the opera management in 1938 Boris returned to the Met as prima ballerina. She was also a charter member of Lincoln Kirstein's Ballet Caravan and during its

first season played the lead in Lew Christensen's modernist ballet *Pocahontas,* to music by Elliot Carter.

In 1943 Boris joined Sergei Denham's Ballet Russe de Monte Carlo. She was the first American ballerina to become a star in that company, and her partnership with Leon Danielian became almost as famous as that of Danilova and Frederic Franklin. Her repertory included a full range of classical parts—Odette, Swanilda, the Sugar Plum Fairy, the Black Swan, Giselle—as well as leading roles in modern works like Ruth Page's *Frankie and Johnny* and in Balanchine's ballets. In one of his *New York Times* Sunday dance columns in the late forties, John Martin remarked on Boris's versatility: "No role to her is merely a vehicle for the display of her talents; her talents

rather become the vehicle for publishing the role's intent. . . . It would be difficult to name another dancer who has so clear a sense of these stylistic differences."

Boris choreographed her first work for the Ballet Russe in 1947—*Cirque de Deux,* to the Walpurgis Night music from Gounod's *Faust,* in which the elements of the classic pas de deux were treated as though they were circus acts. The following year she put together another humorous piece, *Quelques Fleurs.* When she left the Ballet Russe Boris created a work for the New York City Ballet—*Cakewalk,* to Hershy Kay's orchestration of short pieces by Louis Moreau Gottschalk, the nineteenth-century American composer who used Creole and folk tunes in his music. A sort of minstrel show in ballet language, *Cakewalk* was popular with audiences and critics, especially during the company's London season in 1952. Boris made two more short ballets for NYCB. She is the only woman to have created pieces for Balanchine's company. (Martha Graham's section of *Episodes* in 1959 was danced primarily by members of her own group.)

During the fifties Boris appeared in concert performances with her husband, Frank Hobi, and danced with the Royal Winnipeg Ballet. Her career as a dancer ended with the onset of degenerative arthritis. Boris has staged works for the Joffrey Ballet, the Eglevsky Ballet, and the Royal Winnipeg Ballet. Since 1965 she has been a professor of drama and director of dance at the University of Washington in Seattle. She is also a dance therapist.

You said to me that you met Balanchine practically the day he got off the boat in America. How had you heard of him?
When Colonel de Basil's Ballets Russes came to New York in 1933

they did two ballets by G. Balanchine—*Cotillon* and *Concurrence.* It was the first time I had seen Balanchine's name, and I remember thinking how different his ballets were from the other ones. It was also the first time I had seen the Russian dancers—Toumanova, Riabouchinska, Baronova, Alexandra Danilova.

Toumanova made a real impression on me. In fact, a lot of girls started imitating her then. She was especially important to me because basically we're alike—not exactly, because I'm Jewish and she's not, but my father's Georgian. I started holding my head the way she did and wearing my hair like hers, and finally Balanchine came along—later, when I was taking classes from him—and said, "You know, your name is Ruthanna Boris and not Tamara Toumanova, and I wish you would pick up your head because that is one habit I could never make Tamara change. It's not good for your dancing."

But you were studying ballet before Balanchine arrived.

Yes, at the Metropolitan Opera school, for several years. My mother had written John Martin at *The New York Times* asking him what she should do with her insane child who wanted to dance, and he advised her on the alternatives—vaudeville schools, the classical ballet academy taught by Italians at the Metropolitan, and Martha Graham's modern-dance classes. She went to look at them and hated the vaudeville school. No high hats and sequins for her daughter. Martha Graham scared her to death. She didn't know what all those girls were doing on the floor with their crotches open. But she loved the Opera, so I went—three lessons a week for fifteen dollars a month. They took you for a year, and if you were promising you got a scholarship.

Then one Sunday I was reading John Martin's dance column in the *Times* and I saw a notice that Mr. Lincoln Kirstein, the editor of a magazine called *Hound and Horn,* and Mr. Edward Warburg were founding a school and a company and were bringing in Mr. George Balanchine as the artistic director. I went for an audition wearing what we wore at the Metropolitan—pink dresses below the knees, pink tights, pink ballet shoes, and little bows tied so our brassiere straps wouldn't show. In a room at the school on Fifty-ninth and Madison there were two men. One looked Chinese. That was Balanchine. He was young and handsome. Gorgeous. The other man was very austere—Pierre Vladimiroff. He had no English and he gave me my barre. When Vladimiroff sat down, Balanchine started giving me things that flew. I had elevation like a flea. Not much extension at first, but I could jump like a flea. Balanchine said, "You are Italian. Italiansky." His English was charming. Then he said, "Do a double pirouette." But we weren't allowed to do that at the Met, and I told him I could only do single turns. "No," he said, "you will do it. You will see." So I tried and he spanked me and I went around twice and fell down. I looked at him and I knew that this guy was making jokes. And I loved it. I wanted to be taken in. He looked down at me and said, "You remind me of little girls when I was a little boy. So old-fashioned." The other kids were coming to the audition in bathing suits. "You are like from the past. So chubby. I would like to bite your knees. To take a bite out of your knees." He was so adorable.

Did you have a crush on him?

Everybody is in love with Balanchine in a way, because he teaches and works with love. But I'm afraid I don't look at Balanchine the way a woman looks at a man. I look at him

more as an inevitable force—like I would look at lightning, at Niagara Falls, at Mount St. Helens, at cosmic events. I had childhood fantasies about Balanchine—that he would fall in love with me and marry me. But I never expected it to happen. I know kids who used to sit on his doorstep to be there when he got home at night. But I never had the courage to do that. I remember once standing on a street corner waiting for the crosstown bus at Sixty-sixth Street and Balanchine went by in an open car with Holly Howard. Holly was his first love in America. She was the Suzanne Farrell of her day. They didn't see me, but I saw them in the car, and I remember the feeling like it was yesterday. I thought I was going to faint. I would have given anything to be Holly and sit in that car. It was envy of the highest order, and it felt like death to me. Then they drove away. My bus came and I got on and went home.

That was when you were in the American Ballet? Balanchine's first company?

Yes. That whole group of us came from a time so different from the situation kids are in now. We were like the covered wagon of Balanchine's empire. We weren't as technically proficient as kids today. I think Elise Reiman, Gisella Caccialanza, and I were possibly closest to what Balanchine wanted professionally. He wanted speed, precision, legs, feet. And no sentimentality. He can't stand the Russian thing. He said, "Be a cold angel."

Then, in American Ballet Caravan, Marie-Jeanne started getting everything. She was the chosen one, and I was very upset. Balanchine was in love with her legs. Marie-Jeanne scared me to death. When I would get in the elevator at the school and Marie-Jeanne got in at the same time I was petrified. A very cute young Irish guy ran the elevator, and suddenly the lights would go out and there would be giggling. I was a timid little virgin, but I used to wish that I could be like Marie-Jeanne. Everything pointed to the fact that she got parts and I didn't get parts. I came second.

I complained to my mother about this, and she said to me, "I want you to go to Mr. Balanchine and tell him you want to be equal to Marie-Jeanne. That you are as good a dancer and you want solos." So I went to Mr. Balanchine and said those things, and then I started to cry. Balanchine said, "Don't cry, and don't tell me what your mother wants. And don't ask me for solos. Do you know how to make a Caesar salad?" And I said no. So he took my hand and sat me down and it took about a half an hour for him to tell me how to make that salad. "First you go to the market and buy the freshest lettuce, and anchovies . . ." and so forth. Then when he was through he said, "You see how long it takes and how much you have to know and how you have to work to make a Caesar salad? Now go away." He speaks in parables. It's very far out.

Did what he said make you feel better? Because you did work with him again.

We've always been good friends. When he went to work in Hollywood and on Broadway I went to the Ballet Russe, so when he came to do *Song of Norway* and then stayed with the company we were together again. It was great. I remember when he was traveling with us we were in Houston once for Christmas. Krassovska, Danilova, and I shared a suite, and Balanchine was supposed to stay with Mr. Denham, but he hated it, so he asked us if he could be our ghost, and he was sleeping in our little room. Later he took a room in the Rice Hotel, but for days he was there with us like a little gremlin. We were

going to give a Christmas party, but we couldn't get any Christmas-tree ornaments. It was during the war. And Balanchine was making the most delightful things with tangerine skins, cotton, singing and carrying on like one of the Seven Dwarfs. He wasn't fussing around with anybody. At the party everybody was saying, "Oh, Mr. B., oh, what lovely ornaments." He was like the king of the pixies.

Balanchine is charming. I love him. I love his cooking. I love to hear him talk. I love to swap stories with him. During the war we had a whole routine going. I write jingles sometimes, and one day we were sitting in the Russian Tea Room and he said, "Let us write the Russian Tea Roomba. I'll write the music and we'll make a lot of money for the company." I loved that. We had fun.

But what about your professional relationship?

Professionally it was harder. I hurt Balanchine without meaning to—by not going into his company when he asked me. It was 1949 and I was married to Frank Hobi then, a very gifted man and a beautiful dancer. He and Balanchine got along like brothers. He adored Balanchine's choreography and wanted to study more at his school. Meanwhile back at the ranch I had been making my career as a classical ballerina, and I finally had a contract to dance *Giselle*. Now, you can imagine what that meant. I had my *Coppélia,* my *Nutcracker,* my *Swan Lake,* and finally I had my *Giselle.* It had taken me a long time to get there.

Anyway, Frank came home ecstatic one day and said, "Balanchine came to me and offered me a full scholarship at his school. And I can work in his little company." I said, "Marvelous." My contract was signed and my salary was secure, so we could pay the rent.

The phone rang the night before I

Ruthanna Boris as Carmen, 1935.

was to leave on tour with the Ballet Russe. It was George. He said, "Will you meet me for breakfast at Rumpelmayer's tomorrow morning?" So I went to Rumpelmayer's and he was there with Maria. He said, "We are making a little company, and Frank will be with us." I said, "I know, it's wonderful." He said, "I want you." I said, "I can't, I've signed with Mr. Denham." And he said, "What is he? Break the contract." Maria leaned over and said, "Ruthanna, we need you." And it was that "we" that kind of got to me. Tallchief and I had been roommates. But I said, "George, after all these years I will have *Giselle.* Let me finish my contract. It goes to August, and when it's over I'll come to you."

So I thought it was all nice. I resigned from the Ballet Russe in August and flew back to New York. I went to a rehearsal at City Center, and during a break I walked up on stage and said, "George, I'm here." I showed him a copy of my resignation letter to Denham. He read it and then he folded it very carefully and handed it back and said, "I don't need you now. I have the Janet Reed and the Melissa Hayden." It was too late.

The next day I went to see Lincoln and said, "Lincoln?" He said, "You hurt him. And he's never going to forgive you. But hang around. Come to class. Let him see you dancing. You're one of his children, and a wonderful dancer. We need you."

I came in. I was in great shape—dancing up a storm. I was really marvelous. After about a month I went to see George again. I said, "George, can you give me a job? I'm a dancer." He took my hand and looked deep into my eyes and said, "If Anna Pavlova would come back from the grave I have no place."

So I went back to Lincoln and he said, "If that's the way it is, that's the way it is. But look, we need a ballet and you're a good choreographer. Do a ballet and give yourself the leading role in it. Balanchine will see you on stage. I don't care what you do, but use costumes, because if we do one more ballet in leotards the critics will kill us."

And that's how I came to do *Cakewalk*. I didn't give myself the leading role in it, because I used the women who had the qualities I needed. I needed some bombast, Patricia Wilde, and Janet Reed was for the Wallflower Waltz. We ran into some trouble because Balanchine thought that Tanny Le Clercq should only do *Swan Lake* and classical things and didn't want her to do funny things because she was funny enough already. But I told him that the variation I made for Tanny was classical, and very difficult. What is funny is the juxtaposition of certain steps on toe. But if he thought she shouldn't do it, I'd replace her. I said to Tanny also, "If you don't like it, tell me." She said, "I love it!" And George came to rehearsal and said, "All right."

Balanchine kept complaining about the Wallflower Waltz. He kept coming up and saying, "Why does she shoot him with an arrow? Why not with a pistol?" I said because I see it with an arrow. The company went to Europe. The French hated *Cakewalk*—particularly the Wallflower Waltz. So Balanchine wrote for permission to cut it, and I refused. I said, "It's an American ballet, and I'm an American choreographer. Just do it in England. If *they* don't like it, do anything you want with it." And of course they loved it.

Was he angry?

George resented that kind of independence. He's never gotten over it. I was talking back to him. And I think I'm the only woman who has choreographed for his company. I did three ballets. After *Cakewalk* there was *Kaleidoscope,* and then *Will o' the Wisp,* which he made Lincoln take out after eight performances. I think the only reason I worked there at all was because of Lincoln. He threw me in to choreograph *Kaleidoscope* in twelve hours. They had very little money. Balanchine hated the music [Dimitri Kabalevsky]. He said, "It's cheap. He's a rotten composer." And I said I wanted that kind of music. It's silly and that's what I want. I said, "George, I don't use music the way you do. Music to me is part of the scenery and air. Someday I will have music playing like a radio playing in a room and something happening in the street where it doesn't have anything to do with the music at all." That sort of thing drives George up the wall. I was doing experimental stuff without music.

So do you think you've moved in a completely different direction?

I learned from him. I could never do what I've done or will do without George Balanchine. But I don't imi-

tate him. One of the reasons I dig Balanchine is that dancing fills a need in my life as it fills a need in his life. I'm happiest when I'm working with dancers who trust me. I can give myself to them. It's nurturing. It's family in the truest sense. Balanchine is one of the few people I've ever known who trusts his own unconscious almost completely and can go with it. He doesn't censor it. The only thing that ever seems to stop him is if something doesn't work. For me Balanchine has been a guide, teacher, inspiration, friend, and sometimes beloved enemy.

Ballets in Which Balanchine Created Roles for Ruthanna Boris

SERENADE
music: Peter Ilyich Tchaikovsky
costumes: Jean Lurçat
decor: Gaston Longchamp
role: one of two front girls
premiere: March 1, 1935, Adelphi Theater, New York

REMINISCENCE
music: Benjamin Godard, orchestrated by Henry Brant
decor and costumes: Sergei Soudeikine
role: TARANTELLA
premiere: March 1, 1935, Adelphi Theater, New York
American Ballet

LA TRAVIATA, BALLET DIVERTISSEMENT
music: Giuseppe Verdi
role: GYPSY DANCE
premiere: December 16, 1935, Metropolitan Opera, New York
American Ballet Ensemble

CARMEN, ACT IV BALLET
music: Georges Bizet
role: GITANE
premiere: December 27, 1935, Metropolitan Opera, New York
American Ballet Ensemble

Serenade, *1935. From left to right, Annabelle Lyon, Ruthanna Boris, Helen Leitch, Holly Howard, and Elise Reiman.*

LA JUIVE, ACT III BALLET PANTOMIME
music: Jacques Halévy
role: The Imp
premiere: January 11?, 1936, Metropolitan Opera, New York
American Ballet Ensemble

THE BARTERED BRIDE, ACT I BALLET
music: Bedřich Smetana
role: POLKA
premiere: May 15, 1936, Metropolitan Opera, New York
American Ballet Ensemble

MÂROUF, ACT II ORIENTAL DANCES
music: Henri Rabaud
premiere: May 21, 1937, Metropolitan Opera, New York
American Ballet Ensemble

SONG OF NORWAY (operetta)
music: Robert Wright and George Forrest adaptation of music by Edvard Grieg
lyrics: Robert Wright and George Forrest
book: Milton Lazarus from a play by Homer Curran based on the life of Grieg
role: IN THE HOLIDAY SPIRIT
premiere: June 12, 1944, Philharmonic Auditorium, Los Angeles
Los Angeles and San Francisco Civic Light Operas

DANSES CONCERTANTES
music: Igor Stravinsky
decor and costumes: Eugene Berman
role: PAS DE TROIS
premiere: September 10, 1944, New York City Center
Ballet Russe de Monte Carlo

LE BOURGEOIS GENTILHOMME
music: Richard Strauss
libretto: after Molière
decor and costumes: Eugene Berman
role: HARLEQUINADE
premiere: September 23, 1944, New York City Center
Ballet Russe de Monte Carlo

NIGHT SHADOW
music: Vittorio Rieti's arrangement of Vincenzo Bellini
costumes and decor: Dorothea Tanning
role: Blackamoor
premiere: February 27, 1946, New York City Center
Ballet Russe de Monte Carlo

RAYMONDA (choreographed with Alexandra Danilova)
music: Alexander Glazunov
scenery and costumes: Alexandre Benois
role: PAS CLASSIQUE HONGROIS
premiere: March 12, 1946, New York City Center
Ballet Russe de Monte Carlo

... if Balanchine said,
"You can do," no matter
what it was you would
try.

Elise
Reiman

Apollon Musagète, the oldest ballet still in Balanchine's repertory and the work that is acknowledged to mark the turning point in the development of his neoclassical style, was in fact first performed with choreography by Adolph Bolm, who had in the early years of Diaghilev's Ballets Russes been the company's premier character dancer. Bolm settled in America, opened a school in Chicago, and used his students in the first *Apollon* production at the Library of Congress in Washington, D.C., on April 27, 1928. The role of Calliope, muse of poetry, was given to a young dancer from Indiana, Elise Reiman.

Nine years later, Balanchine's version of *Apollon* (which had first been produced by the Ballets Russes in June 1928) was presented at the American Ballet's Stravinsky Festival. This time Elise Reiman, now a student at the School of American Ballet and a member of Balanchine's company, danced the part of Terpsichore, muse of the dance. Reiman had joined the company in 1935 and danced in the first production of *Serenade*. When Balanchine went to Hollywood to make *Goldwyn Follies* in 1938 Reiman stayed in New York, where she danced in Broadway shows throughout the early forties. When Balanchine returned to New York to form Ballet Society she joined that company. She was in the first cast of *The Four Temperaments,* dancing the Second Theme with Lew Christensen, and the Fourth Movement of *Symphony in C* was created for her. Reiman was married in 1951 and retired from dancing. After her husband's death in 1963 she joined the faculty of the School of American Ballet, where she still teaches.

What was Balanchine's company like in the very beginning, when it was the American Ballet?

We were like a family. We were all together most of the time, and it was very cozy. Balanchine was surrounded by artists—painters and writers who came to watch rehearsals—so it was very interesting. Mr. B. is a bit antisocial now, but it was fascinating to be on board there when I was. A wonderful time. I was absolutely frightened to death at first because I had studied with Adolph Bolm and was used to a style that wasn't like what Balanchine was doing. They were rehearsing *Serenade* when I got there, and it was different from anything I had ever seen before.

Balanchine had a very good nucleus of dancers from Catherine Littlefield's school in Philadelphia. Holly Howard came from there. She was Balanchine's first American love. And there were some wonderful-looking women—Daphne Vane in particular. She had come from Radio City Music Hall and wasn't very strong technically, but she was very glamorous. In retrospect I think the early women were all potentially good dancers, but they didn't have the kind of training kids have today.

How did you come to Balanchine?

I was going to school in California, and my sister, who was living in New York, wrote me about an article on Balanchine that had appeared in *Vogue* magazine. So I took a look at it, and thought that what was going on seemed very exciting, and my mother encouraged me to come to New York. When I got here I began taking lessons at the School of American Ballet. I remember very vividly the first time Balanchine came to watch class, because I was so embarrassed about what I was wearing. Everyone else had on a leotard, and I was wearing a sort of

Elise Reiman, Charles Laskey, and William Dollar in Transcendence, *1935.*

Greek tunic made of chiffon, and gold sandals. But Balanchine asked me to be in his company anyway, and I began taking private lessons with Mr. Vladimiroff. I don't think Mr. B. was the teacher then that he is now, but his choreography was incredible.

Balanchine was always so in command. He was always pushing people to do more than they could technically. He would say, "You can do." And if Balanchine said, "You can do," no matter what it was you would try. I remember a performance of *Reminiscence* sometime in the thirties when I was in the wings waiting to go on in my part with Holly Howard, the Pas de Trois with Bill Dollar. The floor was like glass. Two people had already

fallen, and a third fell right in front of Balanchine and me. Instead of getting furious, Balanchine leaned his elbow on the wall and said, "They fall like snow." He never got mad.

When the American Ballet company folded you did a few shows on Broadway, and a film with Loretta Young. But you went back to ballet when Balanchine started Ballet Society in 1946. Was it because of him or just because you wanted to be in a serious company?

Everyone wants to work with Balanchine. I've always been absolutely devoted to him. Ballet Society wasn't very popular, though. It was hard to

get an audience then, in spite of the fact that Balanchine was making some wonderful ballets. He created *The Four Temperaments* for the first Ballet Society program, and I danced the Second Theme. I had the most terrible costume, and a wig that was two feet tall, red, standing up in a point. When I saw the sketch I thought, Oh, how lucky I am. This is a divine costume. A white bodice with a chiffon skirt and then a chic red wig. But it turned out that the wig weighed about four tons. I tried to do a finger turn and couldn't even find my partner. But *The Four Temperaments* is a brilliant work.

I also did *Spellbound Child* on that first program, but I had a terrible part. I think I was being punished. I had to come out of a fireplace carrying two long poles with veils on them. They were almost impossible to handle. I was so miserable that I thought I would just get off the stage a little bit earlier than I was supposed to, and I backed into the fireplace. But there was some sort of obstruction there that prevented me from getting out. So I came on stage again for a while and then thought I'd try again, even though it still wasn't the right place in the music for my exit. And again there was something blocking my way. It turned out to be Balanchine's foot. He knew I didn't like the part, so he put his foot there and made me finish the choreography.

But that wasn't a serious thing, was it? Did you get along with him for the most part?

Oh, yes. That was a very happy time in my life. I only regret that the one ballet in which Balanchine created a big part for me, *Transcendence*, wasn't successful. But Balanchine was wonderful to me. I think he likes me. When he was married to Maria Tallchief I saw them all the time. Actually, Balanchine said to me, "I want you to be Maria's friend." She was very shy and very young, and we did become good friends. They had wonderful parties where Balanchine would do all the cooking. Maria and I remained friends, and we've shared all our traumatic experiences. Of course I'm a good deal older than she is, but we just seemed to click. She helped me through a very bad time when my husband was dying in a clinic in Tulsa. She came with me there.

You stopped dancing when you were married. Was it because you felt you couldn't be married and be a dancer too?

I felt that I hadn't made it, and I was disappointed. So when I got married I thought that was enough. Balanchine, of course, wasn't very enthu-

Apollon Musagète, *1937. Elise Reiman as Terpsichore, Lew Christensen as Apollo.*

siastic. I don't think he really believes in people getting married. He thinks there are more interesting things to do. My husband and I lived in Cuba for a year, and then in Colorado. But then he died suddenly, when he was much too young. And I was absolutely undone. I thought I would commit suicide. I just didn't know what to do. So I went to Balanchine and asked if I could teach at his school. Everyone had told me, "That's ridiculous. Leaving Balanchine is like leaving the Church. Once you leave you're out." But he just said, "Yes, you should start to try to teach." And I've taught now for over twenty-five years. I love it.

Do you teach the way he taught you?

Well, I think so, although one day Suki Schorer was passing by my class and heard me tell the children, "You must present your foot." She said that Balanchine doesn't say that anymore. He says now, "You get your heel forward so you could hold a martini on it."

When I started teaching I just wanted to teach children. I guess I was timid about dealing with the older ones. Sometimes I think I made a mistake by not asking to teach the more advanced classes, but it's not possible now. We have so many teachers that there isn't really a place.

I've had a lot of wonderful students. Gelsey Kirkland was eight years old when she started in my class. I don't think we can take credit for Gelsey. She is self-taught. She was a very difficult child who resisted, but she has an enormous talent and a wonderful body. Then I taught Darci Kistler. She has Balanchine's "You can do" approach. Maybe she could do something and maybe she couldn't, but she would try, no matter how tricky it was.

You've had a very long professional relationship with Balanchine. Are you close personally?

We were once. Years ago, when he was still married to Maria, I was vacationing at home in Terre Haute. Mother had died, and Daddy was still living there. Balanchine and Eddie Bigelow had driven Maria and Nicky Magallanes to St. Louis, and then Balanchine and Eddie came to spend two nights at my home. Daddy by then was quite old and crotchety and demanding. He was very big and German. We were sitting on the front porch rocking when the car drove up, and Daddy said in a very loud voice, "How long are they going to stay?" But Balanchine was absolutely fabulous with him. He did the cooking and everything. He was like a little boy. Whatever Daddy said, Balanchine did. We didn't talk about dancing or anything like that. And I thought, Really, how kind Balanchine is, he's just incredible.

I feel I'm very lucky to have known him, although when I see him now he's not always accessible. Recently he and I went to dinner at the apartment of a friend of mine, and afterward Balanchine took me home in a taxi and I grabbed him and kissed him and told him, "You know, it's so wonderful to see you, because I really miss you." I think it pleased him. I just wanted him to know that I still adore him.

Ballets in Which Balanchine Created Roles for Elise Reiman

SERENADE
music: Peter Ilyich Tchaikovsky
costumes: Jean Lurçat
decor: Gaston Longchamp
role: SONATINA
premiere: March 1, 1935, Adelphi Theatre, New York
American Ballet

REMINISCENCE
music: Benjamin Godard, orchestrated by Henry Brant
decor and costumes: Sergei Soudeikine
role: PAS DE TROIS
premiere: March 1, 1935, Adelphi Theatre, New York
American Ballet

TRANSCENDENCE
music: Franz Liszt, orchestrated by George Antheil
libretto: Lincoln Kirstein
decor and costumes: Franklin Watkins
roles: MEPHISTO WALTZ: the Young Girl; THE MESMERISM
premiere: March 5, 1935, Adelphi Theatre, New York
American Ballet

MOZARTIANA (originally presented by Les Ballets, 1933)
music: Peter Ilyich Tchaikovsky
decor and costumes: Christian Bérard
role: SCHERZANDO
premiere: September 28, 1935, Westchester County Center, White Plains, N.Y.
Students of the School of American Ballet

LAKMÉ, ACT II BALLET
music: Léo Delibes
role: REKTAH
premiere: December 23, 1935, Metropolitan Opera, New York
American Ballet Ensemble

CAPONSACCHI, ACT I BALLET
music: Richard Hageman
role: ADAGIO
premiere: February 4, 1937, Metropolitan Opera, New York
American Ballet Ensemble

LA GIOCONDA, ACT III BALLET
music: Amilcare Ponchielli
role: DANCE OF THE HOURS: Dusk
premiere: February 18, 1937, Metropolitan Opera, New York
American Dance Ensemble

APOLLON MUSAGÈTE
music and book: Igor Stravinsky
decor and costumes: Stewart Chaney
role: Terpsichore
premiere: April 27, 1937, Metropolitan Opera, New York
American Ballet Ensemble

RESURGENCE
music: Wolfgang Amadeus Mozart
role: Teacher
premiere: January 22, 1946, Waldorf-Astoria Hotel, New York (benefit for the March of Dimes)
Students of the School of American Ballet

THE SPELLBOUND CHILD
music: Maurice Ravel
libretto: from a poem by Colette
decor and costumes: Aline Bernstein
role: Fire
premiere: November 20, 1946, Central High School of Needle Trades, New York
Ballet Society

THE FOUR TEMPERAMENTS
music: Paul Hindemith
decor and costumes: Kurt Seligmann
role: SECOND THEME
premiere: November 20, 1946, Central High School of Needle Trades, New York
Ballet Society

DIVERTIMENTO
music: Alexei Haieff
role: one of four supporting couples
premiere: January 13, 1947, Hunter

SYMPHONY IN C
music: Georges Bizet
role: FOURTH MOVEMENT
premiere: March 22, 1948, New York City Center
Ballet Society

Elise Reiman and Herbert Bliss in the Second Theme of The Four Temperaments, *1946.*

> I moved in a very Balanchine way. I don't know if I copied him or if he used what I had. I think it was a combination. He liked twisted, fast movement.

Marie-Jeanne

Marie-Jeanne was the first important dancer to come out of Balanchine's school. During the 1941 American Ballet Caravan tour of South America she was the company's leading ballerina, and Balanchine made two of his most famous ballets for her: *Concerto Barocco* and *Ballet Imperial* (now called *Tchaikovsky Piano Concerto No. 2*). Both ballets showed off Marie-Jeanne's speed and the clarity of her technique. The "terrors" presented by *Ballet Imperial* have been described by Arlene Croce: "No sooner has the ballerina entered than a pit yawns at her feet—the piano cadenza to which she must perform pirouettes of utmost difficulty, including several ground-skimming double pirouettes on quarter-point which, in their problems of traction, momentum, and braking, are practically unique in the ballerina repertory."

Marie-Jeanne, the daughter of a French hat designer and an Italian chef who emigrated to New York, had been accepted into the first class at the School of American Ballet even though she had no previous training. She was fourteen. Within a few months she appeared as one of the girls in the "Preghiera" section of *Mozartiana* during the demonstration performance of the Ameri-

can Ballet at the Warburg estate in White Plains, and in small parts in *Les Songes* and *Errante.* She early on dropped her family name, Pelus, which she said nobody pronounced correctly.

Marie-Jeanne got her first leading parts when she was seventeen, in Lincoln Kirstein's Ballet Caravan. She danced the role of the Rich Girl in Lew Christensen's *Filling Station* and was Billy's Mexican Sweetheart in Eugene Loring's *Billy the Kid.* In 1940 she was the first American ballerina to perform as a guest with a Russian company, the Ballet Russe de Monte Carlo. Balanchine restaged *Serenade* for her then, adding a movement from the score that he hadn't used in the original production, and she danced all the female solos.

After American Ballet Caravan disbanded Marie-Jeanne performed for a short time with Colonel de Basil's Original Ballet Russe. In 1942 she married Alfonso de Quesada, a young Argentinian whom she had met on the tour of South America, and they had a daughter. She danced with the Ballet Russe de Monte Carlo during the period Balanchine was attached to the company as choreographer, and when he made *Night Shadow* he created the part of the Harlequin for her.

Marie-Jeanne became a member of Ballet Society early in 1948. Balanchine gave her a bravura solo in her role as the First Nymph in the choral ballet *The Triumph of Bacchus and Ariadne,* and she remained in the company during the first season it was the New York City Ballet. She left to get married again in 1949, and didn't return to NYCB until 1953, when she danced for a short time before retiring.

Marie-Jeanne lives in Gainesville, Florida, and teaches ballet at the University of Florida.

Marie-Jeanne and Lew Christensen in Apollon Musagète, *1941.*

You developed very quickly as a dancer. Did you think of yourself as especially gifted?

I was just an average kid. I started taking tap-dancing lessons when I was eight, but I had no training in classical dance until I went to Balanchine's school. Right before the school opened my mother dragged me off to see the Ballets Russes at the St. James Theatre, where I saw Toumanova dancing *Cotillon.* I was a natural-born dancer. In a way it was bad, not having to work hard, because I never developed enough discipline or dedication. I knew I had talent, but I wasn't aware of its value.

I don't think the school was as rigorous in the beginning as it is now, although I had wonderful teachers: Dottie Littlefield, and then Vladimiroff. He had the most wonderful arms. Balanchine taught sometimes, and Muriel Stuart. Anatole Oboukoff was one of my favorites. He gave a long, hard barre that really built up your strength.

You appeared right away. In children's parts.

Yes. Balanchine first put me in *Errante,* which had Tamara Geva as a guest artist. She was a great actress and I was very thrilled to appear with her. My job was to do some pantomime and place a flower on the stage. Afterward Lincoln Kirstein ran up to ask my mother, "Where did she learn to act?" Balanchine always made people look marvelous.

Thank God for Lincoln Kirstein. He made me the first ballerina with the first American touring company: Ballet Caravan. But I felt lost when Balanchine ran off to Hollywood. Since I had started with him, I found it difficult to work with anyone else. I always felt that if George had been there the young American choreographers wouldn't have developed

Concerto Barocco, *1941. Marie-Jeanne, William Dollar, Mary Jane Shea.*

Marie-Jeanne, center, in A Thousand Times Neigh! *William Dollar's ballet at the World's Fair, 1940.*

Marie-Jeanne with Lew Christensen in costumes from William Dollar's Air and Variations, *1938.*

then. They wouldn't have bothered. Nothing but *Billy the Kid* ever held up in American choreography.

But then later Balanchine made two great ballets for you.
Balanchine came back to New York, and did *Concerto Barocco* and *Ballet Imperial* for me in American Ballet Caravan. They both went over big. In *Barocco* I had to dance for eighteen minutes straight. To every beat. It was the most demanding role he ever did for me. The way they do it

now isn't quite the same. *Ballet Imperial* was not a masterpiece like *Barocco*, but it was a vehicle for me and delightful to dance.

Balanchine put me in three more ballets on that tour: *Serenade, Apollo*—I danced Terpsichore—and *The Bat.* I loved *The Bat.* It was the first time I danced out of pointe shoes. And then Balanchine whipped up another piece during the tour. We didn't have anything quite right in the way of an upbeat, closing ballet, and I remember Bal-

anchine took the costumes for *Les Songes* and put together *Divertimento.* On the day it opened he made me an adagio and a Tyrolean variation. I had lots of beats and jumps. Everyone had fun things to do, and I often had to dance the Tyrolean Dance as an encore. I could hardly breathe.

It was my greatest dancing. I was twenty-one and just beginning to peak. But then the war came. It was the worst thing that could have happened to me. I didn't have a company to develop with. Balanchine was busy hanging around the Ballet Russe, and I got married, stopped dancing, had my daughter, and stayed in South America. If the company hadn't disbanded I'd never have made that mistake. But my first instinct was always to have children. I used to dream of having them without husbands. I'm a three-time loser in marriage, and that's the way I should have done it—children without husbands.

You were living in Argentina when Balanchine came there to set a piece at the Teatro Colón, weren't you?

Yes. Balanchine came to Buenos Aires and asked me to dance in that production, but I didn't want to. I was trying to get pregnant. Balanchine didn't like that, and I wasn't very diplomatic. My big mouth did me a lot of harm—all my life I was too wild and outspoken, and now Balanchine began to resent me. I had never taken him seriously, because he had so many girlfriends. With me it was short-lived. I was one of a hundred and didn't fall madly in love with him, which wasn't great for his ego. I loved him as an artistic genius.

When I did return to dance, Balanchine put me in the Ballet Russe de Monte Carlo, but it was never quite the same. That's when I lost touch with my first husband. Still, I suppose the variations Balanchine made for me then are feathers in my cap. I moved in a very Balanchine way. I don't know if I copied him or if he used what I had. I think it was a combination. He liked twisted, fast movement. After I did the Harlequin in *Night Shadow* there was never another woman able to do it. He gave my part to a man. In general, though, the dancers then were not nearly as good as they are now. There's so much more competition now.

Why did you stay with the Ballet Russe when Balanchine went to New York to start Ballet Society?

He didn't invite me into Ballet Society. It's too bad, because I would have liked to dance with them. I didn't know where the hell I was. I did dance with the company later, just when it was becoming the City Ballet. And then in 1949 I married my second husband, which was another great mistake. But I was looking for security, and I thought he could be the father of my child. I tried to live in Paris, but that fizzled out. It was a bad period.

But then you were back in Balanchine's company again before you retired.

Balanchine didn't ask me to come back. I started taking classes at the school, and Lincoln, who adored me because I was his first ballerina, asked me if I wanted to return. I said it would take me a year to get back in shape, and he said, "It's now or never." Balanchine wasn't around at the time. But I tried to come back too fast. I turned an ankle in rehearsal, and then we went on tour and one night in Milan I pulled a muscle during *La Valse* and couldn't get off the stage. Balanchine said to me, "You'd better go home. You're like Joe Louis, you can't make a comeback." It was both an insult and a compliment, but I knew then he didn't want me. I went to Lincoln and said, "Does he have a reason?" And Lincoln said, "He doesn't need a reason." That's when I hung up my toe shoes.

People are always afraid of good dancers, and I felt there was a force behind what Balanchine did to me. Balanchine is very easily influenced by the girl he likes at the time. I didn't have enough sense to use Balanchine that way. It never entered my head. I don't blame the others. They were smart and they became

Marie-Jeanne and William Dollar in Ballet Imperial, *1941.*

famous. And Balanchine does have enormous charm, and so much knowledge. He loses interest in personalities, though. For him the steps come first. He's absolutely incapable of putting steps together incorrectly.

After I retired I married again and rushed into having a family. I had two marvelous boys whom I raised all by myself during the sixties, which wasn't so easy. You know, I always wondered what would have happened if my father had stayed in Italy and not come to America. I would have been an Italian mama cooking pasta for twelve kids. For a long time I felt torn between my gifts as a dancer and wanting to have a family. I felt guilty for a long time, but now I've stopped. The family is what life is all about.

Marie-Jeanne and Nicholas Magallanes, posed by Balanchine for George Platt Lynes.

Ballets in Which Balanchine Created Roles for Marie-Jeanne

PAS DE DEUX
music: Wolfgang Amadeus Mozart
costumes: Pavel Tchelitchev
premiere: late 1930s, party in the Persian Room, Plaza Hotel, New York

SERENATA (SERENADE)
music: Peter Ilyich Tchaikovsky
costumes: Candido Portinari
role: RUSSIAN DANCE
premiere: June 25, 1941, Teatro Municipal, Rio de Janeiro
American Ballet Caravan

BALLET IMPERIAL
music: Peter Ilyich Tchaikovsky
decor and costumes: Mstislav Doboujinsky
role: Ballerina
premiere: June 25, 1941, Teatro Municipal, Rio de Janeiro
American Ballet Caravan

CONCERTO BAROCCO
music: Johann Sebastian Bach
decor and costumes: Eugene Berman
role: First Violin
premiere: June 27, 1941, Teatro Municipal, Rio de Janeiro
American Ballet Caravan

DIVERTIMENTO
music: Gioacchino Rossini, selected and orchestrated by Benjamin Britten
decor and costumes: André Derain (from *Les Songes*)
roles: TYROLEAN DANCE; NOCTURNE
premiere: June 27, 1941, Teatro Municipal, Rio de Janeiro
American Ballet Caravan

APOLO MUSAGETA (APOLLON MUSAGÈTE)
music and book: Igor Stravinsky
decor and costumes: Tomás Santa Rosa
role: Terpsichore
premiere: June 30, 1941, Teatro Municipal, Rio de Janeiro
American Ballet Caravan

EL MURCIÉLAGO (THE BAT)
music: Johann Strauss the Younger
costumes: Keith Martin
role: Hungarian Dancer
premiere: June 30, 1941, Teatro Municipal, Rio de Janeiro
American Ballet Theater

NIGHT SHADOW
music: Vittorio Rieti arrangement of Vincenzo Bellini
decor and costumes: Dorothea Tanning
role: Harlequin
premiere: February 27, 1946, New York City Center
Ballet Russe de Monte Carlo

RAYMONDA (choreographed with Alexandra Danilova)
music: Alexander Glazunov
decor and costumes: Alexandre Benois
role: Peasant Girl
premiere: March 12, 1946, New York City Center
Ballet Russe de Monte Carlo

THE TRIUMPH OF BACCHUS AND ARIADNE
music: Vittorio Rieti
decor and costumes: Corrado Cagli
role: First Nymph
premiere: February 9, 1948, New York City Center
Ballet Society

LA TRAVIATA: ACT III BALLET
music: Giuseppe Verdi
role: Lead
premiere: October 17, 1948, New York City Opera, New York City Center
New York City Ballet

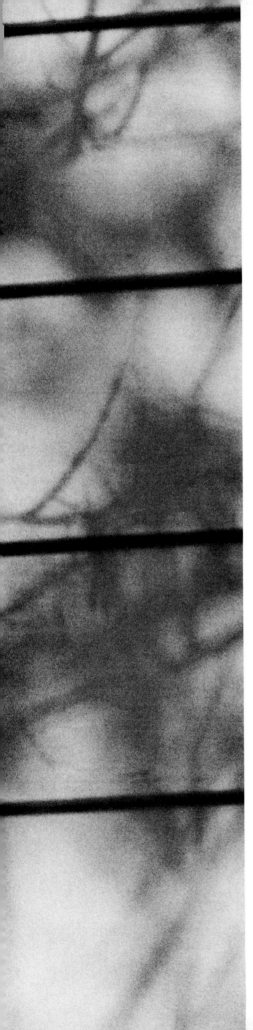

Mary Ellen Moylan

Balanchine created the "Sanguinic" section of *The Four Temperaments* for Mary Ellen Moylan, the de facto ballerina of the first Ballet Society program on November 20, 1946. Ballet Society was the immediate precursor of the New York City Ballet, and *The Four Temperaments* inaugurated a brilliant new period for Balanchine. The ballet looked distinctly modern, yet was based firmly on classical steps. When Moylan performed it she wore the bizarre costume designed by Kurt Seligmann that was shortly thereafter discarded for practice clothes, but under the "bandages" was the role Arlene Croce described much later:

> In the Sanguinic variation, for a virtuoso ballerina and her partner, the vista is wide, the ozone pure and stinging. The ballerina is an allegro technician; she is also a character. She enters and pauses. Her partner is expectant. But she pauses and turns her gaze back toward the wings. For a moment she seems to wear a demure black velvet neck ribbon, and then she is bounding like a hare in the chase, an extrovert after all.

Mary Ellen Moylan was one of the first Balanchine-trained dancers. She grew up in St. Petersburg, Florida, where she took a few dance classes, but she began studying ballet seriously when she was given a scholarship to the School of American Ballet in 1940. Two years later she appeared on Broadway with José Limón in *Rosalinda,* with choreography by Balanchine. At the same time she was performing

Marie-Jeanne's role in a revival of *Ballet Imperial* for the New Opera Company. In the fall of 1943 she joined the Ballet Russe de Monte Carlo as a soloist and danced leading roles in *Serenade, Concerto Barocco, Ballet Imperial,* and *Le Bourgeois Gentilhomme.* During the forties, *Ballet Imperial* was particularly associated with her, and when Edwin Denby wrote about that ballet he described Moylan as "dewy in diamonds, delicate, long, with a lovely pose of the head and a beautiful freedom in her correctness. Her graceful intrepidity and air of candor make me think of those demure ballet heroines who a century ago leaped from the top of a twenty-foot scenic waterfall into the arms of a partner."

On the second Ballet Society program, in January 1947, Moylan danced another new Balanchine work, to Haieff's *Divertimento,* and later that year she did a musical with Balanchine on Broadway, *The Chocolate Soldier.* She then returned to the Ballet Russe de Monte Carlo, where she danced a variety of classical and character roles: the Sugar Plum Fairy, the Swan Queen, Myrtha, Queen of the Wilis, Zobeide in *Scheherazade,* Paquita, Raymonda. When she joined Ballet Theatre in 1950 she danced the Balanchine ballets that belonged to that company's repertory as well as Princess Aurora, the Black Swan, and the *Don Quixote* Pas de Deux. From 1955 to 1957 she was the ballerina of the Metropolitan Opera Ballet. She then retired, married, and had a son. Mary Ellen Moylan now lives in upstate New York with her mother.

You were a student at Balanchine's school in the early forties, when there wasn't really a company. What dancer did you look to as a model?
We were all trying to be like Marie-Jeanne then. She was the epitome of the Balanchine woman—cool, with the longest legs, and a forward thrust of her hips rather than an arched back like the Russians. Marie-Jeanne was special. Very beautiful, with peeled-onion hair and a wonderful face.

Marie-Jeanne was a New Yorker, and knew about Balanchine's school right away, but how did you get to SAB? Your family lived in Florida.
My mother read about the school in a magazine. I wanted to know how I compared with other students, so when I was twelve and thirteen I went to SAB at the intermediate level for one month each summer. My big break came when my aunt invited me to live with her in New York. It was January 1940. We could only afford one lesson a day, but I spent all my waking hours at the school. I would sit on the steps knitting, waiting for it to open in the morning, and then I would practice for an hour before I started watching all the classes. In the professional class there were people like Danilova, Eglevsky, Zorina, Dollar—the leading dancers of the day. I would watch them and then I would practice again until it was time for my class in the afternoon. After taking a class a day for six months I was given a scholarship. I had wonderful teachers—Vladimiroff, Stuart, Oboukoff, Vilzak, Sholler, Doubrovska—but the icing on the cake was Balanchine's class. He taught when he was in New York, when he was not involved in a film or a Broadway show. He was the master, and everyone swooned when he came in, hoping that he would take some notice. In my first class with him Mr. B. corrected me often, which the more experienced girls assured me was a favorable sign. If he corrected you, you were thrilled to pieces, and if he didn't it broke your heart. His classes weren't like regular classes.

He would particularize technique, bringing a single step or gesture into focus. I remember one lesson, for instance, in which the step of the day was glissade. Repeating this simple connecting step in innumerable combinations was exhausting.

How long was it before you appeared on stage?
Two years after I began studying at the school Balanchine choreographed *Pas de Trois for Piano and Two Dancers* for Nicholas Magallanes and me. It was prepared for a benefit for the Russian War Relief. Up to this point I hadn't thought too favorably about appearing on stage, but I loved dancing, and I was absolutely thrilled to be doing this. Pavel Tchelitchev designed the costumes. He hand-painted my skirt and shoulder bow, both of which I still have in my trunk.

Balanchine took me over the hurdle from classroom to stage with that piece, and when I was seventeen I made my professional debut on Broadway in *Rosalinda.* Balanchine really began to have work for his dancers then. He choreographed *Rosalinda* for the New Opera Company, with me and José Limón as principals. Balanchine was putting together *Rosalinda* at the Forty-fourth Street Theatre, and at the same time he was restaging *Ballet Imperial,* also for the New Opera Company, at the Broadway Theatre. *Ballet Imperial* went in to take the place of a Walter Damrosch opera that folded after its first performance, and it turned out that I had to do both shows at once. A few days after rehearsals for *Ballet Imperial* had begun, Nicky Magallanes came to me and said, "Let's learn the pas de deux. You're going to be doing Marie-Jeanne's part." Of course I nearly fainted. Nicky showed me the solo, and I was ready to do it when Balanchine rehearsed us. My first appearance in

Rosalinda was in the second act, so I had time to take a taxi from the theater where *Ballet Imperial* was playing. But can you imagine what it was like to be seventeen and doing both those shows every night? It was awesome just being on the stage in New York City.

The following year you went into the Ballet Russe de Monte Carlo. How did that happen?

I wanted to go with one of the major companies as a soloist, and I felt I was getting on in years. I had just turned eighteen. Balanchine had been talking about my going to Ballet Theatre after the Broadway engagement, but nothing seemed to be coming of that. Then Sergei Denham, the director of the Ballet Russe, came to watch class. He was recruiting, and said he wanted me. Balanchine wasn't too enthusiastic when I went to ask him if I should go, but finally he said, "Go ahead to Ballet Russe, but I will give you a piece of advice. Don't sign a two-year contract." It was very wise. The next year I doubled my salary.

That first year in the Ballet Russe was very hard. We all danced in every ballet and would be so tired we couldn't sleep. Our heads were crammed with steps, and different styles, and parts. It was very demanding, and the travel arrangements during the war years were difficult, especially for exhausted dancers. In the summer of 1944, before the regular season opened, Balanchine made *Song of Norway* for Danilova and the rest of the company. It opened in Los Angeles before moving to Broadway, and as soon as *Norway* had premiered successfully we were called to rehearse daily for a new work, *Danses Concertantes,* for the New York season. These were the days before unions. We worked all day long and loved every minute of it.

Maria Tallchief and Nicholas Ma-

Mary Ellen Moylan in the early forties.

gallanes and I danced a pas de trois in *Concertantes.* She and I were the same size and were often paired in ballets. They called us "the Bobbsey Twins." I remember that during that summer we were eating only fresh fruit for lunch, and we were gorgeously thin. Unfortunately I became sick and couldn't do most of the initial weeks of *Song of Norway*

in New York. This being very thin business is not without hazard.

That September Balanchine formally joined the Ballet Russe as a choreographer. The company was poor and couldn't afford much in the way of new productions, so it was wonderful for them to be given all of Balanchine's things—*Concerto Barocco, Ballet Imperial, Le Bourgeois*

Gentilhomme. I was happy for myself too, because I was a Balanchine dancer. He was my mentor and main inspiration. I was especially glad to have a second chance to dance *Ballet Imperial* after a year's experience in the Ballet Russe. It will always be my favorite ballet.

Did you go directly into Ballet Society from the Ballet Russe?

Not quite. I wanted to broaden my base as an artist, and I spent some time in 1945 studying singing with a teacher from Juilliard and taking acting lessons while I appeared in a Broadway show. Ballet dancers very often become like horses with blinders on—focused in a single direction. In the back of my mind I think I wanted eventually to combine singing, dancing, and acting. Well, I did sing a little song—in a summer-stock production of *The Merry Widow* with Beverly Sills.

At any rate, in 1946 Balanchine and Kirstein formed Ballet Society, which was to be a subscription series featuring opera, drama, music, and dance. The critics were supposed to be excluded, but they wanted to come, and did. I was asked to join the company, and Balanchine made the "Sanguinic" section of *The Four Temperaments* for me. In all my career I have had very few ballets choreographed for me, and this one was really extraordinary. I sensed how great the ballet was even then. My pas de deux had a wonderful feeling of elasticity, fluidity, almost defying gravity. When I saw the ballet from the audience point of view twenty or so years later on TV I was dazzled by it.

How did Balanchine create the part on you?

I could never tell you how Balanchine creates; it would be like trying to hold running water. His creativity seemed to spring like a fountain—so easily. Balanchine was inscruta-ble about any meaning his ballets might have, but he was a prince to work for. He had a sense of humor, and there was a feeling of camaraderie at rehearsals. I always felt that we were sharing a special time. When he choreographed he would show a step quickly, and then I would do what I thought he did. Maybe I didn't do it exactly the way he did it, but it was approximate. That's where a dancer puts a little of herself into the creation. If Balanchine liked what you thought he did, then he would let it stay. So little things that creep in here and there of a dancer's personality, or the way a person moves, become part of Balanchine's choreography. In Balanchine's work the individuality of a dancer always comes into play.

The "Sanguinic" section of *The Four Temperaments* is one of Balanchine's greatest pieces, yet you didn't work much with him after he made it for you. How did that happen?

The last new ballet I did with Balanchine was *Divertimento,* to music by Alexei Haieff. It was a lovely little ballet he made for me and Francisco Moncion. My solo was to a lullaby—very low-key and delicate. That was in January 1947. In the spring I did a musical with Balanchine and Moncion again—*The Chocolate Soldier.* Balanchine gave us a peasant dance, a moonlight ballet in which we wore silver wigs—very romantic—and a can-can number.

Then I remember being invited to lunch by Balanchine and Oliver Smith at the Stork Club later that year. They invited me to join Ballet Theatre because Balanchine was going to make *Theme and Variations* there, and he wanted to create it on me. The two men put this before me, and I rejected the offer. Today I can't tell you why I said no. I can't believe it. I've forgotten the many factors involved, but I guess it was because Ballet Russe was trying to get me back and they promised me so many things. I did return to Ballet Russe, and I was given more scope than I'd had before. I had been typecast as a classical dancer, but I wanted to do other things, like *Scheherezade* and *Le Beau Danube.* And I did my first *Swan Lake* and *Nutcracker*—the old chestnuts. But can you imagine leaving someone whom you had loved as much as I loved Balanchine? I still find it very hard to understand. There are always forks in the road for an artist, and I often wonder what would have happened if I had not taken the road I did.

I think Balanchine was probably disappointed in me for taking off on my own. I didn't mean to appear ungrateful. It probably was a mistake to leave Balanchine in the long run, but I can't undo my life.

In 1950 things were beginning to change in the Ballet Russe, and I approached Lucia Chase about joining Ballet Theatre. They were leaving for a tour of Europe, and I boarded the plane with them without having ever danced a step with the company. I rehearsed for two weeks before I made my debut in London. Two of Balanchine's works—*Apollo* and *Theme and Variations*—were in the repertoire, but the touch of the master was not there. Balanchine didn't come to us until later in the tour. It was so wonderful to see him again and to have him rehearse us. You need him to make your performance correct.

A few years later, you left Ballet Theatre too. Why?

I was having trouble with my ankle—the left one, the pirouette foot, the fouetté foot. I was out for a year and had a hard time coming back; it was the most difficult thing I ever did. Touring seemed too arduous, so when I was asked to join the Metropolitan Opera it seemed like a good

TOP—*Mary Ellen Moylan and Maria Tallchief in* Danses Concertantes, *1944.*

BOTTOM—*Mary Ellen Moylan in costume for the Sanguinic section of* The Four Temperaments, *1946.*

offer. They were going to do new ballets for me, and I had fine partners. I loved being at the Met. Just the smell of the old opera house was exciting. Once in a while, hours before a performance, I would stand on the empty stage and sing one of the arias I had studied years before.

You know, when I was a student Balanchine gave me some advice. He said, "Don't ever get fat and don't ever get married." I noticed at the time that he himself had nothing against marriage, but I could see his point. He would rather have his girls on stage than in the kitchen or nursery. And I knew myself. I was very single-minded about my work. It had to be all or nothing for me. I tried hard not to get fat, and I didn't marry until I stopped dancing. I met my first husband in 1944 while I was doing *Song of Norway,* and I didn't marry until 1957. It was a long wait, but it was a great marriage. I left the ballet with no regrets. By that time, too, there were too many physical problems to keep on dancing—water on the knee, back trouble, and a bad ankle.

I was completely happy being a housewife and mother. We had a lovely son. My husband, Robert, died after we had been married only four years, however, and then four years later my second husband, Read, died. It was terribly sad. I had worked with both of them in their businesses, and I went on to a second career in the business world, which I enjoyed fully.

Didn't you want to teach?
I didn't really want to have my own school of ballet. I taught dance to college students for a year, and I

loved doing that, but I never became quite used to the fact that they were not so dedicated as we had been in ballet school. When I left California I took a trip around the world with my mother, my young son, and a friend. We ended up here in Pleasant Valley, New York, in the country. It's been a wonderful experience for me. I'd never lived in the country before. I love gardening, the birds, and all the little creatures that come into my yard. Except the woodchucks!

Did you ever see Balanchine again?
Many years later I went to see him. He was teaching a class, and he stopped in the middle and introduced me to the company. He said, "This is Mary Ellen. She was the first. . . ." I feel honored that I was one of his dancers. I had tried very hard to show through the movement of my body what it was Balanchine wanted. He's an extremely forceful man. He never raises his voice to anyone, because for him it isn't necessary. If he asked you to do a step that was so difficult technically, one that you had never seen before on land or on sea, you would do it because Balanchine asked you to. Dancing is very dangerous and daring. It's his faith in you that makes you do it.

I've been away from the ballet for more than twenty years, and I still think of Balanchine all the time. He has made an indelible impression on my life. With me I think it was a matter of being in the right place at the right time. I had a great deal of good luck, but I think the greatest good fortune that befell me was the chance to work with Balanchine.

Ballets in Which Balanchine Created Roles for Mary Ellen Moylan

PAS DE TROIS FOR PIANO AND TWO DANCERS
music: Theodore Chanler
costumes: Pavel Tchelitchev
role: Principal
premiere: May 10, 1942, Alvin Theatre, New York
"Music at Work" benefit program for Russian War Relief

ROSALINDA (DIE FLEDERMAUS)
music: Johann Strauss the Younger
decor: Oliver Smith
costumes: Ladislas Czettel
role: Première Danseuse
premiere: October 28, 1942, Forty-fourth Street Theatre, New York
New Opera Company

DANSES CONCERTANTES
music: Igor Stravinsky
role: PAS DE TROIS
premiere: September 10, 1944, New York City Center
Ballet Russe de Monte Carlo

LE BOURGEOIS GENTILHOMME
music: Richard Strauss
libretto: after Molière
decor and costumes: Eugene Berman
role: PAS DE SEPT
premiere: September 23, 1944, New York City Center
Ballet Russe de Monte Carlo

THE FOUR TEMPERAMENTS
music: Paul Hindemith
decor and costumes: Kurt Seligmann
role: SANGUINIC
premiere: November 20, 1946, Central High School of Needle Trades, New York
Ballet Society

DIVERTIMENTO
music: Alexei Haieff
role: Ballerina
premiere: January 13, 1947, Hunter College Playhouse, New York
Ballet Society

THE CHOCOLATE SOLDIER (operetta)
music: Oscar Straus
book: Rudolph Bernauer and Leopold Jacobson
role: Premiere Danseuse
premiere: March 12, 1947, New Century Theatre, New York

Mary Ellen Moylan and Francisco Moncion in The Chocolate Soldier, *1947.*

3. 1948-1983

The
New York
City
Ballet

The New York City Ballet enjoyed a certain *succès d'estime* from the beginning, but it was a very precarious undertaking financially. During the first year, even though the company was in residence at City Center, which provided an umbrella organization, there were only twenty-four performances. The first-season deficit of $47,000 was met by Lincoln Kirstein personally. Kirstein, the general director, and Balanchine, as artistic director (he later changed his title simply to ballet master), received no salaries. Kirstein had an income from his father's estate, and Balanchine was for a time able to live on commissions and royalties from his Broadway and Hollywood projects. Income for the company went to the dancers and for production costs.

Three ballets by Balanchine—*Concerto Barocco, Orpheus,* and *Symphony in C*—made up the company's first program, on October 11, 1948. Several other Balanchine pieces were put on later in the season, including *Serenade* and *The Four Temperaments,* and a new work was premiered, Todd Bolender's *Mother Goose Suite.* In January, NYCB (with a roster of principal dancers that included Maria Tallchief, Marie-Jeanne, Tanaquil Le Clercq, Nicholas Magallanes, and Francisco Moncion) gave a second short season, for which Jerome Robbins made a ballet, *The Guests.* Robbins had been a soloist at Ballet Theatre, had choreographed some ballets there, and was by the late forties something of a celebrity as a choreographer of shows on Broadway. Working for the New York City Ballet gave him an opportunity to make dances free from commercial considerations, and in the fall of 1949 he became the company's associate artistic director.

Balanchine continued to create new ballets and restage old ones, in spite of logistical odds. NYCB even had a box-office hit during its second year—a new *Firebird.* Balanchine's version was simpler than the original 1910 staging by Fokine, and Stravinsky's score was shorter. The company had managed to buy from Sol Hurok the decor and costumes designed by Marc Chagall for the *Firebird* put on by Ballet Theatre in 1945, and they made for a sumptuous production. It was the role of the Firebird that established Maria Tallchief as the company's reigning ballerina, the first Balanchine dancer to become celebrated in the manner of glamorous international dance stars.

In the spring of 1950 Balanchine went to London to stage *Ballet Imperial* for the Sadler's Wells Ballet at Covent Garden. Margot Fonteyn, Beryl Gray, and Michael Somes danced the principal parts, and the ballet was an immediate success. The consequence for NYCB was a contract for a London season in the summer, which gave them the chance to earn a foreign stamp of approval. At the premiere at Covent Garden on July 10 the company took fourteen curtain calls after the last ballet, *Symphony in C.* The English critics, who throughout Balanchine's career were slightly cool toward his work, were sympathetic if not enthusiastic. They didn't much like *Firebird,* and complained of the Americans' "cold, impersonal" qualities and propensity toward "gymnastics," but the company was taken seriously, and had a popular success. The friendliest English critic, Richard Buckle, remarked

The Card Game, *1951. Left to right: Doris Breckenridge, Jillana, Todd Bolender, Patricia Wilde, and Janet Reed.*

in the *Observer* on Balanchine's ability to evoke the mental figures suggested by music: "George Balanchine is the man above all others in the world who can make those impressions and images visible. Like a diver he plunges into the dark depths of music and comes back quietly with a pearl."

Back home, the company had a new champion. John Martin, who had been resisting Balanchine for fifteen years, wrote in *The New York Times* that fall: "At this Thanksgiving season, let us acknowledge with gratitude that we have a ballet company of our own. . . . What more one can ask of any company it would be difficult to say." The newspaper of record was now pretty much on Balanchine's side. Although the company continued to be regularly in desperate financial straits, artistically and critically it was flourishing. Several important dancers from other companies asked to join Balanchine. Diana Adams and Hugh Laing came from Ballet Theatre, and a few months later Nora Kaye followed. Kaye's defection was somewhat sensational because she was in effect the prima ballerina at Ballet Theatre. The virtuoso male dancer André Eglevsky joined the company during the 1952 spring season.

Balanchine and Maria Tallchief separated late in 1950, and their marriage was later annulled, but the break evidently generated little rancor and she remained with the company. When *Apollo* was revived for Eglevsky, Tallchief danced Terpsichore, and she was the Swan Queen in Balanchine's one-act version of *Swan Lake,* the first classical ballet restaged for the company. Cecil Beaton designed the costumes and sets in a style based on late-fifteenth-century German engravings. Although there was initially some public grumbling about the need for another *Swan Lake,* especially in a company dedicated to "pure dance," the production was very popular, and it linked NYCB to ballet tradition in a concrete way.

In the spring of 1952 *Swan Lake* was on the first-night program of the company's first European tour, along with *Serenade* and *La Valse,* Balanchine's ominously beautiful romantic ballet to music by Ravel, in which Le Clercq danced the role of the doomed girl waltzing with Death. The tour opened in Barcelona, to great acclaim. At the end of the engagement, after

Balanchine and Maria Tallchief.

Tanaquil Le Clercq in her Western Symphony *costume.*

a performance of *Symphony in C,* the Barcelonians gave the company an eight-minute ovation, during which rose petals and laurel leaves fell from the balconies, the stage was filled with baskets of flowers, and a flight of doves was released from the ceiling of the theater. Later receptions on the long European tour were not as extravagant, but the company did very well in Paris, Florence, Zurich, The Hague, London, Edinburgh, and Berlin.

That fall in New York Balanchine made a new ballet for Tanaquil Le Clercq, *Metamorphoses,* to a Hindemith score. In Kirstein's memoirs he says there was no money for scenery so they bought three hundred wire coat hangers on Seventh Avenue and hung them like a ladder, then threw a gold light over the whole thing for a "spidery pagoda" effect. The costumes were equally bizarre: masks, antennae, huge wings, tiny sequined bras. Le Clercq's role drew on her theatrical personality. She had a pas de deux with Todd Bolender in which he partnered her while on his knees. Bolender says he did it as if he were a turtle dancing with a butterfly. It was, in any case, one of Le Clercq's most distinctive roles. A few weeks after the premiere, on New Year's Eve 1952, she and Balanchine were married.

The company's first full-length ballet, and the most ambitious project undertaken at City Center, was *The Nutcracker,* which is said to have saved the New York City Ballet from financial disaster. It is still a box-office success, thirty years later. The production included thirty-nine children, a giant tree that rose to the ceiling, snow, and fancifully costumed soldiers, mice, and fairies. When Maria Tallchief danced the Sugar Plum Fairy, Edwin Denby thought her variation the triumph of her career.

Balanchine's versatility and wide-ranging musical interests could be inferred from the new ballets he made in 1954. A few months after staging *The Nutcracker* to Tchaikovsky's lush score, he put on *Western Symphony* to a medley of cowboy tunes. Balanchine had commissioned the arrangement (from Hershy Kay) after a visit to Wyoming. Boys in frontier pants, string ties, and plaid shirts (more or less Balanchine's street attire at the time) danced with music-hall girls on pointe who threw themselves into the arms of cowboys. What made it pure Balanchine and not just another cow-

Caracole, *1952. Patricia Wilde, Diana Adams, Maria Tallchief, Tanaquil Le Clercq, and Melissa Hayden.*

boy ballet was that the steps were strictly classical. The "Westerness" came from the speed and accent and visual emphasis of the choreography. Four nights after the *Western Symphony* premiere the company presented another new piece, *Ivesiana,* very different in tone. *Ivesiana* also had a score from an American composer, six orchestral pieces by Charles Ives, but the music here was somber, eerie—sounds from nature and snatches of popular American music. The dancers wore practice clothes, and their movements were odd and implicitly menacing. A sixteen-year-old corps girl, Allegra Kent, danced the lead in the ballet's central section, the mysterious "Unanswered Question."

By the mid-fifties Balanchine's company could with aplomb handle a large repertory of difficult works. They were dancing regularly, were well received, and had made several tours of Europe. Tragedy struck during the 1956 tour, however, when Tanaquil Le Clercq became ill with polio and was left permanently paralyzed. She was hospitalized in Copenhagen, where Balanchine stayed before taking her to Warm Springs, Georgia for therapy. He was away from the company for a year.

In the fall of 1957 when Balanchine returned to work he created, remarkably, four big ballets in two months. *Agon,* the masterpiece from that period, to a newly commissioned score by Stravinsky, was called by Balanchine "the quintessential contemporary ballet." It was a suite of dances for twelve dancers, spare, rigorous, largely atonal. *Square Dance* was something quite different. The conceit was the relationship between seventeenth-century music and the American square dance. The ballet was very fast, witty, to the music of Vivaldi and Corelli. A small group of fiddlers shared the stage with the dancers, and a real square-dance caller shouted out calls he had written himself after watching rehearsals. (For a revival in 1976 the caller and fiddlers were dropped.) A month after *Square Dance* the company premiered *Gounod Symphony,* a very "French" ballet for a large ensemble, and the following week they put on a big, splashy spectacle, *Stars and Stripes,* to the marches of John Philip Sousa. After five "campaigns" in which the dancers leaped, twirled batons, saluted, performed endless turns,

Balanchine with Melissa Hayden, Suzanne Farrell, Violette Verdy, Patricia McBride.

splits, and lifts, an enormous American flag unfurled, blown vigorously by wind machines. Kirstein says the pas de deux scored for brass instruments, predominantly a tuba, was "a tribute to Dwight Eisenhower, in his senior year at West Point, engaged to Mamie Doud."

The idea that there are no stars in the New York City Ballet, that the choreography comes first, and that the dancers are subsumed into the working organism that is the company was emphasized in 1958 when programs began to list dancers alphabetically. It was a policy that of course never conformed to reality, and audiences always knew who the prima ballerina was—Maria Tallchief and Melissa Hayden, Suzanne Farrell later. But it was also true that NYCB didn't mount "star" vehicles, that the corps dancers were in many cases technically of the caliber of principals in other companies, and that they were asked to do more real dancing than other corps de ballet. The repertory was rich, diverse. Early in 1962 Balanchine added the first original full-length ballet produced in America, *A Midsummer Night's Dream*, with lavish costumes and scenery, extensive use of mime, a complicated plot.

The two big Russian ballet companies, the Bolshoi and the Kirov, had recently appeared in New York, the Bolshoi in 1959 and the Kirov in 1961. Balanchine's company had entertained them both, and in the fall of 1962 the New York City Ballet toured the Soviet Union for eight weeks. Balanchine had not been in Russia for thirty-eight years and was apparently not eager to return now. He was profoundly anti-communist, like many Russian emigrés something of an American patriot, and would not play the role of the Prodigal Son. But he was a very effective cultural emissary for the United States. Early on during the engagement in Moscow, audiences caught on to what had at first puzzled them, and night after night there were repeated curtain calls and cries of "Bal-an-chine." The official critics, although praising the company's brilliant technique, disapproved of the plotless ballets, and complained that the Americans were decadent, had no soul, were trapped in a formalist aesthetic. Then the Cuban Missile Crisis erupted. It was at its height on October 29, the company's closing night in Moscow. Crowds were stoning the American Embassy, and at any moment the Soviet Union and the United States could be at war. But at the end of their performance the New York City Ballet received what attendants at the Bolshoi Theater said was the greatest ovation ever given there.

A contingent of fans followed the company to Leningrad, where performances took place at the Kirov (the old Maryinsky), the theater where Balanchine had first appeared on stage, when he was a child at the Imperial School. The City Ballet's engagement there was sold out. Allegra Kent had become the audience favorite, and her performance of the *Agon* pas de deux with Arthur Mitchell, the only black dancer in the company, was a *succès de scandale*. Balanchine, obviously under a strain, went back to New York for a week's rest while the company went to Kiev, but he rejoined them in Soviet Georgia, his family's home.

One of the members of the corps de ballet on the trip was new to the company—seventeen-year-old Suzanne Farrell, who had come to the School of American Ballet two years earlier, under the first Ford Foundation scholarship program. The season after the Russian tour Balanchine made his first ballet for her, to Stravinsky's *Movements for Piano and Orchestra*, and what later became known as The Farrell Years had begun. Suzanne Farrell in a very short time was dancing more roles than any other ballerina in the company and was Balanchine's chief inspiration for new work. In

Balanchine with Suzanne Farrell on tour.

1963 alone she debuted in *Agon, Liebeslieder Walzer,* as the Bride in *Firebird,* and as Titania in *A Midsummer Night's Dream,* and Balanchine made two ballets for her. Five years later she was the principal dancer in twenty-two of the forty-one ballets in NYCB's working repertory.

The grant that brought Farrell to the company was just the first bit of largesse from the Ford Foundation that made Balanchine's company the "establishment"—at any rate in the eyes of the rest of the dance world. In December 1963 the foundation awarded $7 million to ballet in America. The New York City Ballet got $2 million, and the School of American Ballet got nearly $4 million ($1.5 million of which was to go to scholarships and cross-country surveys). The sense that Balanchine and Kirstein's organization was the dominant force in ballet in this country was strengthened the following spring when the company moved into a permanent home—the New York State Theater, which had been built to Balanchine's specifications by Philip Johnson. Rehearsal rooms were large, with specially woven pine floors designed by Balanchine; there was a big stage and a decent-sized orchestra pit. (Stravinsky said that the orchestra pit at City Center was like a men's room.)

With the move to the State Theater the company took on a new look. Balanchine began to make elaborate new ballets which took advantage of the spacious facilities—*Don Quixote, Jewels, Harlequinade, Coppélia.* And the dancers began to move differently, expansively, in the style of Suzanne Farrell. Her influence was remarkable. In 1965 Maria Tallchief, who had reigned as ballerina since the company's inception, left, saying that Balanchine was paying too much attention to younger dancers. That year Balanchine mounted his production of *Don Quixote,* in which Farrell danced Dulcinea and he himself danced the role of the Don several times. Balanchine described the ballet as being about "the hero's finding an ideal, something to live for and sacrifice for and serve. For the Don it was Dulcinea. . . . I myself think that everything a man does, he does for his ideal woman."

In the spring of 1967 the company had their first new box-office hit at the State Theater—*Jewels,* a plotless ballet in three acts, each act reflecting the qualities of a precious stone: "Emeralds," to Fauré; "Rubies," to Stravinsky; and "Diamonds," to Tchaikovsky. *Jewels* was enormously popular. Clive Barnes in *The New York Times* wrote: "It is open to doubt whether even Balanchine has ever created a work in which the inspiration was so sustained, the invention so imaginative, or the concept so magnificent."

Early in 1969 Balanchine and Tanaquil Le Clercq received a Mexican

Balanchine and dancers, 1968.

Balanchine with Barbara Karinska and Jerome Robbins at rehearsal for Firebird, *1970.*

Balanchine and Danilova rehearsing Coppélia, *1974.*

divorce. At about the same time Suzanne Farrell married a young dancer in the company, Paul Mejia, and moved to Brussels, where she and her husband joined Maurice Béjart's Ballet du XXᵉ Siècle. Farrell was said to have broken with Balanchine because he refused to let Mejia dance in the company after the marriage, but whatever the reasons for the breach, it was a shock to the rest of the company and traumatic for Balanchine. The next three years or so were very much a fallow period for him. Jerome Robbins had just returned to NYCB as a choreographer after a decade on Broadway, and he began producing a series of successful pieces: *Dances at a Gathering, In the Night, Goldberg Variations, Watermill.* Balanchine made the lively and good-natured *Who Cares?* to Gershwin songs, and in the spring of 1971 he produced a ballet which fed rumor mills with evidence that he was through as a choreographer: *PAMTGG,* based on the commercial jingle "Pan Am Makes the Going Great." It was expensive—with elaborate plastic costumes for hippies, airline personnel, stars, clouds, jet-setters. The ballet was quickly removed from the repertory.

Balanchine's abiding choreographic vigor was made manifest the following year in what was probably the company's most ambitious undertaking, the Stravinsky Festival of June 1972, to commemorate the ninetieth birthday of the composer, who had died the previous year. Twenty-two new ballets were prepared for the festival, nine of them by Balanchine (he collaborated with Robbins on one, *Pulcinella*), three of which are among his best works: *Symphony in Three Movements, Violin Concerto,* and *Duo Concertant.* These ballets were prepared in a few intense weeks of rehearsals, for the most part during the company's regular performing schedule, and were presented over seven consecutive days, which produced an effect for the audience, according to Kirstein, of "crowds embarked on a luxurious cruise, crossing an ocean for a gala vacation." Stravinsky was honored and Balanchine vindicated.

Suzanne Farrell returned to the company in January 1975, appearing on the stage for the first time in the Adagio movement of *Symphony in C.* That spring the company put on another festival, for Ravel, this time less concentrated and less of an event. Balanchine's most successful new work was *Le Tombeau de Couperin,* a suite of dances for eight couples. He also made his first new ballet for Farrell in six years—*Tzigane,* a smoldering gypsy dance that caught what seemed to be a new emotional intensity acquired during her years in Europe.

For the U.S. Bicentennial in 1976, Balanchine, always a booster of things American, decided idiosyncratically to mount a huge ballet on British themes, *Union Jack.* In the first section seven "regiments" of ten dancers each marched in to a score derived from traditional Scottish music, shifting around the stage in blocs and performing classical variations based on the Highland Fling, reels, popular dances. After the regiments marched off, a Pearly King and Queen with two children and a donkey cart appeared in front of a scrim in a routine based on turn-of-the-century music-hall songs. During the finale the entire back of the stage was filled with a huge Union Jack, in front of which the dancers in sailors' outfits wigwagged "God Save the Queen" with semaphore flags. As the curtain came down, the theater was filled with the sound of cannon thunder.

Balanchine put on another big ballet the following year, *Vienna Waltzes,* probably the company's most successful production. Every performance was sold out for four seasons. But as an astute critic pointed out, it was not simply a commercial hit, a lavish production number to Strauss. Nearly two

Balanchine with Darci Kistler, 1981.

years after its premiere Arlene Croce thought that *Vienna Waltzes* offered the "pinnacle experience to be had at New York City Ballet."

Balanchine was now in his seventies and was still producing complex, beautiful, intelligent ballets. Early in 1978 he made *Ballo della Regina* to show off Merrill Ashley's speed and precision, and *Kammermusik No. 2,* which is perhaps the only one of all his ballets in which the burden of the dancing falls on the men, here a corps of eight boys. A second ballet was made for Merrill Ashley in the spring of 1980, *Ballade,* to Fauré, and in June Balanchine made one of his last major works, *Davidsbündlertänze,* to eighteen piano pieces by Schumann, in which the composer portrayed himself in many guises: distraught, enthusiastic, passionate. Four couples—Suzanne Farrell and Jacques d'Amboise, Peter Martins and Heather Watts, Kay Mazzo and Ib Andersen, Karin von Aroldingen and Adam Luders—wove in and out of a scene based on the Romantic paintings of Caspar David Friedrich. They were thought to represent aspects of Schumann and his wife Clara. The mood was foreboding, finally elegiac, when in the last episode Luders backed hesitantly offstage, apparently toward death.

The elegiac mood lingered into the company's Tchaikovsky Festival in the spring of 1981. Arlene Croce noted: "The . . . Festival began with Suzanne Farrell, in a formal tutu of solemn black, floating downstage on her long, sensitive pointes, her hands joined in prayer. And it ended pianissimo, with an image of a giant's heart beating its last under a black shroud, followed by the blowing out of a single candle on the darkened stage." The ballet for Farrell was a reworking of *Mozartiana,* and the shroud appeared in a piece to the final section of the Pathétique Symphony, the Adagio Lamentoso, performed by Karin von Aroldingen. The rest of *Mozartiana* was in fact quite lively, as were Balanchine's other new works, *Hungarian Gypsy Airs* and the Garland Dance from *The Sleeping Beauty.* But Tchaikovsky's melancholy and pathos set the tone of the occasion.

The Stravinsky Festival the following year presented the great works of the Stravinsky/Balanchine collaboration, in celebration of the composer's centenary. Balanchine was said to be not well, but he prepared four new pieces: *Persephone; Tango,* for von Aroldingen, and two solos for Farrell, *Élégie* and *Variations,* a new version of a ballet made in 1966.

Shortly after the Stravinsky Festival, Balanchine's ill health kept him away from the company for extensive periods of time. He had not taught company class for some years and now was not available for rehearsals or for the constant adjusting of ballets and fine-tuning of dancers that had been his habit. But the organization he and Kirstein had created was molded to his wishes, and the New York City Ballet remained Balanchine's company even though he was not watching from the wings. The dancers had been trained to his specifications, and they were dancing in a repertory made up largely of his work.

In March 1983, Balanchine, who had been hospitalized for several months with a progressively debilitating illness, was made Ballet Master Emeritus of the New York City Ballet. He died a month later.

Balanchine at the Tchaikovsky Festival, 1981.

Maria Tallchief

Maria Tallchief married Balanchine in the fall of 1946, when she was twenty-one and a soloist in the Ballet Russe de Monte Carlo. They had met when he was touring with the Ballet Russe as resident choreographer. He made the part of the Coquette in *Night Shadow* for her then, and their collaboration continued for many years, long after their marriage had been dissolved. Tallchief was the New York City Ballet's first prima ballerina and the first native-born American to become an international dance star.

She was born in Fairfax, Oklahoma, on an Indian reservation. Her father was the descendant of an Osage chief, and her mother was Scotch-Irish. She was precociously musical, playing the piano by the time she was three and taking ballet lessons, even wearing pointe shoes, when she was four. She and her sister Marjorie also learned to perform traditional Osage dances. In 1933 the family moved to Los Angeles, where she began preparing for a career as a concert pianist and took ballet classes from Bronislava Nijinska. The piano was given up in favor of dance, and in 1940 she appeared at the Hollywood Bowl in Nijinska's *Chopin Concerto.* She was a member of the Ballet Russe de Monte Carlo from 1942 to 1947.

Tallchief accompanied Balanchine to the Paris Opéra in 1947 and was the first American dancer to perform there. Later that year they returned to New York for the third Ballet Society season, in which *Symphonie Concertante* was premiered with Tallchief and Tanaquil Le Clercq as the two female leads. Tallchief's roles later included Eurydice in *Orpheus,* Terpsichore in *Apollo,* and the Swan Queen in Balanchine's version of *Swan Lake,* but it was as the Firebird that she became a star. Walter Terry described her appearance in that role as "breathtaking."

> Balanchine has devised some magnificent movements for her. They are fluttering, flashing, soaring, and at the proper moments they fairly flame with dynamic tension and speed. . . . In their alert, graceful, and sharp exploration of space they define the characteristics of a magical, air-born creature. . . . Tallchief gave a performance of historical proportions.

In 1951 Tallchief's marriage to Balanchine was annulled, but she remained with the New York City Ballet. In the mid-fifties she appeared briefly with the Ballet Russe de Monte Carlo, where she was, according to *Newsweek,* the highest-salaried ballerina in the world. In 1957 she married Henry Paschen, Jr., a prominent Chicago builder, and they had a daughter. Tallchief danced with American Ballet Theatre early in the sixties and was a guest artist with other companies. She was the first American to dance with the Royal Danish Ballet. In 1965 she resigned from the New York City Ballet, saying she felt that too much attention was paid to younger, less-experienced dancers. She was briefly the head of the Hamburg Ballet and then returned to Chicago. In 1975 she became the director of the Chicago Lyric Opera Ballet and in the spring of 1981 started her own company, the Chicago City Ballet. Her sister Marjorie Skibine directs the company school, and Tallchief herself coaches dancers, teaches class, and serves as artistic director.

You began taking ballet classes when you were very young— only four, as I remember reading somewhere—and had a good deal of professional experience before you met Balanchine. Yet you are remembered as being the first great "Balanchine dancer." How did that come about?

Balanchine retrained me completely. I had started too young. In California I studied with Ernest Belcher, and then Bronislava Nijinska opened a school in Los Angeles and my sister and I studied with her. In retrospect I don't think Nijinska was really as interested in training classical dancers as she was in pursuing her own choreography. She did not *insist* upon pure classical training. I could do double fouettés, and big jumps, but I didn't understand the importance of feet and turnout until I met Balanchine.

Other dancers have told me that they never saw anyone work as hard as you did with Balanchine.

I'm glad to hear that the others recognized how hard it was for me, because sometimes I think people assume everything came on a silver platter. Balanchine made me realize what I had to learn, and I was young enough to accept his challenge, but it was a *tremendous* challenge. Even though he never said, "You've got to start all over again." He just said, "Well, you might do this." If one compares various pictures of me in *Ballet Imperial* it's obvious that the shape of my leg was completely different two or three years after I had begun training with Balanchine.

You seem not to have resisted Balanchine at all. Like some of his other dancers did.

I met Balanchine when I was eighteen, and after that it was a complete commitment. There was no doubt in my mind that everything Balanchine said was absolutely right. Even though I always idolized Madame Nijinska, I recognized the true classical genius of Balanchine. Nijinska gave me a great deal—a feeling and love for dance, and a discipline that has lasted forever—but now that I'm working with dancers myself it seems especially clear to me that one must start with the master.

Had you seen any of Balanchine's work before you met him?

I had seen *Serenade* many years before. It was in the repertory of the Ballet Russe de Monte Carlo when they came to dance in Los Angeles. But I was quite young, and I think young people are usually more impressed with dancers than with choreography. When I began to work with Balanchine I was impressed, though. I couldn't believe how musical he was, and how much that affected his choreography. Frankly, I think one reason Balanchine became interested in me is that I was also a musician. We used to play four-hand piano. I think this was intriguing for him.

The first time we worked together was in 1944 when he came to choreograph *Song of Norway* for the Ballet Russe. Mary Ellen Moylan and I were Danilova's understudies, and when she became ill we both performed her roles. Subsequently I was invited to go on Broadway with the show, but decided not to because I wanted desperately to be a ballet dancer. I couldn't be lured by anything else. Balanchine was having a hiatus from films and shows at that point, so he stayed to choreograph for the company, and that's when he made *Danses Concertantes.* It was the first time I danced to Stravinsky's music. And then I danced in Balanchine's *Raymonda* and in *Le Baiser de la Fée,* and he created the part of the Coquette in

Night Shadow for me. The Fairy in *Baiser* was one of the most fascinating roles I ever danced. It had drama, and a beautiful pas de deux. And the music was beautiful.

Balanchine went on tour with the Ballet Russe and set all these ballets on us. I was the second lead in *Ballet Imperial,* and Mary Ellen Moylan had the lead. She was brilliant. A true Balanchine dancer. Mary Ellen and Marie-Jeanne were two typical Balanchine dancers, and it was a revelation for me to see this.

So you had two years of training with Balanchine in the Ballet Russe. And then you were married.

Yes. Balanchine and I were married in August of 1946. Then we went to the Paris Opéra together that spring. It was very difficult for Balanchine in Paris. He was being attacked on all sides. Most of the dancers loved him, although some of the older dancers felt he wasn't using them in his ballets and they resented that. He discovered younger dancers, the *petits rats,* who were beautiful in *Serenade.* He created new stars. Balanchine has always loved the school at the Paris Opéra, and he still does. In spite of the problems he went on to create the glorious *Palais de Cristal* for the company.

But the French were very warm to *you,* weren't they?

They were intrigued that I was an American Indian. At first they were confused—What's this Tall-chief? And then I danced *Le Baiser de la Fée,* which was a very good role for me. It required acting and a very tense kind of dancing. I also danced Balanchine's *Apollon Musagète,* to that wonderful Stravinsky score.

Why hadn't you worked with Balanchine in Ballet Society that first season, before you went to Paris?

Tallchief in the Minkus Pas de Trois, *1952.* BELOW—Apollo, Leader of the Muses, *1951. André Eglevsky with (left to right) Diana Adams, Tallchief, Tanaquil Le Clercq.*

I could not get out of my contract with the Ballet Russe, so I had to go on tour right after we were married. But when we came back from Paris Balanchine created *Symphonie Concertante* for Ballet Society. Then I danced Mary Ellen Moylan's part in *The Four Temperaments*—"Sanguinic." Out of Ballet Society the New York City Ballet was formed, and Balanchine choreographed the *Firebird* for me. A few years ago when Balanchine came out for the opening of the Chicago City Ballet I arranged for my daughter Elise to sit with him, and she told me later that Balanchine said to her, "You know, your mother was wonderful in *Firebird.* It was the New York City Ballet's first great success."

Firebird was very important for you, but were there other roles that didn't seem quite right?

I remember I danced badly my first *Swan Lake.* It was a nerve-wracking experience, and it didn't go well that night. At one o'clock in the morning after the first performance my phone rang and it was Felia Doubrovska. She said, "I just want you to know, Maria, maybe you're not too happy tonight. But it was nerves." And it was true. Doubrovska was always there and very supportive.

She spoke very highly of you in Prodigal Son.

I felt that *Prodigal Son* was my only failure. It was done for Doubrovska, who had extraordinarily long legs. I did as much as I could, but I couldn't handle the cape. You need a large person to do that. The feeling was there, and the desire was there, but I couldn't handle it physically. The photographs of me as the Siren look good because George Platt Lynes was a wonderful photographer. Balanchine put on my makeup.

But *Swan Lake* was made for me, and the Sugar Plum Fairy in *Nut-*

Tallchief as the Firebird, 1949.

cracker, and *Scotch Symphony*. The Sugar Plum Fairy variation was extraordinary. I never said no to anything Balanchine asked me to do. Unless I was injured. I remember I was injured during the first *Firebird* in London and he changed one step. I understand that now if the girls don't like what Balanchine gives them to do they just say they can't do it. But I was there during a different time.

What disturbs me now is the people who think they're dancing the Balanchine way or teaching in a Balanchine way who have never worked with Balanchine. I remem-ber I saw a company perform *Allegro Brillante* and I didn't recognize it. Yet it was done for me. But part of it is Balanchine's mistake: not everyone is qualified to teach his works. To my mind, the dancer who knows as much about Balanchine today as *anybody* is Suzanne Farrell. This lady knows exactly what Balanchine wants. Suzanne is a great dancer now, and one day she is going to be a great, great teacher.

You left New York City Ballet for a short time in the fifties. How did that happen?
Columbia Artists had said they wouldn't tour the Ballet Russe without me, and I was offered two thousand dollars a week, which was unheard of at that time. My picture was on the cover of *Newsweek*. But I shouldn't have done it. It was a mistake, and I was very unhappy. Practically all I danced was *Scheherazade*. And then I hurt my foot. I rejoined the New York City Ballet right away.

You were the prima ballerina of the company at that point, but a few years later it was

designated a "starless" company. How did that come about?

We were scheduled to go on a long tour of Japan and Australia in 1958, but I felt that six weeks was enough time to be away, so I said I couldn't go to Australia. We had a great success in Japan, and then the company arrived in Australia and apparently there were big headlines: "New York City Ballet Arrives Without Its Star." The engagement was a catastrophe. Empty houses for a month. But no one had said to me, "Maria, would you please come and at least open the engagement?" I would have done it. I wouldn't have deserted the company, and my husband could have joined me on the tour. But I didn't think anybody in Australia knew who I was. I would even have come later if they had called. But nobody said anything. When the company came back George started the no-star system of billing. So that if someone can't dance it's not a disaster.

Why do you think it is that Balanchine understands women so well that he gets them to expose their special qualities?

I think Balanchine can bring out the best in any individual, man or woman. He's done some of his best ballets for men—*Apollo, Orpheus,* even *Baiser de la Fée.* Unfortunately not all the men could dance his roles. Eglevsky danced beautifully, and Erik Bruhn was a beautiful dancer. But Balanchine invents for a single person. He would change and change. If something he had done for a dancer didn't look right when somebody else took on the role he would change the choreography so that same effect came through the second dancer's body. For instance, Tanny Le Clercq did *Swan Lake* when I was ill and he changed it completely to get the same effect with her body. This is his genius: to

bring out the best in each person. Something beautiful would come out in class and he would put it in his next ballet. He never did anything that was uncomfortable for a dancer.

When Balanchine was here I said, "Now, George, I teach exactly the way you taught me." And he said, "Maria, that's absolutely right." He was very pleased when he came to see my company. There is a Balanchine technique, but no one knows it unless they have worked with him. You can't just look at the ballets and know. It's not just moving fast. Paul Mejia is working with me in the Chicago City Ballet now. He is Suzanne Farrell's husband and understands the Balanchine technique very well because his wife is the epitome of it. Of course he is a product of SAB too. Paul is an excellent teacher. Watching him, I can see how Balanchine's genius has evolved since I retired as a dancer in 1966.

It's important to believe what Balanchine says. I believed him and I remember everything he ever told me about dancing and every correction he ever made. Sometimes now I have to say to my young dancers, "I don't think you believe what I say is true. But you've got to believe me. You've got to build up your back muscles, and you cannot stand around with your nonexistent stomachs hanging out." My dancers are pulled up and they are going to be even more pulled up. It is the Balanchine look. When a dancer entered the company Balanchine would insist that they hold themselves that way. He never gave great explanations, or talked about ballets. He would demonstrate. I can still see him today, how beautifully he demonstrated.

I was so fortunate to have been around Balanchine. I saw what he wanted and I knew that was the way one had to dance. And finally I had everything, beyond my wildest expectations. But you don't go into the ballet thinking about what might happen. You just go to work, that's all.

Tallchief with Nicholas Magallanes in the Sanguinic section of The Four Temperaments.

Ballets in Which Balanchine Created Roles for Maria Tallchief

DANSES CONCERTANTES
music: Igor Stravinsky
decor and costumes: Eugene Berman
role: PAS DE TROIS
premiere: September 10, 1944, New York City Center
Ballet Russe de Monte Carlo

LE BOURGEOIS GENTILHOMME
music: Richard Strauss
libretto: after Molière
decor and costumes: Eugene Berman
role: DANSE INDIENNE
premiere: September 23, 1944, New York City Center
Ballet Russe de Monte Carlo

NIGHT SHADOW
music: Vittorio Rieti's arrangement of Vincenzo Bellini
decor and costumes: Dorothea Tanning
role: Coquette
premiere: February 27, 1946, New York City Center
Ballet Russe de Monte Carlo

RAYMONDA (choreographed with Alexandra Danilova)
music: Alexander Glazunov
decor and costumes: Alexandre Benois
role: PAS CLASSIQUE HONGROIS
premiere: March 12, 1946, New York City Center
Ballet Russe de Monte Carlo

DIVERTIMENTO
music: Alexei Haieff
role: Ballerina
premiere: January 13, 1947, Hunter College Playhouse, New York
Ballet Society

SYMPHONIE CONCERTANTE
music: Wolfgang Amadeus Mozart
costumes and decor: James Stewart Morcom
roles: ALLEGRO MAESTOSO; ANDANTE; PRESTO
premiere: November 12, 1947, New York City Center
Ballet Society

SYMPHONY IN C
music: Georges Bizet
role: FIRST MOVEMENT
premiere: March 22, 1948, New York City Center
Ballet Society

Tallchief and Jerome Robbins in Prodigal Son.

ORPHEUS
music: Igor Stravinsky
decor and costumes: Isamu Noguchi
role: Eurydice
premiere: April 28, 1948, New York City
Center
Ballet Society

CARMEN: ACT II TAVERN SCENE BALLET
music: Georges Bizet
role: Lead
premiere: October 10, 1948, New York
City Opera, New York City Center
New York City Ballet

AIDA: ACT II, SCENE 2, TRIUMPHAL BALLET
music: Giuseppe Verdi
role: Lead
premiere: October 28, 1948, New York
City Opera, New York City Center
New York City Ballet

PRINCESS AURORA
music: Peter Ilyich Tchaikovsky
decor: Michel Baronoff
costumes: Barbara Karinska after designs
by Léon Bakst
role: BLUEBIRD PAS DE DEUX
premiere: April 2, 1949, Opera House,
Chicago
Ballet Theatre

DON QUIXOTE and SWAN LAKE (BLACK SWAN) PAS DE DEUX
music: Léon Minkus; Peter Ilyich
Tchaikovsky
role: Ballerina
premiere: 1949 Ballet Theatre spring tour

FIREBIRD
music: Igor Stravinsky
decor and costumes: Marc Chagall
role: Firebird
premiere: November 27, 1949, New York
City Center
New York City Ballet

BOURRÉE FANTASQUE
music: Emmanuel Chabrier
costumes: Karinska
role: PRELUDE
premiere: December 1, 1949, New York
City Center
New York City Ballet

PRODIGAL SON
music: Sergei Prokofiev
book: Boris Kochno
decor: Esteban Francés from Georges
Rouault sketches
role: Siren
premiere: February 23, 1950, New York
City Center
New York City Ballet

JONES BEACH (choreographed with Jerome Robbins)
music: Jurriaan Andriessen
costumes: Jantzen
role: HOT DOGS
premiere: March 9, 1950, New York City
Center
New York City Ballet

SYLVIA PAS DE DEUX
music: Léo Delibes
costumes: Karinska
role: Ballerina
premiere: December 1, 1950, New York
City Center
New York City Ballet

MUSIC AND DANCE
music: Léo Delibes
role: WALTZ from NAÏLA
premiere: February 10, 1951, Carnegie
Hall, New York
New York City Ballet and students of the
School of American Ballet

PAS DE TROIS
music: Léon Minkus
costumes: Karinska
premiere: February 18, 1951, New York
City Center
New York City Ballet

CAPRICCIO BRILLANT
music: Felix Mendelssohn
costumes: Karinska
role: Ballerina
premiere: June 7, 1951, New York City
Center
New York City Ballet

À LA FRANÇAIX
music: Jean Françaix
decor: Raoul Dufy
role: Winged Sylph
premiere: September 11, 1951, New York
City Center
New York City Ballet

APOLLO, LEADER OF THE MUSES
music and book: Igor Stravinsky
costumes: Karinska
role: Terpsichore
premiere: November 15, 1951, New York
City Center
New York City Ballet

SWAN LAKE
music: Peter Ilyich Tchaikovsky
decor and costumes: Cecil Beaton
role: Swan Queen
premiere: November 20, 1951, New York
City Center
New York City Ballet

CARACOLE
music: Wolfgang Amadeus Mozart
costumes: Christian Bérard
role: Ballerina (one of five)
premiere: February 19, 1952, New York
City Center
New York City Ballet

SCOTCH SYMPHONY
music: Felix Mendelssohn
decor: Horace Armistead
costumes: Karinska, David Ffolkes
role: Sylph
premiere: November 11, 1952, New York
City Center
New York City Ballet

HARLEQUINADE PAS DE DEUX
music: Riccardo Drigo
costumes: Karinska
role: Columbine
premiere: December 16, 1952, New York
City Center
New York City Ballet

THE NUTCRACKER
music: Peter Ilyich Tchaikovsky
decor: Horace Armistead
costumes: Karinska
role: Sugar Plum Fairy
premiere: February 2, 1954, New York City
Center
New York City Ballet

PAS DE DIX
music: Alexander Glazunov
costumes: Esteban Francés
role: Ballerina
premiere: November 9, 1955, New York
City Center
New York City Ballet

ALLEGRO BRILLANTE
music: Peter Ilyich Tchaikovsky
costumes: Karinska
role: Ballerina
premiere: March 1, 1956, New York City
Center
New York City Ballet

GOUNOD SYMPHONY
music: Charles Gounod
decor: Horace Armistead
costumes: Karinska
role: Ballerina
premiere: January 8, 1958, New York City
Center
New York City Ballet

PANAMERICA
music: Julián Orbón
decor: David Hays
costumes: Esteban Francés
role: SECTION VIII: Cuba
premiere: January 20, 1960, New York City
Center
New York City Ballet

> You make yourself a Balanchine dancer by dancing his ballets. Your legs change, your body changes, you become a filly.

Melissa Hayden

Melissa Hayden was a principal dancer with the New York City Ballet from 1949 until 1973, by which time she had danced with the company longer than any other ballerina, created roles in dozens of ballets, and given hundreds of concerts. As Lincoln Kirstein pointed out, she probably made more appearances before an audience than any other performer of her time. For much of her career she was tacitly NYCB's prima ballerina, although she was never the most favored dancer of Balanchine. She was a womanly figure in a company that revered youth, a dramatic dancer in a choreographic world where the dictum was "Just do the steps." In the last few years of her career she was the only dancer in the company who was invariably greeted by applause when she entered the stage.

What made Melissa Hayden the prima ballerina to so many was, variously, the "clarity of every step she takes," her "unique dramatic thrust," her strength and attack, her swagger and "coiled puma spring," her technique. And her intelligence. She was a solidly schooled classical dancer with a formidable presence. Her training started rather late, when she was already twelve, and it was meant to be nothing more than an extension of piano and swimming lessons—the education of a typical middle-class Canadian child. But while the then Mildred Herman dutifully became the bookkeeper her parents insisted she become, she also became a dancer.

Boris Volkoff was her teacher, and she worked with his Canadian Ballet until she made the inevitable move to New York, where she danced with the Radio City Music Hall corps and took ballet classes during the intervals between shows. Hayden danced for two and a half years with Ballet Theatre, until the company suspended operations in 1948, when she went on a picaresque South American tour with a troupe organized by the Cuban ballerina Alicia Alonso. A cable asking her to come back to New York for the 1949–50 season of Balanchine's new company rescued her. At NYCB she took on major roles in *Apollo, Serenade, Ivesiana, Concerto Barocco, The Four Temperaments, Symphony in C, Orpheus*. . . .

Melissa Hayden with Hugh Laing in
Bayou, *1952.*

During her career Hayden worked with practically every great American choreographer. Her early signature work was William Dollar's *The Duel* (1950), essentially a long pas de deux in which Hayden's Amazonian qualities were emphasized. She played Clorinda, the Saracen girl who disguises herself as a warrior and is killed by her lover in a duel on horseback. Except for a two-year hiatus during which she returned to Ballet Theatre in the early fifties, she danced continuously with the New York City Ballet, where she developed a successful partnership with the somewhat younger Jacques d'Amboise, and was perhaps most famous in Balanchine's *Swan Lake, Firebird, Episodes,* and *Liebeslieder Walzer,* and in Robbins's *The Cage.* She had an international reputation through guest appearances with other companies, in her role as the ballerina in Charlie Chaplin's *Limelight,* and as the Sugar Plum Fairy in a German film version of *The Nutcracker.* She was married in 1954 and has two children. Since 1973 she has been teaching, coaching, and staging Balanchine's ballets for various companies throughout the world.

When you first began to work with Balanchine you were twenty-seven years old and had danced in Canada, and with Ballet Theatre, and with Alicia Alonso's company. What was it like coming into Balanchine's company with all that experience?

I felt that I was surrounded by children. No one there impressed me except Balanchine himself. I looked around and thought, What *am* I doing here?

During our first season—a very spare one, three weeks, Thursday through Sunday—I felt lost in a big ocean. Janet Reed, who had been with me in Ballet Theatre, was the only dancer I could relate to. Mr. Balanchine was not teaching, and I was dancing in ballets I had never seen before. The only woman in the company who knew Balanchine's style was Maria. She was married to him then and had worked with him in Ballet Russe. Maria and Janet taught me the steps of pieces they had danced in, and Lew Christensen, who was the ballet master, showed me the rest and gave me some idea of what Balanchine wanted. This was my initiation into the company.

I had been studying then for some time with Madame Anderson in a little studio on Fifty-sixth Street. When Balanchine found that out he sort of sniffed and said, "Good teacher, but maybe you ought to come to my school." So I dutifully went to the classes there, but kept studying with my own teacher too. What they were teaching at the school really had nothing to do with Balanchine, anyway. Vladimiroff and the others were teaching what they had brought with them from Russia, and Balanchine himself didn't have much time to work with the dancers.

Do you think you transformed yourself into a Balanchine dancer?

The idea that there is such a creature seems simply like good PR to me. He didn't start it, but it's good business and he's a smart businessman. I suppose that what you're in fact talking about is the look Balanchine likes. When he first came to America he went to Hollywood and was very impressed by the glamorous, long-legged girls he saw there. Not necessarily elegant. So the idea was that you could be not only a dancer but also glamorous. He really liked the look of Zorina—long legs, blond, small head. Tanaquil Le Clercq had that look, too. But can you say that Maria Tallchief was not a Balanchine dancer? She's turned in. She doesn't have a typical line. Yet she certainly is a Balanchine dancer. You make yourself a Balanchine dancer by dancing his ballets. Your legs change, your body changes, you become a filly. You're not carrying heavy music or heavy choreography. You're flying.

Fortunately I had studied music, so I responded immediately to Balanchine's choreography. And I had very good classical training. Even in the beginning reviewers would say how perfectly placed I was. So on balance. I had difficulty with the speed at first, but they kept encouraging me. Maria Tallchief was particularly generous. I think she wanted us to feel less alone. She instigated a class with Balanchine for all of us: Janet Reed, Tanny Le Clercq, Yvonne Mounsey, Maria, and

Hayden with André Prokovsky in Brahms-Schoenberg Quartet, 1966.

me. Six weeks of two-hour classes every day. That's where I was really taught the technique. Balanchine is, of course, a marvelous instructor, and a wonderful mime. I remember years later watching him teach Allegra Kent the Swan Queen. He was in street shoes and he did the part more beautifully than anyone else. But he does men's parts beautifully, too. He has wonderful coloration. When he was rehearsing me in *Midsummer Night's Dream* he did the donkey part, and I was splitting my sides. He can do anything. His body speaks.

What were you dancing in those first years with the company?
I was doing the Balanchine repertoire, and I was asked to do new roles by other choreographers: Todd Bolender, Frederick Ashton, Bill Dollar, Jerry Robbins. It was Lincoln Kirstein's idea that other people should be encouraged to do pieces, and he suggested to Ashton that he use me in *Illuminations,* and to Bill Dollar that I be Clorinda in *The Duel,* which became my signature piece

and brought the audience's attention to me. I was dancing all the time and getting training in Balanchine's style by doing roles like *Firebird* after Maria had done it. The leading parts in all those ballets were marvelous, but I thought my purpose in the company was for Balanchine to create on me, and I desperately wanted my own ballet. I had patience, but you know how you get all twisted inside.

Finally, of course, Balanchine gave me opportunities. I was very anxious to please him and to learn from him, and Balanchine must have known that, because for four and a half years, from 1949 to 1953, I had a great deal to do. Then, all of a sudden, I felt there had been a change in the company. Other people were invited in and I thought I wasn't being used enough. I thought the artistic direction of the company had changed, and I felt threatened.

By sheer accident Ballet Theatre was in need of a ballerina then because Mary Ellen Moylan was indisposed and Alicia Alonso was dividing her time between New York and Cuba. So I was enticed back by Oliver Smith and Lucia Chase and had the chance to dance all the roles I dreamed about when I was with them before. We toured a great deal, and as it turned out much of the responsibility for this fell on me. I found myself head of a company, the only ballerina. And I didn't like it! I missed the Balanchine choreography, the atmosphere, the creative process.

It was at this time that you got married, wasn't it?
It was not by accident. I wanted to have a home, and a child. Then I was ready to go back to Balanchine. I knew that other than having a good marriage with someone you trust the most exciting relationship is with him, being the instrument of his creative powers. You bask in that, and

grow in it. So two years after I left the company I let it be known that I was available again. It took two months to get an answer, but finally I had an appointment with Balanchine. I got very dressed up, and there he was, smiling, welcoming me, and in five minutes I was back in the company. With no guilt, no intimidation.

How long did it take you to get back in his good graces choreographically?
Well, about two years. In the meantime I was doing repertory again. It was a very creative period for Balanchine. We were his "family," he said. "I'm making ballets for my family." This was before Tanaquil's accident. I came back the year before she was disabled by polio, on our European tour. That gave me nightmares. Tanaquil loved to dance, and I would dream that she was on stage and that I was excited about her dancing and was congratulating her. She had been so special. It was a tremendous loss to the company, to the shape of the company. I had been struck by her from the very beginning, even when I was skeptical about the quality of the other dancers there. We shared a dressing room, and I thought she was so intelligent, so sensitive, and talented. She had a real feeling of drama about her body, and ballets she felt comfortable in made her glow. I think she was uncomfortable in some of Balanchine's work, but she would always try to figure out what was right about what she was doing. We pulled together very strongly when she got sick and Balanchine left to take care of her. I think most of us felt as if a parent had gone away for a long time. But we knew he would come home. I know I tried harder then, and the personal tensions between people in the company seemed less complicated. Because the competition between

The premiere of Cortège Hongrois, *May 17, 1973. In front, from left to right, Merrill Ashley, Robert Irving, Karin von Aroldingen, Melissa Hayden, Balanchine, and Colleen Neary.*

the women, of course, was always keen.

Balanchine was very giving to the people who kept the company together during that bad time. When he came back, instead of focusing on one woman—which he did with Tanaquil—he started focusing on all the women. Look at the ballets that come from that period! *Agon, Square Dance, Stars and Stripes, Episodes.* . . .

Agon was a breeze for me. I think that when Balanchine saw me in Jerry Robbins's *The Cage* he got the idea that I could do the angular movements he wanted in *Agon.* My variation was not very long—about a minute—and we put it together in about an hour. Balanchine really knew me, what I would respond to. When we went into the studio to start on it the pianist wasn't there, so Balanchine sat down at the piano and played with the timing. He had me count and taught me the music and then suggested I do certain movements. He was the choreographer and the pianist. When the real pianist came, after about half an hour, we'd finished most of the piece. Balanchine eventually changed some of this, but not much. That's the way we worked. The variation in *Donizetti* was also done in a very short time. We always worked quickly, and there was no point in asking Balanchine what the ballet was about. He'd just say, facetiously, "Ten or fifteen minutes." So you listened to the music and danced the choreography as it related to what you heard.

Balanchine didn't seem to visualize me in any one style, but he always thought of me as a technical dancer. When I saw his work with Diana Adams and Bill Carter in *Liebeslieder Walzer* I said, "My God, that's so beautiful and romantic. It's ballroom dancing." And Balanchine said, "Well, yes, but you'll have something more technical." He

would do the most marvelous things for a dancer. But I learned never to question him about what he had in mind, because I knew if I did I wouldn't get an answer. He would get annoyed and be evasive.

It seems that the most satisfying part of your long career with Balanchine was during the decade after you returned to the company from Ballet Theatre. Before the "Farrell years." Was that later period difficult for you?

The Farrell years were difficult for everybody. A number of talented younger people felt especially threatened and were very bitter about Mr. Balanchine's fascination with Suzanne. He was constantly in her company, and it gave him immense pleasure. I think it was somewhat of a lost time for me. The shape of the classes was different, the tutoring of the other dancers in the company was different. For instance, Suzanne had a bad knee, so we hardly ever jumped in class. And if we didn't do any jumps how were we supposed to sustain our technique? He was our coach, teacher, and director, yet he wasn't using *our* bodies to inspire him. It was very hard, but I played by the rules. Fortunately I was in demand for concert work outside the company.

Suzanne Farrell was very young when she came into the company, and NYCB today seems younger than ever. Yet you were always very much an "adult" dancer. Did that cause problems for you?

Of course that got to me, that he chose to have such youthful dancers around him. Balanchine's interest in his choreography and the NYCB and youth is his life's blood. Youthful innocence nourishes him. Before his school was so developed Balanchine was grateful to have dancers

like me and Diana Adams and Pat Wilde. But then there got to be so many little girls vying for his attention, wanting to get into the company. That was very nice for him, but it bored me. Balanchine is childlike. Much of the time I wouldn't even know the names of those young dancers.

Sometimes Balanchine picks a dancer before that dancer is ready, and he doesn't really let her develop properly. Jumping in to dance the lead role in a ballet doesn't feed a dancer. A sixteen- or seventeen-year-old girl doesn't know what choices she should make in a role like that. Gelsey Kirkland, for instance, got too much too soon without the right kind of emotional support. I think that Balanchine gave her opportunities she wasn't ready for. She was very confused and she finally sought support elsewhere, which upset him terribly. But dancers are people. They have emotions like everyone else, and if they aren't nurtured properly and conditioned in a healthy way they'll never make it.

I think finally that Balanchine was very generous to me and that he liked me. Some people have said that I didn't inspire him, but that is a very shortsighted point of view. He needs to have people around him whom he can work with, and I was flexible and versatile and useful to him. He was very tuned-in to me. During my second pregnancy he was wonderful. I danced until I was four and a half months pregnant, because he said no one could tell, and then he had me doing Ford Foundation surveys for him. When I had a huge stomach I was still teaching at his school, but he just said, "Everybody has to know that women are pregnant before they have babies." And then after Jennifer was born I was desperate to come back, and he took me. On the other hand, there was always a distance between me

Hayden in Stars and Stripes, *1958.*

and Balanchine, and he could hurt me. Once he complimented me, and I thought he was open for conversation, so I asked him if I could have back one of the ballets that was created for me. If I could dance in it. And he gave me the most devastating answer: "No, dear," he said, "you're too old."

I don't think I got too old, or that I danced too long, but I did get tired, tired of the pressure I put on myself,

and there came a time when dance wasn't fulfilling for me anymore. I saw that opportunities were being given to younger dancers and that I was not in the mainstream of Balanchine's thoughts. In 1967 I was terribly disappointed when he didn't create a part for me in *Jewels.* Arthur Mitchell and I were to have danced a section called "Sapphires," but instead we were given a token ballet, *Trois Valses Romantiques.* Arthur

didn't like that, and I felt cheated because this big ballet was being done and I didn't have a part. Later I asked Balanchine if I could dance "Emeralds," and he liked the way I did it. He suggested that I do "Rubies" too, but I thought it was too young for me.

Then at the Stravinsky Festival in 1972 I felt left out. I looked at rehearsals of his ballets and I felt I was sitting on the side of a stream watching the water rush by. I got one token ballet, and I danced *Agon,* and *Orpheus,* and *The Cage,* but I wasn't really involved in the company anymore. Even though I was still capable of dancing the most difficult parts, Balanchine didn't think of me in a vital capacity. He in a sense announced my resignation for me. So I told him I was leaving.

But you had lasted a long time with Balanchine, even though you got married and had babies. Why do you think you were able to work with him artistically longer than the others?

I was very turned on by Balanchine. What he was saying choreographically excited me—emotionally, intellectually, physically. That doesn't mean that I ever thought of Balanchine as a father figure, or had fantasies about him as a lover, or thought that if I slept with him I would get another ballet. I love Balanchine dearly, no matter if it's returned or not, and I would always do whatever he wanted. Mr. Balanchine is a very disciplined person, and I responded to that. He would walk into a studio with two hours to work and in two hours he had made something. He didn't wait around for Terpsichore or someone to come to him, and I didn't let anything interfere with the fact that I was a dancer. My family—my children and a focused relationship with my husband—gave me an anchor and kept me from developing a big ego, which helped. I was sometimes impatient, and sometimes bitter, but in the end I was the ballerina of Balanchine's company. In a starless and nameless-ballerina company, I was the ballerina. The audience accepted me as the ballerina, and the repertoire was there for me to present myself as a ballerina.

Hayden in Agon, *1957.*

Ballets in Which Balanchine Created Roles for Melissa Hayden

THEME AND VARIATIONS
music: Peter Ilyich Tchaikovsky
decor and costumes: Woodman Thompson
role: Solo
premiere: November 26, 1947, New York City Center
Ballet Theatre

JONES BEACH (choreographed with Jerome Robbins)
music: Jurriaan Andriessen
costumes: Jantzen
role: SUNDAY
premiere: March 9, 1950, New York City Center
New York City Ballet

CARACOLE
music: Wolfgang Amadeus Mozart
costumes: Christian Bérard
role: Ballerina (one of five)
premiere: February 19, 1952, New York City Center
New York City Ballet

BAYOU
music: Virgil Thomson
costumes: Dorothea Tanning
role: LEAVES AND FLOWERS
premiere: February 21, 1952, New York City Center
New York City Ballet

VALSE FANTAISIE
music: Mikhail Glinka
costumes: Karinska
role: Ballerina (one of three)
premiere: January 6, 1953, New York City Center
New York City Ballet

THE COUNTESS BECOMES THE MAID
(made for television)
music: Johann Strauss the Younger
role: Countess
premiere: February 3, 1953, *The Kate Smith Hour*, NBC-TV

PAS DE TROIS
music: Mikhail Glinka
costumes: Karinska
premiere: March 1, 1955, New York City Center
New York City Ballet

JEUX D'ENFANTS
music: Georges Bizet
decor and costumes: Esteban Francés
roles: THE DOLL; PAS DE DEUX
premiere: November 22, 1955, New York City Center
New York City Ballet

DIVERTIMENTO NO. 15
music: Wolfgang Amadeus Mozart
decor: James Stewart Morcom
costumes: Karinska
role: SECOND VARIATION
premiere: May 31, 1956, American Shakespeare Festival Theatre, Stratford, Conn.
New York City Ballet

AGON
music: Igor Stravinsky
role: BRANSLE GAY; BRANSLE DOUBLE
premiere: December 1, 1957, New York City Center
New York City Ballet

STARS AND STRIPES
music: John Philip Sousa, arranged by Hershy Kay
decor: David Hays
costumes: Karinska
role: FOURTH CAMPAIGN
premiere: January 17, 1958, New York City Center
New York City Ballet

EPISODES
music: Anton Webern
decor: David Hays
role: RICERCATA
premiere: May 14, 1959, New York City Center
New York City Ballet

THE FIGURE IN THE CARPET
music: George Frederick Handel
decor and costumes: Esteban Francés
role: Princess of Persia
premiere: April 13, 1960, New York City Center
New York City Ballet

VARIATIONS FROM *DON SEBASTIAN*
music: Gaetano Donizetti
decor: David Hays
costumes: Karinska
role: Ballerina
premiere: November 16, 1960, New York City Center
New York City Ballet

LIEBESLIEDER WALZER
music: Johannes Brahms
decor: David Hays
costumes: Karinska
role: Second Couple
premiere: November 22, 1960, New York City Center
New York City Ballet

MODERN JAZZ: VARIANTS
music: Günther Schuller
decor and costumes: David Hays
roles: VARIANT 3 (vibraharp); VARIANT 4 (drums)
premiere: January 4, 1961, New York City Center
New York City Ballet

A MIDSUMMER NIGHT'S DREAM
music: Felix Mendelssohn
decor: David Hays
costumes: Karinska
role: Titania
premiere: January 17, 1962, New York City Center
New York City Ballet

PAS DE DEUX AND DIVERTISSEMENT
music: Léo Delibes
costumes: Karinska
roles: VALSE LENTE AND PAS DE DEUX; PIZZICATI
premiere: January 14, 1965, New York State Theater
New York City Ballet

BRAHMS-SCHOENBERG QUARTET
music: Johannes Brahms, orchestrated by Arnold Schoenberg
decor: Peter Harvey
costumes: Karinska
role: ALLEGRO
premiere: April 21, 1966, New York State Theater
New York City Ballet

TROIS VALSES ROMANTIQUES
music: Emmanuel Chabrier
costumes: Karinska
role: Ballerina
premiere: April 6, 1967, New York State Theater
New York City Ballet

GLINKIANA
music: Mikhail Glinka
decor, costumes, and lighting: Esteban Francés
role: JOTA ARAGONESE
premiere: November 23, 1967, New York State Theater
New York City Ballet

CHORAL VARIATIONS ON BACH'S "VOM HIMMEL HOCH"
music: Igor Stravinsky
decor: Rouben Ter-Arutunian
role: Principal
premiere: June 25, 1972, New York State Theater
New York City Ballet

CORTÈGE HONGROIS
music: Alexander Glazunov
decor and costumes: Rouben Ter-Arutunian
role: Ballerina
premiere: May 17, 1973, New York State Theater
New York City Ballet

> He X-rayed all of us. He saw the internal thing that could be elicited. There was such a combustible, explosive atmosphere in those old studios.

Diana Adams

Diana Adams was the foremost interpreter of Balanchine's terse, highly concentrated style of the late 1950s, epitomized by *Agon,* which Balanchine himself called "the quintessential contemporary ballet." The *Agon* Pas de Deux was created for Adams and Arthur Mitchell, who remarked that it was her "nervous intensity that made the whole pas de deux work, because it's not so much the difficulty of the steps or how flexible you are, it's the precariousness."

Adams was born in Stanton, Virginia, and took ballet classes from her stepmother in Memphis, Tennessee. In New York she studied with Agnes de Mille. She made her theatrical debut on Broadway in *Oklahoma!* in 1943, and the following year joined Ballet Theatre, where she soon became a soloist. She created the role of the mother in de Mille's *Fall River Legend* and frequently appeared as the Queen of the Wilis in *Giselle.*

Adams and her husband, Hugh Laing, joined the New York City Ballet in 1950, and John Martin soon after called her "the epitome of the lyric dancer" for her performances in *Concerto Barocco* and *Symphonie Concertante.* She was also celebrated for dramatic roles such as the Siren in *Prodigal Son* and Eurydice in *Orpheus.* Martin pointed out that she could dance so well in so varied a repertory because her "special gift is simply for movement. It is vividly colored by feeling, but its strength lies in the vital continuity of muscular impulse which gives it timbre and substance."

Before *Agon* she had danced in a diverse collection of Balanchine ballets, including *Western Symphony, Ivesiana,* and *Divertimento No. 15.* In 1959, when he made the "Five Pieces" section of *Episodes* for her, Balanchine emphasized what Lincoln Kirstein had called her "cool linear plasticity." At one point in the ballet she was hanging around her partner's neck in such a way that her legs seemed to become antlers. The Ballerina role in *Movements for Piano and Orchestra* was conceived for Adams in 1963, but she never performed it. She left the company during rehearsals when she became pregnant, and her role was taken over by Suzanne Farrell.

Adams taught at the School of American Ballet after her retirement and in 1982 served as an adviser to American Ballet Theatre when they remounted Balanchine's *Symphonie Concertante.* She was divorced from Hugh Laing and later married Ronald Bates, the stage manager of

Diana Adams with Arthur Mitchell in Agon, *1957.*

Adams with Conrad Ludlow in Electronics, *1961.*

NYCB. They have a daughter, Georgina.

When you joined the New York City Ballet in 1950 you had already established yourself as a dancer at Ballet Theatre. Yet when Arlene Croce remarked on the development of the Balanchine style she said that by the late fifties you were the dancer who above all the others had consolidated the Balanchine look for the company. Did you just take to it naturally?

Not at all. I didn't think I fit as a Balanchine dancer. I looked around and saw dancers with tremendous, dizzying, fast technique, and it intimidated me terribly. That's what I wanted to be like—strong and com-pact, with some kind of attack, like the other dancers. But they had all danced in Balanchine's ballets be-fore and seemed to assimilate them in a way that I didn't very easily. I felt like an outsider.

I had seen almost everything that Balanchine had done for Ballet Russe, and I saw Ballet Society a couple of times, which impressed me very much, but I was intimidated because it was so obvious that his dancers had to be very strong tech-nically and I didn't think I was. I knew Balanchine liked me, because he told Lucia Chase to put me into his things at Ballet Theatre. Lucia was trying to get Balanchine in-volved with the company, and he was being elusive, but he came to restage *Princess Aurora* and to do *Theme and Variations*. He coached me in *Sylphides,* and I finally learned *Theme and Variations* and did it on tour a couple of times, al-though I almost fell into the orches-tra pit. I was terrified. Balanchine rehearsed me in the pas de deux and I was nice in it, but those fast first entrances were terribly hard for me.

Joining his company meant a re-training for me. At that time every-body in Ballet Theatre felt that Balanchine would think you were wonderful if you could just get your leg up high and could turn. Antony Tudor had a great influence on Bal-let Theatre dancers, so we all thought you should act when you danced. I had worked hard trying to learn how to "project," and conse-quently I resisted Balanchine's sug-gestions about what I should do because I was afraid that whatever quality I had developed would get lost.

What sorts of ballets did he put you in at first?

Serenade was the first. I was the girl who runs in at the end, and I felt like I had three feet. Then I did *Sym-phonie Concertante*. We used to call it "Symphonie Concentrate" be-cause it was terribly long—three movements, terribly difficult. I wasn't used to working like that, and my feet would bleed during rehears-als, which Balanchine never seemed to notice. It was like a marathon. I almost never slept during that pe-riod, because I was so worried I wouldn't get through these things. I couldn't get through the Finale of *Symphony in C* at all. I kept thinking there must be something wrong with me, because everybody else could do it and I couldn't.

I thought he didn't understand what kind of dancer I was, but he was very nice to me and didn't press me. He thought if I could settle down and work I would be all right. I wasn't given parts where I would fall over my feet. He did nice things for me like *La Valse,* and when I told him that I thought I was awful in the Finale of *Symphony in C,* where everybody else was whirling around with so much aplomb, he said, "I'll change it, I'll change it." But something happens to you when he says that. I felt guilty that he would have to adapt all those marvelous steps to me. It just seemed that I couldn't let that happen.

So how did you finally accommodate yourself to his style?

It's a question of trust. You have to recognize that he sees some kind of intelligence within you, that he understands you. I really resisted for a long time. Poor man, I don't know how he did it. He would tell me the same thing over and over again very quietly and insistently and wait until I realized why he was doing it. In those days Tanny Le Clercq used to resist also. We would argue with Balanchine, "But I can't do it that way!" And he never got angry.

He knows more about dancing and the dancer's body and how dancing happens than anyone. He knows what is physically possible and what is most beautiful. And when you realize that, you have to give up some fantasies about yourself. In the beginning if you had given me a list of ballets that I thought I would be good in and then had shown me a list Balanchine thought I would be good in, there would have been no relation. He X-rayed all of us. He saw the internal thing that could be elicited. There was such a combustible, explosive atmosphere in those old studios. Balanchine had so much energy, yet so much patience.

When he cast people he had a sense of where each one would look good, where all the gifts would best come into play. It used to really confuse me, because there were several

roles that I thought I would be absolutely sensational in and I was never cast in them. I thought I would be fantastic as the Sleepwalker in *La Sonnambula,* and a lot of people in the company danced it, but I don't think he ever thought of casting me in it. I wanted to do the Sleepwalker because there were no pirouettes and I saw myself as a romantic, dreamy dancer. I didn't see myself flashing around like Balanchine did. He kept making me do all those fast and tricky things that technically were very difficult for me. And that annoyed me. I thought for a while he was trying to challenge me, to make me see what I lacked. But he wasn't. He just thought that with my long legs I should move that way. A big girl flashing around the stage looked nice. He saw the kind of movement that best suited each of his dancers, and how they would be perceived by the audience.

So everybody didn't end up looking alike at all, did they? He sometimes is criticized for going for uniformity.

Oh, no. Maria Tallchief, Tanny Le Clercq, and I had very different styles and ways of refining them through Balanchine's training. But there were things he thought were important for all of us—that we have tight fifth positions, and turned-out passé, and that we not lean forward and not be limp and not be sentimental. You don't drift around when you dance. You have to have energy. You must attack with Balanchine. He said, "Don't come on apologetically." That's the quality I think he tried to erase in me more than anything else.

Marie-Jeanne had a tremendous attack. And Maria was the mistress of coming on stage like an electric current. I just couldn't believe that anyone could enter with that kind of presence and confidence. I don't think Tanny thought of herself as a

classical dancer in the way it was understood in those days. She was very comfortable in contemporary things. But she presented herself with tremendous confidence and style.

Did you find that you analyzed Balanchine's choreography?

I don't think I ever analyzed Balanchine's movement. I was always so involved with trying to figure out the technique. In the immediate doing of it, you have to pick up quickly. Balanchine works very fast, and the music is often so complex that you are too involved in the counts and the beats to wonder what he is seeing.

I don't remember ever sitting around discussing dancing with him. Even with something like *Agon,* I tried not to analyze, because then I might give too much significance to a gesture, like when I put my hand on Arthur's wrist. I knew it wasn't meant to be a sentimental gesture. It had to do with part of a movement and I would spoil it if I started to think about it. In *Agon* the movements were so intricate that you really didn't think in terms of whose limb was attached to some other limb. You were just trying to negotiate your bodies. In the Pas de Deux what seems to be terribly intimate is simply one movement evolving from another. It was scientific.

Balanchine started making *Agon* with that Pas de Deux for Arthur and me. I was interested in what he was going to do for us, but I accepted it without thinking much about it. Balanchine rehearsals whip you into a frenzy. Keeping up with him was so difficult. I just tried to get the next step and fit them all together, to make them look like what I thought he wanted to see. We used to have hilarious rehearsals in the first part of *Agon* because we were in three groups and at the end of one section when we cross and go to a different

Adams in Monumentum Pro Gesualdo, *1960.*

Adams leading the Third Campaign of Stars and Stripes, *1958.*

position we were always getting there on a different count. I swore Melissa was one count early each time we arrived at that place, and Balanchine would have to make peace between us.

It was very challenging, and I liked that. It gave me less of an opportunity to brood on whether I was going to be good in something or not. I was involved with just doing it. That's how he works. What you are doing is important, not how your personality is being used. It was all totally fused.

But did you think about the effect of what you were doing?
Well, working it out is very intense. And he doesn't describe. In the last part of *Electronics,* for instance, Balanchine was very concerned about whose hand went where to get the movement right. I didn't think at the time about how this looked from the front. I was too involved in how he wanted it to be done, and it took a while to make it work. I got down on the floor and was very uncomfortable and was trying to do what he wanted. Balanchine was saying, "If you go here would this work?" "And if you put your arm there can he do that?" Then someone said, "Good God. That looks so pornographic!" I guess it looked very sexual, but I hadn't thought about it while I was doing it. And I wore a white leotard in that part, which is the most exposed that you can get, aside from being nude. When I thought about it afterward I realized that of course it looked sexual, and I was never able to do it well again.

You danced for over twelve years with Balanchine. Did you lose your feelings of insecurity and feel comfortable finally?
I was always convinced I wasn't going to be good enough, ever. Balanchine told me I was unbearably dull in *Swan Lake* and *Nutcracker*—two things I should have been nice

in, because they weren't that difficult technically. He didn't mean to be cruel, and I understood this. He wanted me to find some freedom to dance the way I probably could have if I hadn't been so neurotic, so worried about disappointing. At City Center I remember standing in the wings waiting to go on for *Swan Lake,* praying that he wouldn't show up. Because you always knew when he was in the theater. He would come flying in backstage, take off his coat, and go straight out front. I would think, Oh, blast, I was hoping he wasn't coming. But it wasn't the same when he wasn't there. It was less tense. Certainly not the same adrenalin.

John Martin told me that Balanchine said to him in Russia that you epitomized the kind of dancer he wanted.
He didn't get me early enough. If he could have trained me I might have been something else.

Why did you retire finally?
I was out with an illness, a miscarriage. And then when I came back I went on tour and got tendinitis. And I had a bad left knee. I wanted a child, and I think I wanted a different life. Dancing was full of stress for me. I didn't know, of course, that motherhood would be too. After I had my daughter, I stayed for a few years at the School of American Ballet, helping with the students. I was in charge of the scholarship program. But it was hard suddenly to just watch other people dance.

You saw Suzanne Farrell during auditions for that scholarship program, didn't you?
Yes. I saw her in Cincinnati. But that was before I had retired. When we got that first grant the funds were for looking at schools where there might be scholarship material. I was dizzy looking at all the bodies. There was another girl in Suzanne's class who looked more advanced, but she

didn't really seem to have an affinity for dancing. Suzanne was very young, and not very strong, but I thought she had a special quality of movement.

People say she moves like you did.
I don't know that we have anything in common. Maybe we are both a little remote, and concerned with immediacy of movement, but she is much more free and flamboyant than I was. I wasn't often very animated, because I usually was intimidated. I would have given better performances if I had gotten more pleasure out of dancing. Recently I was watching a young dancer in the company, Darci Kistler, who is wonderfully free, never hiding or holding anything back. Suzanne had that quality, too. But I was a rather neurotic dancer, always anxiety-ridden. The feeling comes back even now when I go to a performance. I can't sit still and, as Tanny says, "let it wash over me." I get very tense. You know how difficult it is and you want so much for everything to go well.

Even so, do you have pangs of regret about not dancing? Was it difficult, for instance, to see Suzanne Farrell take over your roles?
I had a tremendous feeling of warmth toward Suzanne Farrell. She was so young and scared when she first came to New York. I wanted very much for good things to happen to her, for her to have a good experience with things that I'd done. It's inevitable that someone will replace you, and she replaced me. One always thinks, though, that the ballets done for you are not the same with other dancers in them. It can be painful.

I'm very grateful no longer to have to face the exposure of dancing, which was so hard for me. But I know, too, that some of the most stimulating moments of my life were the classes with Balanchine.

Ballets in Which Balanchine Created Roles for Diana Adams

WALTZ ACADEMY
music: Vittorio Rieti
decor: Oliver Smith
costumes: Alvin Colt
role: FIRST PAS DE TROIS
premiere: October 5, 1944, Opera House, Boston
Ballet Theatre

PRINCESS AURORA
music: Peter Ilyich Tchaikovsky
decor: Michel Baronoff
costumes: Barbara Karinska after designs by Bakst
role: one of the Six Fairies
premiere: April 2, 1949, Opera House, Chicago
Ballet Theatre

LA VALSE
music: Maurice Ravel
costumes: Karinska
role: FIFTH WALTZ
premiere: February 20, 1951, New York City Center
New York City Ballet

THE SLEEPING BEAUTY: VARIATION from ACT III, AURORA'S WEDDING
music: Peter Ilyich Tchaikovsky
premiere: Summer 1951, Jacob's Pillow, Mass.

APOLLO, LEADER OF THE MUSES
music and book: Igor Stravinsky
costumes: Karinska
role: Calliope
premiere: November 15, 1951, New York City Center
New York City Ballet

CARACOLE
music: Wolfgang Amadeus Mozart
costumes: Christian Bérard
role: Ballerina (one of five)
premiere: February 19, 1952, New York City Center
New York City Ballet

BAYOU
music: Virgil Thomson
decor and costumes: Dorothea Tanning
role: Starched White Person
premiere: February 21, 1952, New York City Center
New York City Ballet

CONCERTINO
music: Jean Françaix
costumes: Karinska
role: Ballerina (one of two)
premiere: December 30, 1952, New York City Center
New York City Ballet

VALSE FANTAISIE
music: Mikhail Glinka
costumes: Karinska
role: Ballerina (one of three)
premiere: January 6, 1953, New York City Center
New York City Ballet

OPUS 34
music: Arnold Schoenberg
decor and lighting: Jean Rosenthal
costumes: Esteban Francés
role: THE FIRST TIME
premiere: January 19, 1954, New York City Center
New York City Ballet

WESTERN SYMPHONY
music: Hershy Kay
role: ALLEGRO
premiere: September 7, 1954, New York City Center
New York City Ballet

IVESIANA
music: Charles Ives
role: OVER THE PAVEMENTS
premiere: September 14, 1954, New York City Center
New York City Ballet

A MUSICAL JOKE
music: Wolfgang Amadeus Mozart
costumes: Karinska
role: Lead
premiere: May 31, 1956, American Shakespeare Festival Theatre, Stratford, Conn.
New York City Ballet

DIVERTIMENTO NO. 15
music: Wolfgang Amadeus Mozart
decor: James Stewart Morcom
costumes: Karinska
role: THIRD VARIATION
premiere: May 31, 1956, American Shakespeare Festival Theatre, Stratford, Conn.
New York City Ballet

AGON
music: Igor Stravinsky
role: PAS DE DEUX
premiere: December 1, 1957, New York City Center
New York City Ballet

STARS AND STRIPES
music: John Philip Sousa, arranged by Hershy Kay
decor: David Hays
costumes: Karinska
role: THIRD CAMPAIGN: "Rifle Regiment"
premiere: January 17, 1958, New York City Center
New York City Ballet

EPISODES: PART II
music: Anton Webern
decor: David Hays
role: FIVE PIECES
premiere: May 14, 1959, New York City Center
New York City Ballet

PANAMERICA
music: Carlos Chávez
decor: David Hays
costumes: Karinska
role: SINFONÍA NO. 5, FOR STRING ORCHESTRA (Mexico)
premiere: January 20, 1960, New York City Center
New York City Ballet

THE FIGURE IN THE CARPET
music: George Frederick Handel
decor and costumes: Esteban Francés
role: SCOTLAND
premiere: April 13, 1960, New York City Center
New York City Ballet

MONUMENTUM PRO GESUALDO
music: Igor Stravinsky
decor: David Hays
role: Principal
premiere: November 16, 1960, New York City Center
New York City Ballet

LIEBESLIEDER WALZER
music: Johannes Brahms
decor: David Hays
costumes: Karinska
role: First Couple
premiere: November 22, 1960, New York City Center
New York City Ballet

RAGTIME (I)
music: Igor Stravinsky
decor: Robert Drew
costumes: Barbara Karinska
role: PAS DE DEUX
premiere: December 7, 1960, New York City Center
New York City Ballet

MODERN JAZZ: VARIANTS
music: Gunther Schuller
roles: INTRODUCTION (orchestra); VARIANT 1 (piano); VARIANT 2 (bass); VARIANT 5 (quartet)
premiere: January 4, 1961, New York City Center
New York City Ballet

ELECTRONICS
music: electronic tape by Remi Gassman and Oskar Sala
decor: David Hays
role: Principal
premiere: March 22, 1961, New York City Center
New York City Ballet

In rehearsal for Movements for Piano and Orchestra, *1963, with Jacques D'Amboise and Balanchine.*

I offer a little suspense
because you never know
if I will appear or not.
Nor do I.

Allegra Kent

In 1954, when Balanchine
used her impassive, sphinxlike
beauty as the subject of the "Unanswered Question" section of *Ivesiana,* Allegra Kent was seventeen.
She appeared to be, in Arlene
Croce's words, "so supple she practically invited a man to turn her into
a docile toy." Imperturbable and still
while being manipulated in all directions by four male dancers who
carried her just out of reach of a
fifth, she never touched the floor,
never moved of her own volition, yet
she retained an indomitable inner
distance.

Allegra Kent's career, which has
been marked by a series of depar-
tures and returns to NYCB, seems to
reflect an unwillingness to be possessed entirely by ballet. She was
born in Santa Monica and was
trained in Los Angeles before coming to the School of American Ballet
as a scholarship student when she
was fourteen. Balanchine invited her
to become a member of the company the following year, but after her
success in *Ivesiana* she left NYCB to

enroll at the University of California at Los Angeles. She returned in a matter of months and was given a leading role in *Divertimento No. 15.* During the European tour of 1956 she filled in for Tanaquil Le Clercq after Le Clercq fell ill with polio. When she was nineteen she was made a principal dancer, and a few months later she left the company again, this time to play a kitten on Broadway in the flop musical *Shinbone Alley.*

Kent returned to take on the role of the Swan Queen, to great acclaim, during NYCB's Australian tour in the summer of 1958. That winter she appeared in *The Seven Deadly Sins,* the recreation of the Balanchine/ Weill/Brecht work made for Les Ballets 1933. She played the silent Annie to Lotte Lenya's singing Annie and was a sensation, "stripped to the legal minimum, borne in on a cellophane-wrapped platter as the most delectable dish in a night club," according to John Martin's description of one scene. The ethereal side of Kent's persona was brought out in 1960 when she was cast as the Sleepwalker in the revival of *Night Shadow,* a role with which she became identified.

Kent married the photographer Bert Stern in 1959, and left the company when she became pregnant with her first child. She returned in time for the 1962 tour of Russia, where she had a great popular success, especially in the *Agon* Pas de Deux, which she danced with Arthur Mitchell. Balanchine made the blatantly sexual *Bugaku* for Kent and Edward Villella in 1963, and she then left the company again to have a second child. She returned during the period when Suzanne Farrell, who shared her sexual/spiritual qualities, had become the central figure for Balanchine. The last role Balanchine made for her was the Andante section of the *Brahms-Schoenberg Quartet,* in 1966. After a

leave of absence for the birth of her third child in 1967, she originated the role of the Girl in Apricot in Jerome Robbins's *Dances at a Gathering.*

Divorced in the early 1970s, Kent moved with her children in 1975 to Scarsdale, where for a few years she had her own ballet school. She has written a book on water exercises and a short reminiscence of the artist Joseph Cornell for a retrospective of his work in 1976. Cornell revered Kent as a Romantic ballerina, and several of his "boxes" were inspired by her.

When did you first become aware of Balanchine?

The first ballet I saw and liked was Balanchine's *Night Shadow.* It was in the Ballet Russe de Monte Carlo repertory. What got me was when the Sleepwalker carried the dead poet offstage at the end. I couldn't believe my eyes. I thought, Did I see that or did I imagine that? But I just kept silent. As a child I didn't like to talk about what I'd seen.

I had never heard of Balanchine then. The first time I saw him was when I came to the school and needed a scholarship. He watched me do some steps—glissade, assemblé, jeté—and I got the scholarship, but I never knew if they were that interested in me. Except for one of my teachers, Felia Doubrovska. She focused on me.

The Sleepwalker became one of your greatest roles after Balanchine revived it in 1960. Since it had been the first ballet you liked, were you particularly attached to your own interpretation?

I always thought other people did it better than I did. But I love to watch other people. I think it was a relief to know that they did it better. Then I was free. I could just do it my way. I tried to do things correctly, but you

don't know how what you're doing looks like from the front. I had ideas of my own about how to do roles, although I tried never to overanalyze, and I trusted Mr. Balanchine if he said I was too extreme.

You were very young and hadn't been in the company very long when Balanchine made something for you—the "Unanswered Question" section of *Ivesiana.* What was that like?

The actual creation was casual. During rehearsals I couldn't figure out what was happening, so I just gathered ideas. I didn't really perform it until we were on stage. I was held aloft by four men, and another man was groping for me on the ground, but I didn't see him. I am momentarily in his hands, like an embryo, but he can't hold on to me.

I don't have a great ballet memory—perhaps I associate dancing with too much pain. I do remember a moment from another section of *Ivesiana,* though. The part called "In the Inn." At the end Tanaquil Le Clercq and Todd Bolender came out of the inn and shook hands and then parted. It was one of the greatest moments in ballet. The way Tanny shook his hand broke my heart. It was a very simple thing but very poignant. Now it has a completely different feeling. There's no pathos. It was a very moving image and now it's lost. But a lot of things are lost.

Ballets don't seem to be the same when they are revived. Some of your most famous roles have been in revivals, though. The Sleepwalker, of course, and the 1958 version of *The Seven Deadly Sins* was also a triumph for you.

But that ballet has become lost again, too. Lotte Lenya couldn't continue to do it, and I had a baby and left for a while. Somehow it wasn't kept in the repertory. It's too bad,

Allegra Kent with Jean-Pierre Bonnefous in Bugaku.

Rehearsing The Seven Deadly Sins, *1958.*

Kent and Edward Villella in Brahms-Schoenberg Quartet, *1966.*

because I loved doing that ballet. I was so young then.

It was a ballet about being manipulated, but in a different way than the manipulation in *Ivesiana.* In *Seven Deadly Sins* two people inhabit one body, which is something I understand. Lenya speaks and makes the decisions, and I try to express my thoughts silently. I understand that type of person. Someone who lives through someone else.

I prepared for the part by listening to the record. I didn't think much about the sins, because they aren't really sins anymore, except maybe gluttony. The ballet seemed to me to be about someone being controlled by their alter ego. And about something becoming insufferable and then you die. It leads to suicide, because you have to get out of it. But actually my suicide at the end isn't really a suicide. It's more of a rebirth.

I had to act in *Seven Deadly Sins* more than in most ballets, and dancing and acting are quite different. But it didn't seem like a problem to me. Walking down the street requires a great deal of acting. Buying something in the supermarket is a great act. So I felt that I could act, but in the end the only things that you can express yourself with are steps. And Balanchine always gave me steps. Boy, was I glad to have some steps. An Arctic explorer said, "Give me winter, give me dogs." I say give me music and give me steps.

A few months after *The Seven Deadly Sins* revival Balanchine made *Episodes* for you, which is very abstract, just steps and movement, with no acting. Yet it too has a sexual quality. How does that happen?

Who knows what is in Balanchine's mind? His abstract ballets use the body as if it weren't human, but since it really is a human body some of the movements take on sexual overtones. In *Episodes* the twisting and turning give an illusion of more flexibility than there actually is. I'm lucky that I had flexibility, since Balanchine wants it in so many of his ballets. The whole second part of my career has been based on flexibility.

Bugaku was a genuinely erotic ballet. Erotic in the way Japanese prints are. Balanchine approached it very casually, and I didn't know what he was getting at when we started working on it. It's very difficult. My face is like a mask and I show very little emotion, which makes the movement important.

Did you ever think about your position in the succession of Balanchine's ballerinas? For instance, were you upset when it seemed that you were being replaced by Suzanne Farrell?

I just did my work, the way I always did. I knew I was Balanchine's favorite for a time, and I suppose I was surprised when Suzanne arrived, but it must have been because I was getting old. Balanchine was still interested in my dancing, but not as interested. I had been very important to the company at one time, particularly when I was twenty-one. I've done a lot of parts in my day. When we were touring Australia in the late fifties I learned thirty roles. I did a lot of roles that were done for other people, and I really had no favorites. I used to say that whatever ballet I had just done was my favorite. To confuse people. But I danced everything, two and three ballets a night, and eight ballets on the weekend. For a while there were only three principal women—Melissa Hayden, Patricia Wilde, and me. So we danced an amazing number of things. The other dancers were very helpful. They showed me steps, and helped me with technique. Sometimes you just had to learn the steps and figure out the rest during a performance. Interesting things can come out of being thrown into a ballet.

Your career has been very long, even though you started doing fewer things in the mid-sixties. But there were a lot of stops and starts. Does it seem to you that your professional life has been a series of comebacks?

Perhaps, although nothing I've done has been intentional. My comebacks are based on personal things. My mother made me leave the company the first time, so that I could go to college, and I guess Balanchine understood that, because he accepted me back. Then other things in my life took me away briefly, and I'd prolong the absence, which made it much harder to come back.

But I can't dance when I'm unhappy. I did come back after my third baby, and I think I danced very well.

I offer a little suspense, because you never know if I will appear or not. Nor do I. I know as little as anybody else until I actually appear. Sometimes it becomes so difficult for me to dance that I can't contemplate doing it. I think I'll never dance again, and then I break the ice and am able to dance for a while, until I can't continue again. It's difficult to come back when a year or two has passed and the body is that much older and the mind that much more set.

I always did what I wanted to do. I wanted three children, so I had them. I love creeping babies. Some part of me wanted to have an ordinary life. Other dancers are strong and can have children and come back immediately—like Melissa Hayden, or Merle Park, or Natasha Makarova. But I would start wondering whether I wanted to come back at all. I adored working, but dancing was such an effort that I didn't know if I could go through with it.

Sometimes I think that I didn't enjoy my career as much as I should have. Dancing to music is very important to human beings, and I always felt most alive if after a class I had worked so hard that I was almost raving with delirium. That's my style. But forcing yourself to make the effort to get to that point of intensity is hard.

What will you do when it's over?

I may want to teach, but mostly I just like to read books all day long, and swim in the ocean. Any ocean, but preferably the Indian Ocean. When I danced I always knew that it was a fleeting thing, that there would be a time when I wouldn't dance. That's the way things are. There will be another time and other dancers. You can't hold on to the past.

Ballets in Which Balanchine Created Roles for Allegra Kent

IVESIANA
music: Charles Ives
role: UNANSWERED QUESTION
premiere: September 14, 1954, New York City Center
New York City Ballet

DIVERTIMENTO NO. 15
music: Wolfgang Amadeus Mozart
decor: James Stewart Morcom
costumes: Karinska
role: FIRST VARIATION
premiere: May 31, 1956, American Shakespeare Festival Theatre, Stratford, Conn.
New York City Ballet

STARS AND STRIPES
music: John Philip Sousa, arranged by Hershy Kay
decor: David Hays
costumes: Karinska
role: FIRST CAMPAIGN: "Corcoran Cadets"
premiere: January 17, 1958, New York City Center
New York City Ballet

THE SEVEN DEADLY SINS
music: Kurt Weill
libretto: Bertolt Brecht, translated by W. H. Auden and Chester Kallman
decor and costumes: Rouben Ter-Arutunian
role: Anna II
premiere: December 4, 1958, New York City Center
New York City Ballet

EPISODES: PART II
music: Anton Webern
decor: David Hays
role: CONCERTO, OPUS 24
premiere: May 14, 1959, New York City Center
New York City Ballet

NIGHT SHADOW
music: Vittorio Rieti, after Vincenzo Bellini
decor: Esteban Francés
costumes: André Levasseur
role: Sleepwalker
premiere: January 6, 1960, New York City Center
New York City Ballet

BUGAKU
music: Toshiro Mayuzumi
decor: David Hays
costumes: Karinska
role: Ballerina
premiere: March 20, 1963, New York City Center
New York City Ballet

BRAHMS-SCHOENBERG QUARTET
music: Johannes Brahms, orchestrated by Arnold Schoenberg
decor: Peter Harvey
costumes: Karinska
role: ANDANTE
premiere: April 21, 1966, New York State Theater
New York City Ballet

La Sonnambula with Erik Bruhn.

> You are alone on the stage, and when I was dancing Balanchine's work I felt that I was carrying a better solution for that moment.

Violette Verdy

When Violette Verdy joined the New York City Ballet in 1958 she was twenty-five years old and a fully formed dancer with a dramatic style. She had been trained by Russian teachers in Paris and had been appearing for over a decade with French, English, and American companies. Her adaptation to Balanchine—and her adaptation of his choreography to her own highly inflected personal style—made for a unique career at NYCB.

Violette Verdy was born Nelly Guillerm in the medieval town of Pont-l'Abbé-Lambour in Brittany. Her father died when she was an infant, and she was raised by her mother, an elementary-school teacher who was to guide her daughter's career and remain her companion for many years. Madame Guillerm arranged for Nelly's music and ballet lessons, and when the child was nine they moved to Paris. She made her professional debut at the age of twelve with Roland Petit's Ballets des Champs-Élysées and danced with that company until it was disbanded three years later. Nelly Guillerm became Violette Verdy in 1949 when she starred in the film *Ballerina*. She also appeared in Jean-Louis Barrault's production of Montherlant's *Malatesta*.

In 1954 Verdy toured the United States with Petit's Ballets de Paris and gained a good deal of attention for her performances as the Bride in *Le Loup* and in the title role of his version of *Carmen*. Following the tour she went to Hollywood to make a film with Leslie Caron, *The Glass Slipper*, and then joined the London Festival Ballet, where she danced leading roles in *Swan Lake, The Nutcracker*, and *Les Sylphides*. She underwent surgery for a ruptured Achilles tendon in 1956, but was able to dance with Ballet Rambert in London the following year, performing *Giselle* and *Coppélia* for the first time. She came to New York again in 1957 to dance with American Ballet Theatre. She had been chosen by Birgit Cullberg to dance the title role in Cullberg's production of *Miss Julie* for ABT, and she also appeared in Balanchine's *Theme and Variations*.

Violette Verdy in the Tchaikovsky Pas de Deux.

When American Ballet Theatre disbanded temporarily, Verdy was asked to join the New York City Ballet. She made her debut in *Divertimento No. 15,* and was soon plunged into more difficult Balanchine territory with the creation of the first section of *Episodes,* to a twelve-tone Webern score. In March 1960 Balanchine choreographed the *Tchaikovsky Pas de Deux* for Verdy and Conrad Ludlow, and John Martin noted in *The New York Times* that she was "obviously the key to its charm. Balanchine has built it upon her beautiful phrasing, and her capacity for lyric gaiety." That No-

vember she and Nicholas Magallanes were one of the four couples in Balanchine's Brahms masterpiece, *Liebeslieder Walzer.* Another great role followed in 1962, the Act II Divertissement of *A Midsummer Night's Dream.*

Unlike most of Balanchine's ballerinas, Verdy continued to appear in the nineteenth-century classics as a guest artist with other companies. She danced *The Sleeping Beauty* for the first time in 1964 with the Royal Ballet, but soon afterward a serious foot operation caused her to take off more than a year from dancing. When she returned to NYCB Balan-

chine made several roles which emphasized her French qualities. In April 1967 she led the elegant "Emeralds" section of *Jewels,* to music by Fauré; in 1968 she was the inspiration for *La Source,* to Delibes; and in 1975 Balanchine opened the Ravel Festival with *Sonatine,* created for Verdy and Jean-Pierre Bonnefous, in a French-accented evening at which Balanchine received the Légion d'Honneur.

Verdy reduced her performing schedule after she underwent a third operation on her foot in 1973, and finally retired from dancing in 1976, when she became the first woman to direct the Paris Opéra Ballet. She left the Opéra after three years of bureaucratic entanglements, and since 1980 has been associate artistic director of the Boston Ballet. Verdy was married to Colin Clark, son of Sir Kenneth Clark, in 1961. They were divorced in 1969.

When Balanchine took you into the company you were still quite young, but you had been dancing for over a decade and had developed a style. You were also the first European to dance with NYCB. Why do you think he wanted you?

You forget that at that time, in the late fifties, the company had dancers with personalities. Balanchine had Patricia Wilde, Diana Adams, Jillana, Melissa Hayden—dancers with distinct identities. Now it's different because the accent is on the shapes. Everybody is a greyhound. And Balanchine takes people when they are not yet formed, when they are buds, like Darci Kistler. I think that he wanted me then because he saw that I could bring things to his company that it didn't have, details of style that no one else had, and also because he felt that I was still young enough that he could develop things in me that had not yet been brought out.

Balanchine once told me that he knew my pedigree very well. He's always liked France, and the Paris Opéra is a landmark that excited him. I was French, with typical French qualities—a clear, clean technique and articulated feet, with refined pointe work. And I had been schooled in the Russian style. You know, my Russian teachers gave me something which helped me very much when I began dancing for Balanchine. They made me aware of a performance as a great drama, almost a question of life and death. Going from the black wing of a curtain into the light of the stage is

something incredible, indescribable. A performance is not something out of normal life. You are alone on the stage, and when I was dancing Balanchine's work I felt that I was carrying a better solution for that moment. His choreography is the best solution.

But you never felt that he wanted you to be anonymous? To suppress your personality?

Even he says you can never get rid of the human person. When people say his ballets are abstract he replies, "How can you say 'abstract' when it deals fundamentally with human bodies?" A dancer directs her attention first to the work, to the choreography, but it is unavoidable that her accent will remain—humor, behavior, the atmosphere of her personality. It is a package deal. You can't avoid it. After I had been in Balanchine's company for a while I began to realize that he needed a gallery of dancers because he had within him so many possibilities to express. He needs differences between the dancers.

I think that Balanchine worked with me in a way he didn't with other people. John Martin once wrote about me that I analyzed each role I took on and made each one different. He said that was a very French quality. We analyze the problem and look for solutions. When Balanchine and I worked together he would just throw the choreography at me. He never said anything like "Put the accent here," or "Don't run too much there because you'll be too far for the diagonal," or anything like that. He knew that I would take what he gave me and say, "OK, now what is this? A flute? So I can't stamp too hard." Or "This is a cello, so I have to look more serious." He never bothered to tell me too much, because I would analyze it anyway. However, when he worked with other women he would tell them

everything. There were even sessions in which he would act out the girl's role. He would say, "OK, darling, now you run here," and he would mime what the dancer should do. Sometimes I would watch this and think, My God, what is he doing? He knew that the fastest way to obtain what he meant was just to act out what he wanted and then they could copy him. With me he knew he might as well leave me alone and then later he could correct what I did if he didn't like it.

Balanchine made a lot of ballets for you, but you also took on many roles that had been created for other dancers. Did you mind doing things that had been made for women whose style was unlike yours?

No, and I'm not selfish about having my roles taken over by other dancers. I think that sometimes Balanchine starts with an idea and it changes later, when other people come along. The Divertissement in *Midsummer Night's Dream*, for instance, was made for me, but then Allegra Kent was very beautiful in it, and the lines changed a bit. And a ballet that wasn't made for me, but for Maria Tallchief, the *Gounod Symphony*, was absolutely clearly explained when I danced it. It was conceived like a beautiful French garden, like some of the big gardens of Versailles. It had a courtlike quality that I could handle well. I think it is one of Balanchine's most beautiful ballets.

The *Tchaikovsky Pas de Deux*, which became practically my signature piece, was not meant for me at all. It was for Diana Adams and Jacques d'Amboise, but Diana hurt her foot, and Conrad Ludlow and I were understudies, so we were the first ones to do it. I think Diana became injured before the solo was completed and Balanchine finished it on me, which of course made it somewhat mine. I couldn't resist giving it some of those little phrasings and accents that I had been taught by the Russians. Balanchine didn't mind. I've always especially liked dancing to a violin, because it gives a sensuous quality to the way you use your muscles. You have to sustain the movement.

But I'll tell you, no matter how divine it is to dance Balanchine's ballets even after they've been done by twenty-six other people, nothing can compare with working with him and seeing him create something in front of you, for you. Seeing how he solves the problems that come up with the music, and how simple and right his solutions are. It happens with no one else in that way.

Have you been able to figure out how he does it? Do you think you got to know him well enough to know how he approaches a problem?

There is a great deal about Balanchine that I think I will never know. He has a mysterious creative aspect that I cannot put myself into. I can't tell how he assimilates himself into a situation, or how he interprets things. He always surprises me, which is very rewarding, of course. But I can't analyze him. I can't even tell you what he saw in me, although he made me discover things about myself that I didn't know. He was in some ways like a big mirror for me. There is a lot of reflection from the mirror, you see yourself, you catch yourself at moments being something you didn't know you were. The mirror knows what you are, but you know nothing of the mirror.

Frankly, I had a hard time thinking of Balanchine as a person. I was brought up in a very traditional, European way, with a clear sense of the different positions in life. There are distances between people because of rank and age that are to be respected. I would never have been able to call Mr. Balanchine George. I suppose an American psychologist would say that I saw him as a father figure, which would make sense, because I didn't have a father, and Balanchine was a rich replacement. But Balanchine also represented to me the most extraordinary creative aspect of the world of dance, about which I had many dreams and aspirations. I suppose I was afraid to discover too much about him because I didn't want to lose my illusions.

Balanchine was probably annoyed that I put him on a pedestal. Now, much later, I've gotten over those fantasies to a certain extent and I've discovered that I like Balanchine. I agree with him on most things, and I know what he's up to. He's a very principled man. But for a long time he was primarily a mythical or symbolic figure for me.

You seem to have thought of him as a guru. Do you think that during your greatest creative period as a dancer with Balanchine, in the early sixties, you were able to give yourself over to him in the way one aspires to with a guru?

I suppose that in the dance Balanchine is more of a guru than anyone else, but his offer is still on the human level. I discovered much later, when I went to a real guru, how it is possible to address the question of giving yourself up in a serious way. I think that the person who has come closest to surrendering to Balanchine is Suzanne Farrell. She has managed that kind of wonderful surrender that is also a glorification of the self. Suzanne has a sincere faithfulness to Balanchine; she is completely invested of only his intentions. There she is with that beautiful body, executing what Balanchine wants by doing those wonderful things. Sometimes I see pure Balanchine when I watch her.

I was not physically able to sustain my commitment, which is a form of treason. The final reluctance to give myself over translated itself into injuries. I looked like a victim, someone you could feel compassion for, but the truth was, I think, that it had become impossible for me to realize myself as a Balanchine dancer. It was not meant to be. It's a very mysterious thing.

Someone who maintained herself on a different level is Melissa Hayden. Melissa did it for herself. She knew that Balanchine was so much the best she had ever known that to elevate herself to her best she should stay with him. She stayed there no matter what, and he repaid her beautifully for it. She always danced, and in fact if Melissa did not have enough he would take things away from me and give them to her. She deserved something from Balanchine because of her faithfulness, her work, and her incredible determination.

I sometimes felt that he was unfair, because it seemed to me that I was better for certain things than she was. But I understood about seniority, although I also had a certain ordinary, aggressive ambition in me. Balanchine knew what he was doing and he knew what I was thinking. He would tap me on my cheek and say, "That's a nice Christian girl for you." Because he knew I wasn't going to say anything, that Melissa in any case would squash me if she needed more, and that I would take it on some remote sort of Christian terms.

Don't forget that Balanchine, apart from his beautiful creativity, is also a director running a company, and he knows his animals. He has to deal with a zoo. When you have a pelican and you have a hippo, and you have this one and that one, the bigger animal is going to eat the little one next door when you open the gate. And sometimes it's necessary to let that happen. The big animal

Verdy with Conrad Ludlow in the Divertissement of A Midsummer Night's Dream, *1962; with Jean-Pierre Bonnefous in* Sonatine, *1975; and (BELOW) in the Geneva Ballet Production of* Episodes, *1973.*

has what he needs, and the little animal . . . well, never mind, you'll find another one next year.

But you stayed with Balanchine. Was it because you didn't realize then that your collaboration was not going to be everything that you had hoped for?

No, I knew. I realized after a while that I had disappointed him a little here and there. But he was so faithful to me in spite of it that I stayed. I had been taught that you don't run to discover; you stay and find out. And I knew that I wasn't going to be any better for anybody else and that nobody was going to do better things for me than Balanchine did.

There were other considerations too. My mother was becoming old and ill, and I needed a stable situation for her. I didn't feel that I could move around a great deal. And also, of course, the condition of my feet was rather precarious. I did a great deal of free-lance work, but I didn't think it was a good time to commit myself solely to that. I knew my horoscope too. Again and again Saturn will strike me down just when I am beginning to free myself and fly.

I continued to dance lovely things, though, and I certainly don't regret staying on. *La Source,* for instance, was really beautiful, and a joy for me to dance. Balanchine made it in order to put my partner, John Prinz, on the map. He told me,

Verdy with Balanchine before a performance of Symphony in C.

"You know, dear, it will be difficult, but I'm going to force John to do this, and you will be a nice French girl and take care of him." In the process I got a ballet that was just right for me, with the kind of dancing that I was best at—with articulated feet, and elegance, and character. *Sonantine* too was an exquisite piece made for me.

You disappeared from the company very quietly when you left to become director of the Paris Opéra Ballet. Was that the way you wanted it? You didn't want a gala like Melissa's?

Oh, no, no. I wanted to disappear. I thought it was just right for Melissa to have her evening, but not for me. I had already gone in and out, and this time I was really out. Anyway, I view the whole thing as a continuous form of service, in which I am a dancer or a teacher or whatever. I couldn't refuse the Opéra, so I had to go. Sometimes you can't refuse a decoration, and you can't refuse the Opéra.

Now I'm directing the Boston Ballet, and I teach my dancers what I absorbed from Balanchine, but I cannot imitate him. My background is not the same as other New York City Ballet dancers who apply his methods exclusively. I'm still a little bit of an original, even if it is not an enormous original. A good friend of mine tells me that there is a monument in Paris that makes him think of me. It is a small carousel in the Jardin des Tuileries, across from the Palais-Royal. Through that tiny carousel, which is pink with beautiful little horses, like a Philippine shell, you can see at the end of the Champs-Élysées the big Arc de Triomphe. My friend says I am really like that little carousel. One can only be what one can be.

Ballets in Which Balanchine Created Works for Violette Verdy

EPISODES: PART II
music: Anton Webern
decor: David Hays
role: SYMPHONY, OPUS 21
premiere: May 14, 1959, New York City Center
New York City Ballet

THEME AND VARIATIONS
music: Peter Ilyich Tchaikovsky
costumes: Karinska
role: Ballerina
premiere: February 5, 1960, City Center
New York City Ballet

TCHAIKOVSKY PAS DE DEUX
music: Peter Ilyich Tchaikovsky
costumes: Karinska
premiere: March 29, 1960, New York City Center
New York City Ballet

THE FIGURE IN THE CARPET
music: George Frederick Handel
decor and costumes: Esteban Francés
roles: THE SANDS OF THE DESERT; THE WEAVING OF THE CARPET
premiere: April 13, 1960, New York City Center
New York City Ballet

LIEBESLIEDER WALZER
music: Johannes Brahms
decor: David Hays
costumes: Karinska
role: Fourth Couple
premiere: November 22, 1960, New York City Center
New York City Ballet

ELECTRONICS
music: electronic tape by Remi Gassmann and Oskar Sala
decor: David Hays
role: Principal
premiere: March 22, 1961, New York City Center
New York City Ballet

A MIDSUMMER NIGHT'S DREAM
music: Felix Mendelssohn
decor: David Hays
costumes: Karinska
role: ACT II DIVERTISSEMENT
premiere: January 17, 1962, New York City Center
New York City Ballet

JEWELS
music: Gabriel Fauré
decor: Peter Harvey
costumes: Karinska
role: EMERALDS
premiere: April 13, 1967, New York State Theater
New York City Ballet

GLINKIANA
music: Mikhail Glinka
decor, costumes, and lighting: Esteban Francés
role: POLKA
premiere: November 23, 1967, New York State Theater
New York City Ballet

LA SOURCE
music: Léo Delibes
costumes: Karinska
role: Ballerina
premiere: November 23, 1968, New York State Theater
New York City Ballet

PULCINELLA (choreographed with Jerome Robbins)
music: Igor Stravinsky
decor and costumes: Eugene Berman
role: Girl
premiere: June 23, 1972, New York State Theater
New York City Ballet

CHORAL VARIATIONS ON BACH'S "VOM HIMMEL HOCH"
music: Igor Stravinsky
decor: Rouben Ter-Arutunian
role: Principal
premiere: June 25, 1972, New York State Theater
New York City Ballet

SONATINE
music: Maurice Ravel
role: Ballerina
premiere: May 15, 1975, New York State Theater
New York City Ballet

Patricia McBride

In his memoirs of his years with the New York City Ballet, Lincoln Kirstein noted about Patricia McBride: "A product of our school, she came up through the ranks of our company. In good times and bad she never failed to use steps as sparks that have kept us bright; there have been times when she could properly be thanked for having kept our entire ensemble in focus."

McBride was born in Teaneck, New Jersey, in 1942. She began taking ballet lessons when she was seven, and by the time she was thirteen was coming to New York regularly to study at the School of American Ballet. When she was fourteen she was given a scholarship to the school, and she made her professional debut a year later with André Eglevsky's Petit Ballet Company, dancing the difficult Bluebird Pas de Deux from *The Sleeping Beauty*. McBride became an apprentice in the New York City Ballet in 1958 and joined the corps the following year. Balanchine made his first role for her, in *The Figure in the Carpet*, in 1960. She was also dancing such ballets as *Liebeslieder Walzer* and *Concerto Barocco*, and was elevated to principal-dancer status in the fall of 1961. She was the youngest principal in the company. In 1962 Balanchine created the role of Hermia in *A Midsummer Night's Dream* for McBride, and cast her as the lead in the restored *La Valse*. She danced the Swan Queen the following year.

McBride had danced with Edward Villella as early as 1958, when they performed the Bluebird and *Nutcracker* Pas de Deux at the Jacob's Pillow Festival. Their partnership, which was to become one of the most celebrated in ballet, was given Balanchine's imprimatur in 1964 when he made the tricky, very fast pas de deux *Tarantella* for them. In 1965 McBride was Columbine to Villella's Harlequin. The following year she was paired with the much taller Conrad Ludlow in the ravishing Intermezzo of the *Brahms-Schoenberg Quartet*. Arlene Croce wrote that "the Intermezzo unfurls in a continuous line indistinguishable from the line of McBride's body; the dance just seems to grow out of the curve of her deeply indented lower back. . . ."

Her performances in Jerome Robbins' *Dances at a Gathering* in 1969 and, especially, in Balanchine's *Who Cares?* the following year firmly established McBride as a star. Perhaps her greatest triumph was in one of Balanchine's few full-length ballets, *Coppélia*, which, Nancy Rey-

nolds noted, "reinforced, although this point needed no underlining, the position of McBride as first ballerina of the company."

Since then she has had important roles in *Vienna Waltzes*—in the only section set on pointe—and *Union Jack.* She was Mikhail Baryshnikov's principal partner when he was a member of the New York City Ballet in the late 1970s. McBride was married in 1973 to Jean-Pierre Bonnefous, then a principal dancer with the company and now retired due to an injury. They have an adopted daughter and a son born in 1982.

You are a product of Balanchine's school and have been in the company since you were sixteen. What's your relationship with Balanchine?

I've seen Balanchine practically every day for over twenty years. I'm part of his family. But it doesn't seem to me that he's so much a father figure as simply a force that is there. His talent is overwhelming. You just can't imagine where it comes from. He continuously does the most amazing things in a completely natural way. I think the relationship we all have with this man is very unusual. He's always there, our light and our hope. I'm still awed by him after all these years, which I think he must hate. He would like to be treated like a normal man.

Balanchine is the boss. It's a dictatorship. It's his company, and he does exactly what he wants, like deciding what roles a dancer will be seen in. To a certain extent this means that you know where you stand, but on the other hand he can surprise you. You're never quite sure what he's going to do next. Sometimes if you speak to him about something he will do exactly the opposite of what you think he's going to do. When he does a ballet for you, though, you fall in love with him all over again. He's so easy to work

Patricia McBride with Jacques D'Amboise in Who Cares?

with, so patient. He'll come into the room and whip off a variation in forty-five minutes and it will be done. That's possible because he knows what you can do before you do it. And he has great taste.

What was it like for you in the beginning, when you first got into the company?

I was very shy. I'm not an aggressive person at all, and I could barely utter "Hello" to Balanchine at first. He used to give us two-hour classes on how to hold our fingers, and he said that my hands looked dead. So I went around holding a little rubber ball to make them right. I would take my rubber ball into class and do the barre with it. Balanchine told me that I had to immediately change all my bad habits. He never gave many corrections to any of us, though. You mostly just watched Balanchine and tried to duplicate what he did and hoped for the best. The older dancers were very nice to me and gave me advice.

I was trying to do the best with what I had, and I think that Balanchine liked me. It was hard work, but I always had a lot of ballets, and if someone was injured I was usually there to fill in for them. I danced a lot.

Your partnership with Edward Villella, which was one of the most famous in the history of the company, started when you were very young. How did that happen?

I was seventeen when I started dancing with Eddie. Balanchine needed a partner for him, and I was chosen. He made a lot of ballets for us. We seemed to fit together naturally. Eddie told me that no one wanted to dance with him and that everyone wanted to dance with Jacques d'Amboise. I don't know whether that was really the case, but I loved having those ballets. Eddie and I grew together in our partnership. I always did feel, though, that Balanchine's creations were for Eddie and not for me. Eddie and Jacques were exceptions to the rule that said Balanchine made ballets for women and not for men.

The first time that Balanchine seemed to be making something especially for me was when he made the *Brahms-Schoenberg Quartet.* He asked me if I wanted to dance with Eddie or with Conrad Ludlow, and I didn't want to be the one to decide, because I thought it should be up to him. So he said, "Maybe Conrad. It will be something different." I wanted Balanchine to make those decisions. I didn't always see myself the way Mr. B. cast me, but then sometimes he challenges a dancer and gives her roles so that she has to work on certain things. If he feels you should work on extension he'll give you something like *Bugaku.* When he made "Rubies" for me it was very difficult because I'd never had a modern ballet. Most of my things had been classical. "Rubies" was a killer, but I loved it. It was full of jazzy movements and was absolutely exhausting to do. It seemed like an endurance race. When we ran through the whole piece for the first time it was so hard that Balanchine cut out some of the move-

With Edward Villella in Tarantella.

TOP RIGHT—With Rudolph Nureyev in Le Bourgeois
Gentilhomme, *1979.*

LEFT—*With Balanchine at a
rehearsal for a televised version of
the* Tchaikovsky Pas de Deux, *RIGHT
—with Mikhail Baryshnikov in*
Harlequinade, *1979.*

ments and let us run off stage for a breather and then we came running in again.

Your career got going just a few years before Suzanne Farrell came into the company. Were the "Farrell Years" hard on you?
I survived better than the other dancers, because I had Eddie Villella. He was my strength during those years. Then when Suzanne left Jerry Robbins came on the scene, and he was my savior. I had a very interesting time with Jerry. He showed me a different way of moving. A lot started happening in my personal life at that time, too. I met Jean-Pierre Bonnefous, who was to be my husband, and I was very happy. Mr. Balanchine went through an unhappy time when Suzanne left, and he didn't seem to like the fact that Jean-Pierre and I were together, but Mr. B. is known to disapprove of his ballerinas getting married, and it was to be expected that he would act that way. I survived. I tend to just work hard and get through the bad times.

Having Jean-Pierre for a partner must have been great.
Dancing with him was hard at first. We were in love with one another, but we never danced together. It didn't work on stage for us. It took a few years to work out our personal and our dancing relationship. I loved it afterward, though. The problem was that neither Balanchine nor Jerry would put us together, and I never got a chance to dance with Jean-Pierre except when someone was out sick. We didn't have a new ballet to work together in. I remember that when I did my first *Tchaikovsky Pas de Deux* with him I had just danced *Liebeslieder Walzer* and came off stage and someone said, "Melissa hurt herself and you're going to have to dance Tchaikovsky with Jean-Pierre." I changed my hair, threw my toe shoes on, we re-

With Peter Martins in Coppelia.

hearsed about two steps, and then we did it. It was Jean-Pierre's first performance with the company.

Now that Jean-Pierre has retired I miss him a great deal. I miss dancing with him. He was such a great dancer, and his career was over so suddenly, because of a tragic accident. It's too bad.

You've had wonderful partners, though. Eddie Villella, and Baryshnikov, and Nureyev.
I've had a good career. It was a dream to dance with Nureyev in *Le Bourgeois Gentilhomme* revival. He's a very warm partner. I never expected these things to happen to me. I heard that Baryshnikov was

joining the company, and I thought, Oh, I'll never get to dance with him. But of course who else could dance with Misha? Everyone was too tall. Our partnership was wonderful in the beginning. He has such wonderful technique, and the experience was a thrill, but the thrill wore off.

I've been very fortunate to have been around at this time, and around Balanchine. He's a little older now, and he's not always in the first wing with his elbow hanging over it. But, you know, we still do everything for Balanchine. We all dance for him. Recently I've felt that I want to enjoy myself, and I dance for myself as well. But I'll always dance to please Balanchine.

Ballets in Which Balanchine Created Roles for Patricia McBride

THE FIGURE IN THE CARPET
music: George Frederick Handel
decor and costumes: Esteban Francés
role: Duchess of L'an L'ing
premiere: April 13, 1960, New York City Center
New York City Ballet

A MIDSUMMER NIGHT'S DREAM
music: Felix Mendelssohn
decor: David Hays
costumes: Karinska
role: Hermia
premiere: January 17, 1962, New York City Center
New York City Ballet

TARANTELLA
music: Louis Moreau Gottschalk, reconstructed and orchestrated by Hershy Kay
costumes: Karinska
role: Ballerina
premiere: January 7, 1964, New York City Center
New York City Ballet

HARLEQUINADE
music: Riccardo Drigo
decor, costumes, and lighting: Rouben Ter-Arutunian
role: Colombine
premiere: February 4, 1965, New York State Theater
New York City Ballet

DON QUIXOTE
music: Nicolas Nabokov
scenery and costumes: Esteban Francés and Peter Harvey
role: RITORNEL
premiere: May 28, 1965, New York State Theater
New York City Ballet

BRAHMS-SCHOENBERG QUARTET
music: Johannes Brahms, orchestrated by Arnold Schoenberg
decor: Peter Harvey
costumes: Karinska
role: INTERMEZZO
premiere: April 21, 1966, New York State Theater
New York City Ballet

JEWELS
music: Igor Stravinsky
decor: Peter Harvey
costumes: Karinska
role: RUBIES
premiere: April 13, 1967, New York State Theater
New York City Ballet

GLINKIANA
music: Mikhail Glinka
decor, costumes, and lighting: Esteban Francés
role: DIVERTIMENTO BRILLANTE
premiere: November 23, 1967, New York State Theater
New York City Ballet

DIANA AND ACTAEON PAS DE DEUX
(made for television)
music: Cesare Pugni?
role: Lead
premiere: June 2, 1968, *The Ed Sullivan Show*, CBS-TV

WHO CARES?
music: George Gershwin, orchestrated by Hershy Kay
decor: Jo Mielziner
costumes: Karinska
roles: THE MAN I LOVE; FASCINATIN' RHYTHM; CLAP YO' HANDS
premiere: February 5, 1970, New York State Theater
New York City Ballet

DIVERTIMENTO FROM *LE BAISER DE LA FÉE*
music: Igor Stravinsky
costumes: Eugene Berman
role: Ballerina
premiere: June 21, 1972, New York State Theater
New York City Ballet

TCHAIKOVSKY PIANO CONCERTO NO. 2
music: Peter Ilyich Tchaikovsky
costumes: Karinska
role: Ballerina
premiere: January 12, 1973, New York State Theater
New York City Ballet

BEGIN THE BEGUINE (one of five sections of Edward Villella's *Salute to Cole*)
music: Cole Porter
costumes: Peter Wexler
role: PAS DE DEUX
premiere: May 31, 1973, Philharmonic Hall, New York

COPPÉLIA (choreographed with Alexandra Danilova)
music: Léo Delibes
libretto: Charles Nuitter, after E. T. A. Hoffmann
decor and costumes: Rouben Ter-Arutunian
role: Swanilda/Coppélia
premiere: July 17, 1974, Performing Arts Center, Saratoga Springs, N.Y.
New York City Ballet

PAVANE
music: Maurice Ravel
role: Solo
premiere: May 29, 1975, New York State Theater
New York City Ballet

THE STEADFAST TIN SOLDIER
music: Georges Bizet
decor and costumes: David Mitchell
role: Doll
premiere: July 30, 1975, Performing Arts Center, Saratoga Springs, N.Y.
New York City Ballet

UNION JACK
music: Hershy Kay
decor and costumes: Rouben Ter-Arutunian
role: Pearly Queen
premiere: May 13, 1976, New York State Theater
New York City Ballet

THE SLEEPING BEAUTY: AURORA'S SOLO, VISION SCENE
music: Peter Ilyich Tchaikovsky
decor and costumes: Peter Farmer
role: Princess Aurora
premiere: April 14, 1977, Hofstra University, Hempstead, N.Y.
Eglevsky Ballet

ÉTUDE FOR PIANO
music: Alexander Scriabin
costumes: Christina Giannini
role: PAS DE DEUX
premiere: June 4, 1977, Spoleto Festival USA, Charleston, S.C.

VIENNA WALTZES
music: Johann Strauss the Younger
scenery: Rouben Ter-Arutunian
costumes: Karinska
role: VOICES OF SPRING
premiere: June 23, 1977, New York State Theater
New York City Ballet

LE BOURGEOIS GENTILHOMME
music: Richard Strauss
decor and costumes: Rouben Ter-Arutunian
role: Lucille
premiere: April 8, 1979, New York State Theater
New York City Opera and students of SAB

Suzanne Farrell

Suzanne Farrell is the paradigm of the Balanchine ballerina, in her size and speed, her physical proportions and beauty, the spontaneity and musical sensitivity of her performances. Arlene Croce called her "probably the most important dancer who ever entered Balanchine's life."

Farrell was born Roberta Sue Ficker in Cincinnati in 1945. Her mother sent her to parochial school and to ballet classes at the Cincinnati College Conservatory of Music. When she was ten she played Clara in the Ballet Russe de Monte Carlo's touring production of *The Nut-* *cracker*, and five years later she was seen by Diana Adams, who had been sent to scout for young talent under the first major grant for ballet from the Ford Foundation. Farrell was given a scholarship to the School of American Ballet after Adams suggested that she audition for Balanchine in New York.

She joined the company in 1961 and took on her first solo role, the Dark Angel in *Serenade*, ten months later. In 1963 she replaced Adams at the premiere of Stravinsky's *Movements for Piano and Orchestra*, in which she revealed, as Croce wrote, that she "could do anything Balanchine asked of her—and do it on a grander scale, at greater speed, and with a silkier recovery and sense of control than anyone else." A stream of new roles followed: the romantic pas de deux *Meditation,* the lead in the revival of Balanchine's arduous *Ballet Imperial,* the central role of Dulcinea in his full-length *Don Quixote.* She became a principal dancer with *Don Quixote* and, at the age of nineteen, the center of Balanchine's attention and inspiration.

Among the many aspects of Farrell that were shaped and revealed by Balanchine during the period that followed were the gypsy exuberance of the *Brahms-Schoenberg Quartet* and the classical grandeur of "Diamonds." By 1969 her repertory included thirty-two roles. In February of that year she married Paul Mejia, a soloist with the company, and in the middle of the spring season they left NYCB. Farrell was taken on briefly by the National Ballet of Canada, where she danced a full-length *Swan Lake* and *La Bayadère.* In 1970 she and Mejia joned Maurice Béjart's Ballet of the Twentieth Century in Brussels.

On January 16, 1975, Farrell returned to Balanchine's company in the Adagio movement of his grand *Symphony in C.* She resumed her place as the company's tacit prima ballerina and Balanchine's inspiration. Kirstein wrote that "Farrell's appearance marked a rise in the company's spirits, another chapter of growth." For the Ravel Festival that spring Balanchine choreographed his first new work for her, the blazing gypsy *Tzigane.* The following year he made *Chaconne* for Farrell and Peter Martins, who had come to the company in 1969 to dance with her; their collaboration blossomed into one of the most important partnerships in contemporary ballet.

The delicate sensuality and rococo elegance of *Chaconne* was followed a few months later by Farrell's performance as leader of the hip-swinging "Wrens" section of *Union Jack,* and in 1977 Balanchine choreographed a solo that is a celebration of yet another aspect of her dancing: the expressive ports-de-bras that are the subject of the *Rosenkavalier* section of *Vienna Waltzes.*

For the 1981 Tchaikovsky Festival Balanchine rechoreographed *Mozartiana* for Farrell, and Croce wrote: "Thus does the master choreographer aggrandize the gifts and presence of a ballerina. Thus does he reveal her, sovereign in her kingdom of ballet." Almost all of Balanchine's last works—*Davidsbündlertänze, Mozartiana, Élégie,* and *Variations*—were made with Farrell, and the final two, both for the 1982 Stravinsky Festival, with her and for her only.

Were you aware of Balanchine's work from very early on? Did you, for instance, have any kind of Balanchinian model in the late fifties when you were a student in Cincinnati?
Companies didn't tour much then, so for the most part I knew only what I got out of books, and I had never seen photographs of Balanchine's work. I knew more about English companies, because in the fifties most dance books were published in England. And when the Royal Ballet came to Cincinnati I was the Mouse in *Sleeping Beauty.* I also had a few ballet records, though, and one of them was Robert Irving's New York City Ballet recording of Tchaikovsky's *Serenade,* so I assumed Balanchine had done a ballet to that music.

What happened when Diana Adams came to audition you for the School of American Ballet?
It was a typical class. Diana had been going around the country scouting for dancers, and my mother had read about this in *Dancemagazine* and asked my teacher to get someone to come to look at me. There was another girl there who was thought to have some talent too, so an audition was arranged. I had always been the big fish in the little pond, but I was very nervous. This was a very important thing for me. Diana arrived looking elegant and austere, and everything seemed to go all right. We had a pretty good class under the circumstances. Afterward I went up to Diana and asked for her autograph, and she gave it to me and said, "Good luck." So I was encouraged. I didn't get a scholarship right away, but I did get a chance to go to New York and audition, which was good enough for me. I would have been willing to start anywhere.

You were in the school only for about a year, weren't you?
Yes, I guess it was about a year. You lose track of time when you're taking classes day in and day out. I was taking a special class from Doubrovska, with about ten other girls, and once in a while Diana would teach, but I was just dying to be on stage. When I was little I had danced in operas in Cincinnati, and I felt that unless you can do a performance people aren't going to know that you're better on stage than in classes. I always thought I was.

Then they came to take apprentices for *Nutcracker,* and I wasn't chosen. I knew that I hadn't been at the school very long and that I should be thrilled just to have a scholarship, but the fact that other people in my class had been chosen and I wasn't made me very upset. The chosen ones got to do the Spanish Dance or be Flowers or Snow. I in fact got to be an Angel, which pacified me for a while. In those days they had big Angels in Act Two. I learned the whole second act just in case anybody got sick. And I spent all my time at the theater and was very diligent with my makeup. Mr. B. chose me to push the throne in, so I thought, Aah, he's got his eye on me! I doubt that he did, but I had to fasten the hook onto the ring in back of the throne, and I wrote in my diary that this was a big responsibility. I took my part very seriously.

Lincoln Kirstein said that when you were a child you had incredible discipline. That you had no distractions, and didn't even go to the ballets that you might someday be in.

That was because I couldn't afford to. I loved to go to the ballet when I was young, but I didn't have the nerve to sneak in. And I was a young girl alone, with few friends. I didn't know anybody I could go with. My mother worked at night. We lived in a one-room apartment, and my sister was busy. We'd do things together sometimes, but that meant more expense for my mother. Actually, though, I like to dance, to have the music, steps, and special feeling going through *my* body. It's not the same watching. I was aware of this early on.

When you were made a member of the company your life must have changed. Did you realize what extraordinary progress you were making?

I wasn't anything special when I got into the company. The ballet masters gave me a hard time, and I was very nervous. I made my debut in Todd Bolender's *Creation of the World* and in *Stars and Stripes.* In our section of *Stars* you do some piqué turns around the solo girl, and I remember that after the performance Janet Reed came back and said, "If you can't learn how to do piqué turns better than that you're going to get thrown out!" And I was devastated. It was the night of my premiere, and I thought I turned rather well.

Do you think she was just giving you a hard time?

No. I suppose my piqué turns were bad. I was just mad because she hadn't told me in rehearsal that they weren't good enough. I would have worked on them.

Jacques d'Amboise told me that he was the one who brought you to Balanchine's attention. When you took over Diana Adams' part for the premiere of *Movements for Piano and Orchestra* in the spring of 1963.

It's possible. Jacques always liked me. He likes to take young girls and mold them. Sometimes it works and sometimes it doesn't, but he means well. He used me in lecture demonstrations and concerts, so he knew I picked things up quickly. He and Diana were working on the leads in *Movements* when she became pregnant and couldn't dance, and I guess Jacques thought it would be easy for him to work with me. I don't imagine that anybody else already established wanted to step into the ballet under those circumstances. It was thought of so much as Diana's ballet. Nobody else looked like her, so they couldn't take her place visually. The whole ballet would have taken on a different atmosphere.

I read much later that Patty McBride was Diana's understudy, but I didn't know that then. I wonder if Patty knows I didn't know. And what that situation did to our relationship. If I had known that there was an understudy I wouldn't have done the ballet. I didn't think I could learn it under the circumstances. It was so bizarre. Diana had to teach me the part in her house, while she was lying down. I remember that the floor was slippery. But you just couldn't think about all the things going against you. I was hired as a dancer, and it never occurred to me not to try to learn the ballet.

The next ballet Balanchine made for you was very much yours. *Meditation.*

We started working on that during the winter, and it went very fast. For some reason Balanchine didn't need a lot of time to work with me. He told me years later that he knew I understood what he wanted, even though I might not be able to produce it on the spot. I could never get the entrance in *Meditation,* though. I still rarely do it right. He says you have to come in and step up on pointe and hold on to the air. It's true that air has weight, and substance. I tell my students to hold on to the air. But it's still a difficult entrance to do. After I had tried and tried to do it Balanchine finally said, "Well, let's pretend you're in." And that, of course, made me feel really inadequate. So we took it from where I'm in already and Jacques is on his knee, and we started to do a little more dancing.

***Meditation* is very different in mood from the things Balanchine had been doing before. It's much more sentimental and romantic than *Movements,* for instance. Does it seem to you that it's a very personal work?**

I suppose it might be significant that Balanchine always asked Jacques to put gray in his hair. So perhaps he did identify with the role of my partner.

After you did *Movements* and *Meditation* you had a new ballet almost every year. Sometimes two. So you became the company's leading dancer very quickly.

It's funny, but no matter how many nice things were happening to me, I

Suzanne Farrell rehearsing with Balanchine, 1968. BELOW—*With Arthur Mitchell in* Metastaseis and Pithoprakta, *1968.*

With Sean Lavery in Movements for Piano and Orchestra, *1982;* BELOW—*with Peter Martins in* Diamonds, *1982.*

always lived in fear of getting fired. I put a lot of pressure on myself. The whole first year at SAB I was afraid I would lose my scholarship.

But surely you must have begun to feel more secure after Balanchine made *Don Quixote* for you.
Well, then things changed.

Your partnership with Peter Martins is one of the most famous in the history of the company. When he talked about you in his autobiography he called you "the last of her kind" and implied that young dancers now think of themselves more like athletes and don't share your attitude toward being a ballerina. Do you think this is true?
I think Peter is right. But it just seemed normal to me to want to do things the way I did them. And I never thought of myself as a ballerina in the demanding sense. I never questioned casting or refused it. I never ask for anything. If I can't get it simply because I deserve it I'm not going to ask for it. I don't get temperamental, because it upsets me too much and I can't function when I'm upset.

I do see a difference in younger dancers, though. It's especially apparent to me when I teach. I was noticing yesterday in class how much people were concentrating on steps. I concentrate also, but you have to be aware that you're performing something, that you're showing how beautiful it is. There is a very high level of technical proficiency in ballet today. I sometimes wonder how much better dancers can get. But the problem with the girls is that they seem to look alike. If you were to get everybody in a room doing a step, just the legs, it would be difficult to know what face

went with what pair of legs. Everyone works the same way.

I don't look like dancers do now. I'm not structured the same way, and I haven't developed the same muscles they have. I don't have muscular legs like theirs. The younger girls are thin, but they're very sinewy. You see the calves. They have tension in the neck, and muscular arms. I don't look like that, yet I'm a disciple of Mr. B.'s. I worked the same way. People now seem to worry a lot about being strong. Naturally you need the strength to get through a ballet, but you also need to be feminine. And so many dancers work on building up strength to the point where they become unfeminine. Tough. Yet ultimately our job is to entertain. To be beautiful to look at.

Women dancers now seem to be competing with men. So perhaps that accounts for the androgynous look.
You have to be many things, but I think a woman should be idolized. Balanchine idolized women. His whole idea of a pas de deux is to extend what the woman can do. But it's not a competition. My partners are very important to me. Naturally I adore dancing with Peter, because it's easy and pleasurable for us. When I dance with him it feels even. For instance, I've done "Diamonds" with several other people. When Sean Lavery had to learn it quickly, I dominated because he didn't know the ballet and I had to take it into my own hands. But that's not something you want to continue, because ultimately it's two people and they're both important. It doesn't matter if you're in front or in back. If I were a boy I would think it was a wonderful thing to show this person off. She couldn't do it without me. On the other hand, I don't like to rely on another person too much. I try to be

both dependent and independent. To have both qualities.

When I dance something like the *Tchaikovsky Pas de Deux* with Peter, we do the pas de deux, which is very nice and elegant, and then he does his variation, which always brings down the house, and I'm happy for his success, but I feel superfluous; it's not necessary for "little me" to do my passés. Then I think, Come on, Suzy, and I try to rise to the occasion. And I suppose Peter thinks, Well, she held her own there, so I'm going to go out in the coda and do something smashing. That's what makes a ballet build. But it's not exactly competition.

I can understand why boys might not like to partner. No boy wants to be treated like he's just there to hold the ballerina up. But that works both ways. I've danced with people who when they look at you they're not really looking at you. They are playing both parts. I remember dancing with someone like that once, a wonderful dancer who I liked, but I always felt that he didn't think I was enough. Even though there I was, in the flesh, She.

When you left NYCB in 1969 you went to Brussels to dance with Maurice Béjart's company. People always say that he is a choreographer for men. And that Balanchine, of course, is the central choreographer for women. Was it hard for you to make that move?
I think that I adapted very well. Principally because I was determined to survive. I always felt that Balanchine was the best, but I didn't have that anymore and I needed to dance. I didn't know anything else. I hadn't even graduated from high school. Béjart wasn't as technically challenging to me as Mr. B. He didn't have the same ballet concept. But in a way it was good for me because

he emphasized an area in which I was deficient. And I chose to give everything to him, because that's the way I am. I'm not afraid to go out on a limb—to become committed. I didn't have any trouble learning his ballets. I could do them, and I wanted to extend myself, even though it was an extension that some people felt was a step down. I gained a lot there and came back a better person. Of course, Béjart admired Mr. B. very much and was devoted to the ballets he did especially for me. I think, too, that several of Béjart's things could have been done by a woman as well as a man. *The Wayfarer* or *Firebird* could have been done by either.

Your break with Balanchine is very well known. But how did the reconciliation come about? What happened that led you to rejoin NYCB?
In 1974 I did *Meditation* in Brussels with Jorge Donn. Balanchine had given the ballet to me as a gift—legally—in 1966, and I wrote to his secretary asking if Mr. B. would mind if I did it in Brussels. Jacques came to teach it. It was the first time I had done a Balanchine ballet in many years. And Jacques went back and told Mr. B. that I was in good shape, and how nice it had been for us to work together again.

Then that summer Paul and I were spending our time off on the island we own near Saratoga, where NYCB is the company in residence in July. With Béjart we had six weeks off every summer, but for the first two years I couldn't get myself to go see the company, although I kept up on what was happening. Then finally it was the third summer and we thought it would be fun to go. There was a good program with *La Valse* on it, and that brought back memories because I had enjoyed doing it so much. Of course there were ru-

mors that I was in the audience, and those who were happy were happy and those who weren't weren't. Anyway I thought, How can I be so close and not go see my friends? I didn't go with any preconceptions, and I didn't even know if Mr. B. was there. But I ran into him and we went into his office to talk for a very short while. It was a bit strange, but I felt comfortable. He knew what I was doing and he knew I knew what he was doing.

I went back to the island and decided to write Mr. B. a letter, for what it was worth. I said, "As wonderful as it is to see *La Valse* it is even more wonderful to dance. Is this impossible?" Then a few days later I was practicing outside and Paul came out to tell me Barbara Horgan, Mr. B.'s secretary, was on the phone. She said, "I know you have to go back to Brussels soon, but why don't you stop in New York and see George before you go?" So I went to his apartment in New York. He opened the door, and we sat on the couch and I didn't say, "May I come back?" and he didn't say, "Would you like to come back?" It was "When do we get to work?" I was committed to Béjart until December, and Maurice said he was sorry to lose me, but he knew how important Mr. B. was to me. He knew this had to be. Of course it was hard to give everything to Maurice when I knew I was going to go back where I belonged, but when I returned I felt what had happened before was over.

The first thing Balanchine did for you when you got back was *Tzigane,* a sort of gypsy ballet. How did it feel to work with him again?
When I first got back I did a ballet for Jerry Robbins, and another one for Jacques, both during the Ravel Festival. I was happy to be with the

The Rosenkavalier section of Vienna Waltzes.

company, but I wanted to work with Mr. B. *Tzigane* was for the festival, too, but the other ballets opened first, and Mr. Balanchine left the creation of our ballet until a couple of days before the premiere. I was feeling good, and thin and healthy and new. And I was curious about what he would do. Then the first thing he asked me to do in *Tzigane* was just to schlepp on. And I said, Gee, but people are expecting me to dance, to wow them. People are curious to see what Balanchine and I will do after all this time. They're not going to be prepared for this. And it bothered me, until I realized what he was up to. Of course they were not going to be prepared. That's good! There's no point in doing something people expect.

I hadn't had to put my faith in Balanchine for five years. But you have to have faith in your partner whether he's your physical partner or your choreographer. Or your husband or your friend. You have to let them know you trust them, and they will come through for you. I realized that Balanchine saw that I was different after having danced with Béjart. And *Tzigane* was a reflection of that. Of course he had made *Brahms-*

Farrell and Balanchine in Don Quixote, *1965.*

Schoenberg for me, which was also a gypsy dance, but this was a different kind of gypsy.

You are said to be perhaps the most musical dancer on the stage. Are you aware of that quality?

I realize now that I'm very musical even though I can't read a note of music. Which always disturbed me. But I think that some people who are said to be musical do things that look, to me anyway, just very precious. You know they're always going to accentuate the crescendo. It's not spontaneous. I think it's important to hear different things in the music at different times. In *Chaconne,* for instance, a ballet I've done often, I usually dance to the strings. They are plucking away, and those are the counts that my steps are structured to. Then one summer

Peter and I were doing a guest appearance in Chautauqua, and the orchestra was in front of us, outdoors, and the woodwinds and brass were very close to the stage. Their sound carried in our direction, but I couldn't hear the violins, although I knew the music very well and I could see the conductor. But I had never heard the horns going boom, boom, boom, boompa, counterpoint to the violins. And I realized I could dance to that also, without changing any of the counts of my choreography. It just becomes a different accent. You move differently. So that performance I danced to the brass. It changed the way I felt, and I assume the way I looked.

Did the audience notice?

No, but most of them had never seen the ballet before. I thought it was very interesting, though. And when I

danced *Chaconne* again in a theater I looked for that quality I had found in Chautauqua. Acoustics in different theaters vary, too, and what goes out to the audience is different than what comes back to the stage.

And I suppose more subjective factors affect your performance.

Different emotions influence a performance. I'm not saying that my private life enters into what I do, but on the other hand it does. If my whole world is falling apart, if I'm unhappy or depressed, it's going to affect what I do. Maybe I will go on stage and give my best performance. Lots of times I've given a wonderful performance simply because I *was* depressed. Perhaps it added to the solemnity of the ballet or something. But I think you should use everything that happens to you in your work. With no regrets. There's too little time. However, I'm a professional dancer, and I'll always give my best.

Since so much of your life goes into your dancing, how do you view the inevitability of retirement?

I don't know at what point in my career it will happen. Whether I'll be forced to retire or will have the luxury of choice. I don't know what it will be like for me if I have to dance without Balanchine sometime. That would be less exciting, and I've just come to realize that it will happen. I know I want to remain involved with ballet, but I would be a fool to think that whatever I do when I retire will give me the thrill that dancing does. Even though I have other things in my life, and I'm very happy, there will be nothing as meaningful to me as dancing. After all, it has comprised most of my life, been the most constant factor.

In the last few years, since you came back from Europe,

With Balanchine at a rehearsal for Davidsbündlertänze, *1980.*

Balanchine has made some wonderful pieces for you—*Chaconne, Vienna Waltzes, Davidsbündlertänze*. . . . How have you felt about these ballets? About *Davidsbündlertänze*, for starters.

I was in the dark longer with that piece than with anything else. Until zero hour. He did all of the sections separately, and I was in the dark practically until the night of the performance. I know people think it's a very schematic ballet, and full of references to Schumann's life, but I really don't think—and I've never asked Mr. B. about this—that we are all little Clara Schumanns running around at different points in her life and that the men are all Schumann. I don't think that's what Balanchine had in mind.

It's a strange ballet to dance,

though, because usually in a ballet there is a central figure. In this piece you have practically four separate ballets going on at once, with four different couples. And then all of a sudden you all get together. People are either physically in your way or mentally in your way or visually in your way. You have your little ballet worked out for you, and then all of a sudden somebody comes in at the end of your thing. You've worked out this atmosphere, and somebody interferes. It's like being in a dream that is intruded upon.

The ballet he made for you the following year, *Mozartiana*, for the Tchaikovsky Festival, was quite different. It was a revision of the earlier *Mozartianas*, wasn't it?

It was a completely new work. Even the sequence of music was different.

I love it. *Mozartiana* has changed my life. I've never felt so calm on stage as I do in that ballet. And given all the things you have to do, and all the technical things that could go wrong, you shouldn't feel so calm. Starting out with the "Prayer" section is wonderful. If one were to know what Heaven is like, it would be *Mozartiana*.

It seems very holy. You come out and hold that balance and then come down. . . .

It seems very right. It's not contrived and it's not a trick. If you were singing and holding your breath it would be the same thing. It seems right to hold that arabesque.

Then for the last Stravinsky Festival he revived *Variations* for you. Something you had done in another version sixteen

chine thought that he hadn't had *Variations* pegged right in the beginning. It was very successful then, but he seemed to think he understood the music better now. So he liked our new version, and he told me so.

Your collaboration with Balanchine has been a long one, and you seem to have given one another so much. Violette Verdy told me that when she watches you dance it's like seeing pure Balanchine.

I think I was born at just the right time. I have the benefit of Mr. B.'s old ballets, plus the new ones. And I can share all the things that happened to him in his life. I know I have a wonderful repertory. I couldn't ask for another facet. But you can be anything. I tell my students to do something and they say, "Oh, we've never done it that way." And I tell them that doesn't mean it's not possible. Or even that it's difficult. It's just different. Whether you like the ballet, or like what the choreographer is doing, as soon as he says, "This is what I want," it becomes valid. You have to accommodate to what he wants. And that's what's fun.

I like dancing because I like the work that I put into it. Feeling that I am able to do something or coping with not being able to do it. Not being able to turn in class in the morning and yet being able to get out there on stage and turn. I don't get a thrill out of seeing someone else being able to do it or not do it. Even when I watch myself on films I don't get a thrill. It's not like doing it. I'm bored to death watching tapes of myself, even if it's a wonderful performance. And yet I felt excited at the time.

I always feel that I'll never have this moment again when I dance. I know that I'll probably do the ballet again, but I will never be the same as I was during the breath I just took.

years earlier. What was working on that like?

Strange. I was upset that I didn't remember more of the old choreography. Only the beginning and the last couple of measures are the same. Balanchine wasn't well, and he was having a hard time getting started, and it kept being postponed. Most of his time was spent on *Perséphone*, which was very elaborate. But Balanchine was in control of the whole thing, and knew exactly what he wanted. It's not the same choreography, because he's not the same person he was before. It took me a couple of days to realize he didn't *want* the old version. We'd changed. All those years had gone by and neither one of us was the same. So we have another version, and I enjoy doing it.

We were listening to an orchestra rehearsal of the piece, sitting in the audience, and Mr. B. said to me,

"You know, I realize this is the most difficult music he's done." More advanced than Webern. More advanced than any of Stravinsky's other things. When we did it in 1966 it was terribly dancey. Lots of steps. Which I think is in a way a problem that people have in choreographing to Stravinsky. The music makes you nervous, and you start putting something on every count, moving to everything that he's written. This time it was just the opposite. There are places where you go in slow motion or you don't do much of anything.

The whole concept of Balanchine's choreography to Stravinsky's music has changed. Now he underplays the music instead of matching it note for note. It takes a lot of nerve to just stand still, like they do in *Symphony in Three Movements* at the end, while the orchestra is playing away like mad. I think Balan-

Ballets in Which Balanchine Created Roles for Suzanne Farrell

MOVEMENTS FOR PIANO AND ORCHESTRA
music: Igor Stravinsky
role: Principal
premiere: April 9, 1963, New York City Center
New York City Ballet

MEDITATION
music: Peter Ilyich Tchaikovsky, orchestrated by Alexander Glazunov
costumes: Karinska
role: Ballerina
premiere: December 10, 1963, New York City Center
New York City Ballet

CLARINADE
music: Morton Gould
role: CONTRAPUNTAL BLUES
premiere: April 29, 1964, New York State Theater
New York City Ballet

BALLET IMPERIAL (TCHAIKOVSKY PIANO CONCERTO NO. 2)
music: Peter Ilyich Tchaikovsky
decor: Rouben Ter-Arutunian
costumes: Karinska
role: Ballerina
premiere: October 15, 1964, New York State Theater
New York City Ballet

DON QUIXOTE
music: Nicolas Nabokov
decor, costumes, and lighting: Esteban Francés
role: Dulcinea
premiere: May 28, 1965, New York State Theater
New York City Ballet

VARIATIONS
music: Igor Stravinsky
role: Solo
premiere: March 31, 1966, New York State Theater
New York City Ballet

BRAHMS-SCHOENBERG QUARTET
music: Johannes Brahms, orchestrated by Arnold Schoenberg
decor: Peter Harvey
costumes: Karinska
role: RONDO ALLA ZINGARESE
premiere: April 21, 1966, New York State Theater
New York City Ballet

ÉLÉGIE
music: Igor Stravinsky
role: Solo
premiere: July 15, 1966, Philharmonic Hall, New York
A Festival of Stravinsky: His Heritage and His Legacy

RAGTIME (II)
music: Igor Stravinsky
premiere: July 15, 1966, Philharmonic Hall, New York
role: PAS DE DEUX
A Festival of Stravinsky: His Heritage and His Legacy

JEWELS
music: Peter Ilyich Tchaikovsky
decor: Peter Harvey
costumes: Karinska
role: DIAMONDS
premiere: April 13, 1967, New York State Theater
New York City Ballet

METASTASEIS & PITHOPRAKTA
music: Iannis Xenakis
role: PITHOPRAKTA
premiere: January 18, 1968, New York State Theater
New York City Ballet

SLAUGHTER ON TENTH AVENUE
music: Richard Rodgers, arranged by Hershy Kay
scenery and lighting: Jo Mielziner
costumes: Irene Sharaff
role: Strip Tease Girl
premiere: May 2, 1968, New York State Theater
New York City Ballet

REQUIEM CANTICLES
music: Igor Stravinsky
costumes: Rouben Ter-Arutunian
role: Principal
premiere: May 2, 1968, New York State Theater
New York City Ballet

TZIGANE
music: Maurice Ravel
costumes: Joe Eula and Stanley Simmons
role: Lead Gypsy
premiere: May 29, 1975, New York State Theater
New York City Ballet

CHACONNE
music: Christoph Willibald Gluck
costumes: Karinska
roles: SECOND PAS DE DEUX; CHACONNE
premiere: January 22, 1976, New York State Theater
New York City Ballet

UNION JACK
music: Hershy Kay
decor and costumes: Rouben Ter-Arutunian
roles: RCAF; WRENS
premiere: May 13, 1976, New York State Theater
New York City Ballet

VIENNA WALTZES
music: Richard Strauss
scenery: Rouben Ter-Arutunian
costumes: Karinska
role: ROSENKAVALIER WALTZES
premiere: June 23, 1977, New York State Theater
New York City Ballet

WALPURGISNACHT BALLET
music: Charles Gounod
role: Ballerina
premiere: May 15, 1980, New York State Theater
New York City Ballet

LE BOURGEOIS GENTILHOMME
music: Richard Strauss
libretto: after Molière
decor and costumes: Rouben Ter-Arutunian
role: Lucille
premiere: May 22, 1980, New York State Theater
New York City Ballet

ROBERT SCHUMANN'S DAVIDSBÜNDLERTÄNZE
music: Robert Schumann
decor and costumes: Rouben Ter-Arutunian
role: Second Couple
première: June 19, 1980, New York State Theater
New York City Ballet

MOZARTIANA
music: Peter Ilyich Tchaikovsky
scenery: Philip Johnson and John Burgee
costumes: Rouben Ter-Arutunian
roles: PREGHIERA; THEME AND VARIATIONS
premiere: June 4, 1981, New York State Theater
New York City Ballet

ÉLÉGIE
music: Igor Stravinsky
role: Solo
premiere: June 13, 1982, New York State Theater
New York City Ballet

VARIATIONS FOR ORCHESTRA
music: Igor Stravinsky
role: Solo
premiere: July 2, 1982, New York State Theater
New York City Ballet

Kay Mazzo

Kay Mazzo, a waiflike
young soloist at NYCB during the
sixties, was in the spring of 1969
called upon virtually overnight to
take a leading place in the company.
Suzanne Farrell, Balanchine's favorite
ballerina, resigned on Thursday,
and Mazzo was dancing Farrell's
role in the "Diamonds" section of
Jewels at the Sunday matinee. Many
of Farrell's other roles became Mazzo's
soon after, including those created
for Farrell's very different gifts.
It was an extraordinary challenge,
especially for a dancer whose chief
characteristics seemed to be, in
Clive Barnes's words, "shy grace"
and a "flickering incandescence."
Critics were generally indifferent,
but audiences were responsive to
her, and Balanchine went on to
show off Mazzo's own qualities in at
least two roles of genuine greatness.

Mazzo was born in Chicago in

Kay Mazzo with Balanchine in a rehearsal for PAMTGG, *1971.*

1946. She began taking ballet lessons when she was six, and four years later appeared in the New York City Ballet's production of *The Nutcracker* when it was mounted in Chicago. She spent two summers at the School of American Ballet, and when she was thirteen she came to New York to study there on a regular basis. Mazzo joined Jerome Robbins's touring company, Ballets: USA in 1961, winning special acclaim for her performance in *Afternoon of a Faun.* Ballets: USA disbanded, and Mazzo joined the corps of the New York City Ballet in 1962. Two years later, when she was eighteen, she danced her first principal role in a Balanchine work, *La Valse.* She became a soloist in 1965 and was given a number of principal roles during the next few years, from the *Tchaikovsky Pas de Deux* and *Liebeslieder Walzer* to Merce Cunningham's *Summerspace.*

Mazzo became a principal dancer in 1969, shortly after Farrell's departure. In May of that year she originated the role of the Girl in Mauve in Robbins's *Dances at a Gathering.* That summer she danced Terpsichore in *Apollo* for the first time, in Monte Carlo, and was rumored to be Farrell's successor. In such roles as Dulcinea in *Don Quixote,* in "Diamonds" and in the Adagio section of *Symphony in C,* which demand expansiveness of movement, the delicate Mazzo did not claim that succession. In other roles—in the new pastel-colored version of *Donizetti Variations,* in the Divertissement of *A Midsummer Night's Dream,* and as Titania—the extraordinary lightness of filigree ports de bras were distinctively her own.

In 1972 Balanchine made the *Stravinsky Violin Concerto* and *Duo Concertant* for Mazzo, partnered by Peter Martins. The beauty of her roles in these ballets, and of the last role Balanchine made for her, in *Davidsbündlertänze,* affirm her place in the company's history. Mazzo was married in 1978 to Albert Bellas, a New York businessman and a member of the board of directors of the School of American Ballet. They had a son in 1981, and Mazzo retired from the company. She teaches children's classes at the School of American Ballet.

When you were a child you danced in Balanchine's *Nutcracker* in Chicago, but your first professional experience was with Jerry Robbins's Ballets: USA. Did you feel early on that you wanted to dance for Balanchine, or didn't it matter to you?

Oh, I very much wanted to dance for Balanchine. I went to the audition Jerry Robbins gave for his company simply because I was curious. I was fifteen and I hadn't been to an audition since I was nine. Most of the girls in my class at SAB were older than I was, and they were going to auditions because they wanted a job. At that time at the school they let people stay on, so in the advanced group there were girls in their twenties or late teens. I didn't even know who Jerry Robbins was, but he needed a ballet dancer, a naïve-looking person for *Afternoon of a Faun,* and I was chosen. I was an apprentice to NYCB at the time, but I was told that Mr. B. wasn't going to use the apprentices that year in *Nutcracker* and that it would be OK if I went with Jerry's company. I wouldn't have gone if I had thought I would lose my place.

When I came back from the tour we had a season in New York and I went back to school. I was just waiting to get into Balanchine's company. If he didn't take me, if going with Jerry had ruined my chances, it would have broken my heart. But I guess Balanchine knew I wanted to dance for him, and he took me and two or three other girls.

Did you feel that he was especially interested in you?

He was looking at everybody. I remember that he would come into a class at school, before I got into the company, and just peruse, but there wasn't much communication between us. He's shy. Mostly I remember that everything we did was wrong. He would say, "Where did you study?" even though he knew we came from his school. And then he would say, "Terrible training," but of course he didn't mean it. He still does the same thing with the young girls. I danced in some of his ballets, like *La Valse,* but I also was in Jerry's *Interplay,* and in things by Todd Bolender and Antony Tudor. The problem with being thrown into Balanchine's things was that no one would rehearse you. I found it very difficult to learn a ballet when I was fifteen or sixteen without any coaching. But Balanchine was busy.

Were you affected when he began directing most of his attention to Suzanne Farrell?

Well, I wasn't a principal, so I didn't have roles taken away from me. I was still dancing in ballets every night, and I learned very quickly. After one day of rehearsal I would be ready to dance a ballet, and Balanchine needed dancers who could do that. Dancers like Mimi Paul and Pat Neary, principals, had a more difficult time than I did. They were getting nothing new, and their old parts were being given to Suzanne. Eventually I wasn't doing much either, but I still felt that NYCB was the place I wanted to be, that I wouldn't be happy at Ballet Theatre doing the classics. There was no other choreographer like Balanchine. So I waited. I was young, and there wasn't much point in being upset, but if I had had roles taken away from me I would have felt differently.

And then when she left you

became the chosen one.

All of a sudden I got to dance everything I wanted to dance. He had been doing everything for one person, and now he needed someone else, and I was it. It was pure luck. I was the right age and in the right place at the right time. But I felt that he needed other dancers too.

I suppose Balanchine thought of me primarily as a lyrical dancer, but he put me through all different kinds of things. Once he even put me in *Firebird.* That wasn't right for me at all, but it was a challenge. Melissa Hayden was so dramatic and sharp as the Firebird, and I remember when I went out to do my variation I fell flat on my rear end. It was not my ballet.

What was it like having Balanchine make ballets for you? For instance, what were the rehearsals like for *Chopiniana,* his version of *Les Sylphides?*

That was very confusing, because we were rehearsing with three people—Balanchine, Danilova, and John Taras. You'd rehearse with Balanchine and he would say, "Do this," and Danilova would change it, and then John would come in and change that. Then you'd get back to Balanchine. Then you'd get all three and you didn't know which version to dance. Balanchine's idea was that the beautiful steps should be shown off, so we wore leotards and short skirts, but I would rather have had a flowing tutu for that.

A few months later there was the Stravinsky Festival, in June of 1972, and that was spectacular. Balanchine made three new ballets for me—*Violin Concerto, Scherzo à la Russe,* and *Duo Concertant.* He works incredibly fast, but for *Violin Concerto* he was going a little slower than usual. The music was complicated, of course, and he had a few problems with a group of four peo-

Mazzo with Peter Martins in Stravinsky Violin Concerto.

ple. He liked Karin von Aroldingen's dancing, and he liked me then, so he put us together. In *Duo Concertant* Peter Martins and I just did the same thing over and over. Balanchine said that's what the music does. He always says his ballets have nothing to do with his emotions, but you never know. It is the music that seems to be the most important thing for him, and I could never get into what other people said these ballets mean. I don't understand interpretations. I just see it as dancing.

Those two Stravinsky ballets he made for you are among his best works, but a few years later, when Suzanne Farrell came back, he seemed to stop focusing on you. What was it like working for him then?

When Balanchine started doing the big ballets, *Union Jack* and *Vienna Waltzes,* it was fun. It wasn't challenging, but Balanchine was in a good frame of mind and everybody was in them and nobody felt left out. *Davidsbündlertänze,* which was the last thing he did for me, was odd. Ib Andersen, my partner, was wonderful, a very nice person. There was no problem with his personality, which one sometimes gets. But none of us could figure out what the ballet was like. Usually if you are in a ballet you know if it is going to be good or bad or whatever. But not with this one. There was a strange feeling about that ballet, but we all got together and really wanted to dance well.

Do you have any regrets about your career?

I think I was very lucky. I wouldn't have wanted to be anywhere else, do anything else. To have worked with Balanchine is exactly what I wanted. Everyone gets replaced finally, and I knew that would happen. You have to accept it. Balanchine is Svengali for any fe-

With Peter Martins in Duo Concertante *(left) and* Vienna Waltzes.

male dancer in his company, and I think the women who say that's not so aren't being truthful. I have a mind of my own. I'm stubborn and I won't do what I don't want to do. But Balanchine is the greatest choreographer in the world. Where do you go from Balanchine?

I teach younger children at the school now. It's odd to be out of the company, though. Being in Balanchine's company gives you a feeling of security, especially when it's been your life for such a long time. Now I go to the theater and get so nervous when I watch a performance. You're supposed to sit there and relax and enjoy it, but I still know everybody and know what's going on. It would be hard not being in Balanchine's company if I didn't have a child.

If your child were a girl would you want her to go to Balanchine?
If she were good. It's a wonderful life.

Ballets in Which Balanchine Created Roles for Kay Mazzo

DON QUIXOTE
music: Nicolas Nabokov
decor and costumes: Esteban Francés
and Peter Harvey
role: COURANTE SICILIENNE
premiere: May 28, 1965, New York State
Theater
New York City Ballet

SUITE NO. 3
music: Peter Ilyich Tchaikovsky
decor and costumes: Nicolas Benois
role: VALSE MÉLANCOLIQUE
premiere: December 3, 1970, New York
State Theater
New York City Ballet

PAMTGG
music: Roger Kellaway
decor: Jo Mielziner
costumes: Irene Sharaff
role: Principal
premiere: June 17, 1971, New York State
Theater
New York City Ballet

VIOLIN CONCERTO
music: Igor Stravinsky
roles: TOCCATA; ARIA II
premiere: June 18, 1972, New York State
Theater
New York City Ballet

SCHERZO À LA RUSSE
music: Igor Stravinsky
costumes: Karinska
role: Principal
premiere: June 21, 1972, New York State
Theater
New York City Ballet

DUO CONCERTANT
music: Igor Stravinsky
role: Ballerina
premiere: June 22, 1972, New York State
Theater
New York City Ballet

SHÉHÉRAZADE
music: Maurice Ravel
role: Principal
premiere: May 22, 1975, New York State
Theater
New York City Ballet

UNION JACK
music: Hershy Kay
decor and costumes: Rouben Ter-
Arutunian
roles: DRESS MACDONALD; ROYAL NAVY
premiere: May 13, 1976, New York State
Theater
New York City Ballet

VIENNA WALTZES
music: Franz Lehár
decor: Rouben Ter-Arutunian
costumes: Karinska
role: GOLD AND SILVER WALTZ
premiere: June 23, 1977, New York State
Theater
New York City Ballet

ROBERT SCHUMANN'S
DAVIDSBÜNDLERTÄNZE
music: Robert Schumann
decor and costumes: Rouben Ter-
Arutunian
role: Fourth Couple
premiere: June 19, 1980, New York State
Theater
New York City Ballet

Kay Mazzo with her son Andrew.

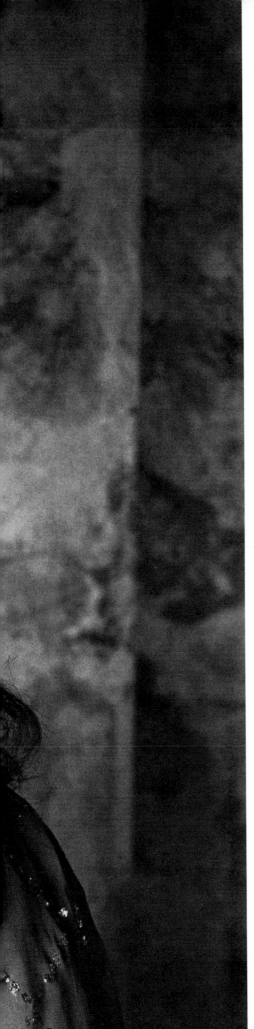

> It took a long time for me to please Balanchine. ...I never was the ballerina type.

Karin von Aroldingen

Karin von Aroldingen's physical strength and unusual dramatic qualities were lent to much of the repertory of the New York City Ballet during Balanchine's later years. She was important to Balanchine as a personal friend as well as an instrument of dance, and between 1970 and 1982 he created roles for her in seventeen new ballets.

Von Aroldingen was born in Greiz, in what would become East Germany, in 1941. Her father died in German-occupied Czechoslovakia when she was an infant, and with her mother and two sisters she moved to West Berlin, where she grew up and where she began taking private ballet lessons. She danced with the American Festival Ballet (based in Bremen, Germany) for six months and then, in 1959, with the Frankfurt Opera Ballet. When she was eighteen she performed the Dancing Annie role with Lotte Lenya as her singing counterpart in the Frankfurt production of the Balanchine/Weill/Brecht *The Seven Deadly Sins.* Lenya spoke of her to Balanchine, and in 1962 von Aroldingen auditioned for him while he was staging a work in Hamburg. Shortly afterward he accepted her as a member of his corps de ballet.

Von Aroldingen went through a long period of adjustment at the New York City Ballet, although she danced some soloist roles, such as Hot Chocolate in *The Nutcracker* and the Coquette in *La Sonnambula,* almost immediately. She moved on to dance the second leads in *Concerto Barocco* and *Scotch Symphony,* and in 1967 she was promoted to the rank of soloist. Her real rise in the company came, however, upon the departure of Suzanne Farrell in 1969, when Balanchine's interest shifted to other dancers. The first role created especially for von Aroldingen was in *Who Cares?* in 1970. Arlene Croce said that the ballet made her look like "a cheerful, beer-drinking American college girl—and makes her look like a star, too." In 1972 Balanchine choreographed the *Violin Concerto* with von Aroldingen and Jean-Pierre Bonnefous as one of the two principal couples. Her part demanded speed and force, and revealed her at her athletic best. She became a principal dancer that year, and in each successive year throughout the seventies she was given a part in a new Balanchine ballet. In 1976 her fierce dance to unaccompanied drums in the tartan processional of *Union Jack* was one of the piece's high points.

Balanchine revealed von Aroldingen as a dancer capable of romance and emotional warmth in the Tales of the Vienna Woods section of *Vienna Waltzes* in 1977, and a few years later she also took on the glamorous Merry Widow role in that ballet. In 1980 she was the central figure in Balanchine's melancholy homage to Robert Schumann, *Davidsbündlertänze.*

Von Aroldingen was married in 1965 to Morton Gewirtz, a New York businessman, and they had a daughter, Margo, the following year.

You are one of the few European women who have had a big career with the New York City Ballet, and one of the few dancers in the company now who weren't trained by Balanchine. What special quality do you think you bring to his ballets?

Well, Balanchine uses my acrobatic nature, for one thing. When I was little I was more on my hands than on my feet. On the street I did cartwheels. When Balanchine made *Violin Concerto* for me he asked me if I could do a bridge, and I did one, and then he said, "Where do you fall from there?" So I twisted myself out of this very strange bridge which I remember doing as a child. It was easy for me, and he liked it and put it in a ballet. He does that a lot when he choreographs. It's like a suit being tailored to you.

I joined the company in 1962, when it was less unusual for Balanchine to take a girl from outside his school. There are so many girls now, but then it was good for him to get new blood, new temperaments. And I think Balanchine is drawn to Germans. He likes the Rhineland, and he loves German food. Perhaps another reason Balanchine liked me was that I have a dramatic flair. I can't help it. Even though few of Balanchine's ballets require drama, I

think he liked that quality in my dancing.

I did have to rearrange my body for him, though, and unlearn everything. It took a long time for me to please Balanchine. I had to go back to the basics. My body is modern, sculptured. I never was the ballerina type. I couldn't have been a dancer in Russia a hundred years ago. People have put me down for looking cold and hard, and masculine, although I feel very much like a woman. In Berlin they called me a "Three-Star Frigidaire." That sort of thing hurts me, but Balanchine said, "What's wrong with it? You don't like ice cream? What do you want to be? Hot stuff?" My body is not liked by the critics at all, so I just don't read the critics anymore. They wrote horrible things about Balanchine throughout his life, and now they say he's a genius. If I do read a review that says something bad about me I feel not so much personally hurt as hurt for Balanchine's ballet.

But it is very unusual that someone with your background, with training so different from ours, would end up with Balanchine. How did you manage to do it?

I saw the company when it was touring Europe in 1957, and I thought, This is it. I was fascinated. My schooling was Russian, and my first love was the Bolshoi, but when I saw the New York City Ballet I knew I wanted to be with them. And I had seen a lot of ballet by then. I had seen Ulanova dance in East Berlin. I wanted to go to New York, but I never really thought it would happen. Then in 1959 I played the Dancing Annie in *The Seven Deadly Sins* in Frankfurt with Lotte Lenya. She had done it with Balanchine the year before in New York, and she talked a lot about him, told us what he had suggested. And she said to me, "Wouldn't you like to come to Amer-

ica?" I said I would, but how? And she said, "I can talk to Balanchine." I gave her some pictures, but I never thought I would hear from her. I did actually go to New York for five days about a year later. I saved all my money and went on a holiday there. I saw *The Nutcracker,* and I meant to see Balanchine, but I was too nervous, so I went back to Germany without speaking to him.

Lotte Lenya and I had kept up a correspondence, and when Balanchine came to Hamburg to stage *Eugene Onegin* she set up an audition for me. My first and last. I didn't even know what you were supposed to do in an audition, and I didn't speak English, but I wouldn't have understood Balanchine's English anyway. It took me years to understand his English. Anyway, it was a private audition, and he asked me to do turns, and I fell off every one. I was wearing new shoes which were very hard. Then he asked me to jump. It was a disaster, and he said, "Well, I can't take you as a ballerina," but I didn't expect that. I just wanted to perhaps get a scholarship to study in his school. So he took my hand, and checked to see how flexible my feet were. Evidently he saw possibilities, because a few weeks later I got a letter asking me to join the corps de ballet. I was in heaven.

I didn't know what to do at that point, because I had a year more to finish on a contract, and it's hard to get out of a German contract. It was complicated, too, because I wasn't twenty-one, and my mother had to sign for me. But I felt I had to go to Balanchine, and so I went up to the director and said that I was going to get married in the States. I just lied. I would never do it today. When you are young you do all kinds of daring things.

As soon as I joined the company we took a tour across the country by train, and then we went to Russia. I still had a passport from Berlin, but they made special arrangements for me. Being in the company scared me totally. All the teachers were against me. It seems that Balanchine had come up to Doubrovska one day and said that he had found a new German girl with good feet. My feet were awful, and I can't imagine what he was thinking, but he felt that I had possibilities. Doubrovska hated me.

I was so scared of Balanchine that I couldn't say a word to him for seven years. It's hard to imagine how our friendship finally developed, because I thought he didn't care for me. He left me alone and never corrected me like he did the other girls. He never gave me any attention. Much later I asked him about that, and he said, "I knew you would do it yourself." And I worked. But after a year I thought, My God, what have I learned? Nothing. I could hardly do a tendu right. Then the second year came and it was just as bad. It took me a long time.

I was in the corps for five years, although I was dancing solo roles from the beginning—the Spanish Dance in *The Nutcracker,* and the Coquette in *Sonnambula.* I took several of Suzanne Farrell's corps parts when she became a principal. She was the preferred dancer, and Balanchine did a lot for her, which was hard on the other dancers. It didn't affect me as much as it did the other girls, though. Suzanne's technique is strong in a different way from mine. I had more elevation. She never had elevation.

You've been Balanchine's closest friend in the company for several years, but that relationship seems to have taken a long time to develop. How did it come about?
It wasn't forced. It just became. When I got married he was against it, and then I was surprised to realize that he really liked me. The day after

Von Aroldingen in Tango, *1982.*

I got married he began making remarks to me like "Do you wash your husband's socks?" So then I knew he cared about me.

I got pregnant shortly after my marriage, and no one knew. The ballet mistress was also pregnant at that time. She was farther along, and all the girls would come up to touch her and say, "Does it kick?" I wanted to say, "Mine kicks too. I know what it feels like." But I was afraid to say anything. Getting pregnant had been an accident, and I thought I had ruined my dancing career just when I had started to get parts. I was doing *Monumentum/Movements* in my fifth month and dancing three ballets a night. Then I had to play the mother in *Apollo*. We still danced the beginning section at that time, where Leto gives birth to Apollo, and I didn't want to give birth to Apollo, because I was pregnant myself. It choked me up. It seemed too ironic. So I went up to Balanchine and asked him if another girl could do the mother. And he said, "Oh, you don't care anymore now that you're married," and I felt awful. So I decided to go up to him again and explain. But this time he said immediately, "I know what it is, you're pregnant." He just guessed. He almost fell over, though, when I told him that I was in my sixth month. I was very small.

I was afraid that Balanchine wouldn't let me come back after I had the baby, but he just said, "Well, I'll leave it up to you. It depends on how you feel." One week after I had my child I was back. I didn't miss the New York season. I was thinner after the child than before, and a year later I was promoted to soloist. I'm glad I got it over with when I was very young.

Balanchine and I started becoming friends a few years later, in 1969, when the company was in Monte Carlo. I had a personal problem which was upsetting me very much,

TOP—*Von Aroldingen with Bart Cook in* Stravinsky Violin Concerto.

CENTER—*Leading the MacDonald of Sleet regiment in* Union Jack. BOTTOM —*With Adam Luders in* Hungarian Gypsy Airs, *1981.*

and I didn't know whom to turn to, so I consulted Balanchine. There were three girls in my family, and I had never had a father or a brother, but I went to Balanchine for advice. A close friend of his was with him then, Lucia Davidova, and we all ended up having dinner together. Balanchine got to know me and realized that I am a dancer first, and not Mrs. So-and-So. He saw that I wanted to dance for him, and he became open to me. Because he thinks that the husbands take their wives away from dancing.

That was right after Suzanne Farrell left, then.

Yes. Suzanne's leaving was hard on Balanchine. But he's a person who can get out of things. Nothing can really affect Balanchine. He seems superior to emotion. He must hide it, because you can see from his ballets that he's emotional. It comes out in his ballets. In a sense it was better for the company that Suzanne left, because we all got more attention from Balanchine afterward. But you cannot blame him for needing someone. Everyone has his favorite girl somewhere.

When Suzanne left, Kay Mazzo took over most of her roles. She and Suzanne are both lyrical types. Everyone figured that Kay Mazzo was his new girl, but someone had to take over Suzanne's parts. He chose the one who would be suitable to his ballets. I did two of Suzanne's roles, *Liebeslieder Walzer* and the Fourth Movement of the *Brahms-Schoenberg Quartet*.

And then Balanchine started making ballets for you. Wonderful roles in *Who Cares?* and *Suite No. 3* and *Violin Concerto.* How did that feel?

I was thrilled, and I worked very hard. I had been depressed when I didn't get things the way I wanted, because I felt my body could make

Balanchine's technique work. But then it all began to happen.

Some of the parts Balanchine made for you were quite different from his other ballets, and complicated. Like *Variations pour une Porte et un Soupir,* and *Kammermusik.*

Variations pour une Porte et un Soupir used an electronic sound that I had no way of counting. I had to be ready to move to the timing of the sound. It was maybe a little annoying, that sound, but amazing. The ballet was about a man who tries to enter a door, which is me. It was a visual thing. Balanchine doesn't analyze his work.

With *Kammermusik No. 2* I have a love-hate affair. We call it Crooked Kammercomputer. Everything is off balance. It's like a computer in the sense that you can never lose the concentration of the piece. You never stop moving. You have to be precise and speedy, and there's always tension because you're so worried you won't get through it.

The ballet he made for you after that, to Schumann's *Davidsbündlertänze,* was very romantic.

It's hard to talk about that ballet. I play Schumann's wife, Clara. After I danced the piece I read about her, and I see a lot of things now. Balanchine must have known a great deal about Clara, because it's amazing how he drew out the essence of her life and her character in the ballet. She was an incredible woman.

Balanchine told me that would be his last ballet, because he wants to retire. He deserves to live a bit, but I thought how horrible it would be for him to retire. He has so much to give. Then he did the Tchaikovsky Festival, and I realized that he can't retire. This is his world.

I was injured during the Tchaikovsky Festival, but Balanchine had

asked me to be in a piece he made to the section of the Pathétique Symphony that was Tchaikovsky's requiem, Adagio Lamentoso. If I had had a broken leg I would have done it. I felt privileged. I'm nobody in it, but it was something special to do that for Balanchine.

Do you think about your own retirement?

I'm phasing myself out. But it seems that now that I'm at the end things are coming easier. There was a point when I felt that I comprehended what Balanchine wanted, and during the last few years I've been very much on top of what I dance. I don't force anymore. Balanchine is the one who suggested that I not drop out too quickly. He said to ease out, and he's right. But it's hard. It has to happen sooner or later, and I don't want to hear people say, "Oh, she's still pretty good for her age."

You are more fortunate than many of the other dancers because even when you do retire you won't have to leave Balanchine. You will still have your personal relationship.

I'm really lucky, because Balanchine has become my mother, my father, my boss, my best friend. And he became friends with my husband. They do a lot of things together. He accepted the child, who adores him —my daughter. It's a little bit like a family with the four of us. He likes the German food I cook, and I've learned to make Russian things. Balanchine has taught me so much, and he has such wonderful memories of his old times. He can talk about the most banal thing in the world and it's still fascinating, and you can hear the stories about his life over again and they're never boring. He's unique. I hope I don't take him too much for granted.

Ballets in Which Balanchine Created Roles for Karin von Aroldingen

WHO CARES?

music: George Gershwin, orchestrated by Hershy Kay
decor: Jo Mielziner
costumes: Karinska
roles: I'LL BUILD A STAIRWAY TO PARADISE; WHO CARES?; CLAP YO' HANDS
premiere: February 5, 1970, New York State Theater
New York City Ballet

SUITE NO. 3

music: Peter Ilyich Tchaikovsky
decor and costumes: Nicolas Benois
role: ÉLÉGIE
premiere: December 3, 1970, New York State Theater
New York City Ballet

PAMTGG

music: Roger Kellaway
decor: Jo Mielziner
costumes: Irene Sharaff
role: Principal
premiere: June 17, 1971, New York State Theater
New York City Ballet

VIOLIN CONCERTO

music: Igor Stravinsky
roles: TOCCATA; ARIA I
premiere: June 18, 1972, New York State Theater
New York City Ballet

SCHERZO À LA RUSSE

music: Igor Stravinsky
costumes: Karinska
role: Ballerina
premiere: June 21, 1972, New York State Theater
New York City Ballet

CHORAL VARIATIONS ON BACH'S "VOM HIMMEL HOCH"

music: Igor Stravinsky
decor: Rouben Ter-Arutunian
role: Principal
premiere: June 25, 1972, New York State Theater
New York City Ballet

CORTÈGE HONGROIS

music: Alexander Glazunov
decor and costumes: Rouben Ter-Arutunian
role: Principal character lead
premiere: May 17, 1973, New York State Theater
New York City Ballet

VARIATIONS POUR UNE PORTE ET UN SOUPIR

music: Pierre Henry
decor and costumes: Rouben Ter-Arutunian
role: Principal
premiere: February 17, 1974, New York State Theater
New York City Ballet

GASPARD DE LA NUIT

music: Maurice Ravel
decor and costumes: Bernard Daydé
role: LE GIBET
premiere: May 29, 1975, New York State Theater
New York City Ballet

RAPSODIE ESPAGNOLE

music: Maurice Ravel
costumes: Michael Avedon
role: Principal
premiere: May 29, 1975, New York State Theater
New York City Ballet

UNION JACK

music: Hershy Kay
decor and costumes: Rouben Ter-Arutunian
roles: MACDONALD OF SLEAT; ROYAL NAVY
premiere: May 13, 1976, New York State Theater
New York City Ballet

VIENNA WALTZES

music: Johann Strauss the Younger
scenery: Rouben Ter-Arutunian
costumes: Karinska
role: TALES FROM THE VIENNA WOODS
premiere: June 23, 1977, New York State Theater
New York City Ballet

KAMMERMUSIK NO. 2

music: Paul Hindemith
costumes: Ben Benson
role: Principal
premiere: January 26, 1978, New York State Theater
New York City Ballet

ROBERT SCHUMANN'S *DAVIDSBÜNDLERTÄNZE*

music: Robert Schumann
scenery and costumes: Rouben Ter-Arutunian
role: First Couple
premiere: June 19, 1980, New York State Theater
New York City Ballet

HUNGARIAN GYPSY AIRS

music: Sophie Menter, orchestrated by Peter Ilyich Tchaikovsky
costumes: Ben Benson
role: Principal
premiere: June 13, 1981, New York State Theater
New York City Ballet

SYMPHONY NO. 6 (PATHÉTIQUE): FOURTH MOVEMENT, ADAGIO LAMENTOSO

music: Peter Ilyich Tchaikovsky
costumes: Rouben Ter-Arutunian
role: Principal
premiere: June 14, 1981, New York State Theater
New York City Ballet

TANGO

music: Igor Stravinsky
role: Principal
premiere: June 10, 1982, New York State Theater
New York City Ballet

PERSÉPHONE (staged by Balanchine, John Taras, and Vera Zorina)

music: Igor Stravinsky
production design: Kermit Love
role: Spirit of Perséphone
premiere: June 18, 1982, New York State Theater
New York City Ballet

Karin Von Aroldingen and Balanchine rehearsing Davidsbündlertänze, *1980.*

Merrill Ashley

Merrill Ashley is a technical virtuoso of great speed and clarity. When Balanchine made *Ballo della Regina* to show off these qualities Lincoln Kirstein remarked on her "high-soprano" dancing: "She was now revealed as a fantastic mistress of *allegro,* moving with more speed, cutting her profiles with greater diamond-edged sharpness, intensity, precision, and strength than almost any dancer within memory." Fast and cool, she is the model for the new breed of Balanchine dancer.

Ashley was born Linda Merrill in 1950 in St. Paul, Minnesota, and grew up in Rutland, Vermont. She received a Ford Foundation scholarship to the School of American Ballet when she was thirteen and joined the corps de ballet of NYCB four years later. Since at that time there was another dancer in the company named Linda Merrill, she became Ashley. She danced her first solo role when she was eighteen, but was not promoted to soloist until 1974, six years later. A great surge of progress was visible in her dancing when she took on the "Sanguinic" variation in the 1975 revival of *The Four Temperaments,* and two years later when she danced the lead in the revived *Square Dance* Arlene Croce cited Ashley for having given "the performance the ballet has been waiting for—full of sharp, bright photoflash pictures."

In early 1978 Balanchine created *Ballo della Regina* for her. Anna Kisselgoff in *The New York Times* had described Ashley's performance in *Allegro Brillante* as "so secure in the difficult choreography that a partner could even have seemed superfluous," and on opening night of the 1980 season, when her partner was injured at the beginning of *Ballo,* Ashley, somewhat remarkably, completed the ballet alone.

During that same spring season Balanchine revealed a very different aspect of Ashley in *Ballade,* a technically difficult yet romantic work to music by Fauré. Croce wrote that "*Ballade* slows her down, softens her edges, amplifies her presence and stretches her range—all through its pursuit of the legato phrase." Shortly after the debut of *Ballade* Ashley was absent from the company for many months due to a slow-healing hip injury. In September 1980, during her period of recovery, she married Kibbe Fitzpatrick, an interpreter at the United Nations.

You are now the paradigm of a certain kind of Balanchine dancer, but you seem to have developed more slowly than other people in the company who became principals. Why do you think that happened?
It may have taken me longer than it did for some people, but I was young and weak when I got into the company, so I didn't expect anything to happen. I got in much sooner than I thought I would—probably too soon, in fact. Balanchine started working with me about two years later, giving me little things to do, but there was a period when I didn't have anything new.

Balanchine gives young people lots of chances, and then if it is too soon he backs off and waits awhile. Then he may give you another chance, depending on how you react. If you stop working because you aren't being given things, which is what happens to many people, then you won't get your second chance. He let me be for a while, and I said to myself, What's wrong? Why isn't he using me? I had gained weight, and he never said to me, "Lose weight." Every now and then he would give me a little hint. I remember after I had danced something, *Who Cares?*, I think, he said, "It's better, but now you have to work on your legs." He made a gesture of stretching, as though I should make them longer. I thought maybe my muscles were bunching, and I

wondered how I was going to change that, but I realize now he was saying that he wanted me to lose weight. He never spoke directly, but he was fantastically patient.

I wasn't like Darci Kistler, who Balanchine really loved from the instant he saw her. I certainly wasn't as strong as she is when I joined the company, and I didn't have any stage presence whatsoever. But I have lots of ambition, and I'm very willing to work hard. I think that that above all is what started to draw his attention. I was intense and tried to understand what he wanted. Balanchine uses his classes for experimenting. He tries to see how much more he can get out of his dancers, and some people find it depressing that he is so exacting. But I loved the challenge. I couldn't live without the challenge of those classes. They were my only nourishment. I couldn't bear it when he didn't teach. He's very tough on the body, and you have to warm up a lot before, but I thrived on it.

Did you realize that you were being asked to do something out of the ordinary? To be an Olympic champion of sorts?
I had very little exposure to other teachers, because I came from the sticks as far as ballet is concerned —Vermont. I thought, This is what they ask for in New York? Well, all right. But of course no one else asks for the kind of speed and clarity that Balanchine does. He carries it much farther. Quick things always appealed to me, but if I had been left to my own devices, I probably wouldn't have developed the speed that I have. Balanchine made me realize that I like it.

How did you fix on the way you were going to present yourself as a dancer? Did you have a particular model?

I never looked at one person and said, That's what I want to be like. I liked some people in some things and others in other things. In many ways I'm glad I didn't have one person who was my ideal. I took a little bit from everyone and came up with something that was my own. Balanchine gives very little direction about how you are to perform. He says you should present yourself, entertain. And after that it's pretty much left up to you. One of the things I like best about the company is that you develop as an individual dancer. You can see several different people in the same role and get an idea of how it developed from his mold, when he first created the role. You have great freedom to develop in your own way. Especially because there aren't any stories. You can go anywhere. Stories can be confining.

What was your relationship with the other people in the company during the time you were developing as a dancer? Did you feel there was a great deal of competition?
Suzanne Farrell was still in the company when I came, but she left two years later, and the atmosphere of the company seemed a little odd. Balanchine wasn't himself for a while, which didn't affect me, because I wasn't ready to do much. Then things worked to my advantage, because he started looking at everyone. I became involved in a sort of race with Colleen Neary. We had always been together, even at school, and we were both strong technically, so the roles we were considered for were the same. Balanchine didn't discourage the competition. There was a period when we were neck and neck and it was getting more serious because the roles were getting bigger. One time one of us would get it and the next time the other. For a while I definitely felt that she was getting more

than I was, and then somehow the tables turned. I felt I was a good competitor, yet I also felt sorry for Colleen. She got heavy, and it was obvious that it wasn't going to happen for her. We shared a dressing room, which in a funny way I liked. She was quiet and neat and I threw everything everywhere and she didn't seem to mind. There was a lot of pressure when I started going ahead and she was getting less. But we never talked about those things.

As far as my relationship with Balanchine went, he's not someone you go to talk to and say, What do you think about this role or that role? He doesn't want to talk about it. And I kept at a distance because I felt I wanted to make it on merit and didn't want to appear to be trying to get ahead by being friendly to him. So although I wasn't aware of it I wasn't even friendly in a normal way. Partly, of course, because I was in awe of him. I think that he was confused by me a little, and that he felt I didn't like him and didn't care about what he was trying to teach. I was aloof, and I didn't show my emotions. He's hard to pin down too, because sometimes he's there taking care of you like a mother, being patient, trying to explain, and then the next minute he's not paying any attention to your feelings, and saying, "Now! Do it now! Come on!" Basically I've learned that although I don't agree with everything he says, especially when he first says it, time inevitably proves him right. I have tremendous faith in his taste and believe that he won't ask me to do something that wouldn't be right for me or the ballet.

What was it like when he finally made a ballet for you? When he made *Ballo della Regina*.
I got into a conversation with Balanchine about some virtuoso role when we were in Nashville setting the first program for the *Dance in*

Merrill Ashley and Ib Andersen in Ballade, *1980.*

America television series. He was saying, "Now, who do you think I should put in it? Peter Martins is too busy, and Peter Schaufuss is leaving." I had no idea he was talking about a ballet for me. He didn't say. He never says. So I didn't answer. And then I went on vacation, and when I came back someone in the elevator told me that I had been made a principal. Then someone else congratulated me about the new ballet. Then the first day we had class I went up to say hello to Balanchine and he said, "Well, dear, I'm going to do a ballet for you. We'll start tomorrow." It was the first time I had come back from a layoff out of shape. The next day I was hopping on pointe and trying impossible steps.

Balanchine was in very good spirits, and I think it was inevitable that he would do something fast for me. He wanted to push me and see how far I could go. He didn't say that to me, but to other people. "I kept giving her harder things to do, and I couldn't believe she could do it." There were some things I couldn't do which eventually got changed, but when he makes a ballet for you it's comfortable. He knows how to make one step flow into the next. They're difficult, but you're not forcing your body into an unnatural pattern. Now *Ballo* is like my second skin. I have fun with it.

The second ballet Balanchine made for me, *Ballade,* is more of a mystery to me, partly, of course, because I was injured before I got a chance to perform it very often. It came as a surprise to me that Balanchine was doing a ballet for me that time too. We were having dinner after his heart attack, and I said, "Do you feel well enough to work now? Have you been listening to music?" I didn't expect him to say he had anything in mind for me, but then he said, "Well, as a matter of fact I have a piece of music I've been listening to for a long time. I thought I might do something for you. A beautiful ballet." I was embarrassed, because I thought I'd forced him to say that.

I think Balanchine made *Ballade* partly to encourage me to develop in certain ways that I hadn't. He said after I had performed it, "It's so nice. You just do it. You haven't added

anything." I worked very hard on it and tried to use my upper body more than I had. It's an exhausting ballet, and some of the steps are difficult, but I don't think of it as a ballet with steps. It's a ballet about love, but every time I would try to do something romantic Balanchine would say, "Don't do it." Right toward the end my partner and I would get close, holding hands, and I would look at him. And Balanchine would say, "No, don't look at him." The main correction I get now is, "Don't look at your partner. You're not in love with him. Just dance."

What do you think Balanchine values most in you? Is it the speed?

Yes, but I think too that I can in general do what he wants better than most people. I understand how he wants certain steps done. There are very few people who can second-guess him, and sometimes in class I know what's coming when everyone else is lost. I'm attuned to the way he thinks, and that's a part of me that I treasure. I'm good at picking up steps, and I'm reliable. Balanchine likes that. I work hard, I don't make scenes.

Of course it is the speed that he's more and more interested in as time goes on. But it's a combination of speed and clarity. He wants to see everything. I think I had the clarity, and then he wanted to see how fast I could go and still be clear. He's experimenting. Balanchine likes extremes. He likes to do things ultra-slow and ultrafast. He has people that excel at the slow things. I'm at the fast end.

Ballets in Which Balanchine Created Roles for Merrill Ashley

CORTÈGE HONGROIS
music: Alexander Glazunov
decor and costumes: Rouben Ter-Arutunian
roles: PAS DE QUATRE; VARIATION III
premiere: May 17, 1973, New York State Theater
New York City Ballet

COPPÉLIA (with Alexandra Danilova)
music: Léo Delibes
decor and costumes: Rouben Ter-Arutunian
role: Dawn
premiere: July 17, 1974, Saratoga Performing Arts Center, Saratoga Springs, N.Y.
New York City Ballet

BALLO DELLA REGINA
music: Giuseppe Verdi
costumes: Ben Benson
role: Ballerina
premiere: January 12, 1978, New York State Theater
New York City Ballet

BALLADE
music: Gabriel Fauré
decor and costumes: Rouben Ter-Arutunian
role: Ballerina
premiere: May 8, 1980, New York State Theater
New York City Ballet

Ashley in Ballo della Regina.

> It's almost like a survival course with Balanchine. That's a funny way of putting it, but you have to learn to do it yourself.

Darci Kistler

Darci Kistler is the last ballerina whose career was anointed by Balanchine. She became his protégée and the favorite of audiences soon after she appeared as the Swan Queen in the School of American Ballet's 1980 workshop performance. She was fifteen years old.

Kistler was born in Riverside, California, the youngest child in a family that includes four older brothers, all wrestlers. A natural athlete, she began taking ballet lessons when she was eight, and enrolled in three summer courses at SAB, after which she was asked to attend the regular session. When she was fourteen she

was given a scholarship to the school, and the next year, following her workshop debut, she became a member of NYCB's corps de ballet. That autumn she danced the Swan Queen in the company's opening-night performance at the Kennedy Center in Washington, D.C., and later in the season in New York she had a great success in the Adagio of *Symphony in C,* a privileged ballerina role in the Balanchine repertory. She also took the roles of supporting soloist in *Walpurgisnacht Ballet* and the Scherzo in the Tchaikovsky *Suite No. 3,* and soon was dancing the Sugar Plum Fairy in *The Nutcracker* and roles in *Divertimento No. 15* and *Who Cares?*

In December 1981 Rudolf Nureyev described her gifts to *The New York Times:*

"Have you seen that new one —seventeen years old—Darci Kistler with the New York City Ballet? Such aggression in her legs, such attack; you are hypnotized by her legs, by her feet. There are four other top ballerinas on stage and she's the one you're looking at, and she's not terribly pretty. But there's that devil inside. She already knows how to move to make everybody watch."

Darci Kistler was promoted to the rank of principal dancer in June 1982, when she was eighteen.

You came into the company very quickly after you began studying at SAB, and seemed to have missed the typical period of anxiety about whether or not you would get to dance with Balanchine. When were you first aware of him?

I studied with Irina Kosmovska in Los Angeles, and she also teaches at

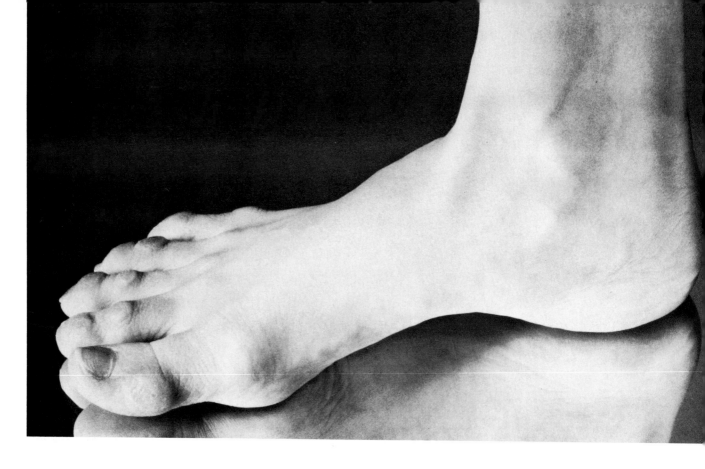

SAB, so everything she taught us was "Balanchine says . . . , Balanchine says. . . ." Just like at the school. All I had in my head was Balanchine. But I had never seen him until three of us were called into a rehearsal of *Le Bourgeois Gentilhomme.* One of us was going to be picked as an understudy, and I knew it wouldn't be me because I had just come and everybody else was a hundred times better than me. I couldn't do a step. Everyone was there: Balanchine, Nureyev, Jerry Robbins, Peter Martins, Patricia McBride—just everybody. And I couldn't sit still. I was very nervous. So way in the back, in a corner, I started to practice to the music, thinking no one could see me. But I kicked my leg up so high that my bottom leg went out from under me and I fell down. It made the loudest noise, and every one of those people looked at me and laughed. I was so embarrassed I wanted to crawl out of the room. At that young age you

just want to please, and falling in front of Balanchine was the worst thing that could have happened.

But the next time you saw Balanchine he picked you out to be an apprentice, didn't he?
Yes. And by then I wasn't even nervous. He came to watch our class for a long time—twenty-eight minutes. I was sure I wouldn't get in. But that very day I heard that I got it. As soon as you get one thing, you want something more, though.

The first ballet I was in as an apprentice was *Ballade,* which he was making for Merrill Ashley. He had to teach all us little girls how to dance. He would push us and say, "Do it," but he was very patient. There were times when someone just wouldn't get it, and you would think that Mr. B. was going to blow up, but he never did. He's a very impersonal teacher, which I like. Most people can't deal with it. It's almost like a survival course with Balanchine.

That's a funny way of putting it, but you have to learn to do it yourself. Even if you have a mother pushing you she isn't going to dance for you on the stage. Even if you have a coach, finally you have to do it yourself.

My father was very strict about work. My mother was completely the opposite, so it was a perfect arrangement. My brothers were wrestlers, and Dad was always cracking the whip for them. He was like the ballet mothers, but with the boys. I think that if I had been a boy I would have been rebellious, but my dad was never interested in what I was doing. At an early age I had to learn how to outsmart my brothers because everything was always a challenge, and they would try to kill me. We were all very athletic—water skiing, snow skiing, and now they send me shirts for ballet class that say, "Kill-em, Sis." I developed self-discipline just by watching them. They developed discipline because of my fa-

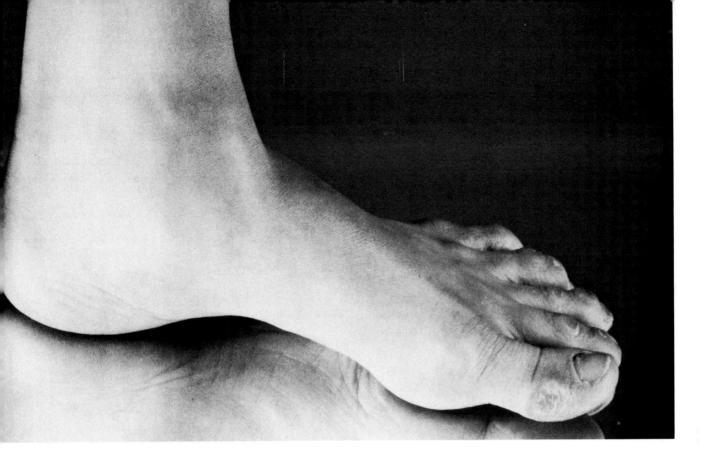

ther, but I developed it for myself. I've always been a loner, and I'm in competition only with myself, so when I got into the New York City Ballet it didn't seem different. When Balanchine isn't around you just learn from watching his ballets. I used to sneak into the theater when I was a student, and I'd always get thrown out.

What else did you do when you were an apprentice?
I danced in the corps in the Fourth Movement of *Symphony in C.* But I would always goof. When I got out on stage it was like someone who's never seen television before, one of those people they bring back from the wild who asks, "What do you do with a fork?" If you're not dancing all the time in that ballet you have to count, or else you don't know where to go. I never counted. I'd just go when the big music came, because I wanted to dance to the big music. But it was always when the principal

was going, but not the corps. I would move, and then I would have to move back again. I remember calling home, crying, and saying, "I'll never get into the company, because I goofed so bad."

But you did get in.
Yes. I think the thing is that Balanchine's choreography is so good you could put anybody in there and they would look good. He's choreographed it so well that it's safe to throw anyone in, even if they're not ready.

When I was thirteen I saw Suzanne Farrell dance the Adagio in *Symphony in C,* and I fell in love. It was my favorite part in the world. And then when I hadn't been in the company that long I was called to a rehearsal to learn Suzanne's role. I died when I found out what I'd be doing. I giggled and laughed all the way down the street and couldn't sleep, I was looking forward to the rehearsal so much. I could only re-

member one thing: Suzanne touches her head to her knee in that arabesque. So when I was learning that part, just practicing the Adagio, I tried it. Of course I fell over and did a complete somersault and knocked my partner over. They told me not to try it again, but now I can do it!

I never think when I'm doing that role, Oh, Suzanne Farrell does this. If you think like that you go on stage and try to become Suzanne. I've seen so many people do that. You have to be you. That's what Mr. Balanchine told me. When I did *Swan Lake* everyone said, "You have to grow up, you have to be more of a woman, more of a ballerina, more this, more that." People were telling me a hundred different things, and I wanted to be as good as Makarova or Suzanne. Then Balanchine got me in rehearsal and he said, "Where did you learn to dance? Alaska? What happened?" The night before I went on he took me aside and said, "Someone's been helping you." I

TOP—*Darci Kistler with Peter Martins in* The Nutcracker. BOTTOM—*With Sean Lavery in the Second Movement of* Symphony in C.

was in tears. I looked at him and said, "Yes," and he said, "You will find your own way. Don't act. Just dance." I went out in the performance and did exactly what he had told me to do. It was so easy, so natural, and such a weight off my shoulders. He said, "Don't emote. Listening to the music will put you in the mood. If you do any more it's ridiculous."

How does it feel to be doing all these extraordinary parts?
It's so incredible to work with Balanchine. You walk around on a cloud for days afterward. I could be really down, and then I look at Mr. Balanchine and something happens. I laugh and giggle. There are so many people better than me. I even tell them that I shouldn't be doing this role or that role, but you have to trust Mr. Balanchine's judgment. And I have fun doing them. I feel guilty picking up a paycheck. I'm not working; this is what I enjoy. Most people come home every single day and say they hate their job. They're stuck. I never want to get stuck. That's why I'm easygoing. I just want to live each day and dance.

Who do you think the ideal Balanchine dancer is?
The ideal dancer is someone who can just dance and yet show her own personality, not a made-up one. For me it's a combination of Suzanne Farrell, Merrill Ashley, Gelsey Kirkland, and Allegra Kent. It's like a family tree, and I dream that someday it will fork down to me. That's what I dream about.

Darci Kistler with Alexandra Danilova, 1981.

CHRONOLOGY OF BALANCHINE'S LIFE

January 22, 1904	Georgi Melitonovich Balanchivadze born in St. Petersburg.
1913	Enters the Imperial Theater School.
1919	First choreography created for Theater School concerts.
1921	Graduates from Petrograd Theater School and enters the ballet company of the State Theater of Opera and Ballet.
1922	Organizes the Young Ballet company. Balanchine and Tamara Gevergeva married.
1924	Leaves Russia with small troupe, the Principal Dancers of the Russian State Ballet. Engaged by Serge Diaghilev as dancer and choreographer for the Ballets Russes. Changes name to Georges Balanchine.
March 21, 1925	Premiere of Ravel's *L'Enfant et les Sortilèges,* Diaghilev's first major assignment to Balanchine.
June 12, 1928	Premiere of *Apollon Musagète* with Diaghilev's Ballets Russes at the Théâtre Sarah-Bernhardt in Paris.
May 21, 1929	Premiere of *Le Fils Prodigue* at the Théâtre Sarah-Bernhardt.
August 19, 1929	Diaghilev dies, and the Ballets Russes ceases to exist.
1932	Balanchine acts as ballet master to de Basil's Ballets Russes de Monte-Carlo.
1933	Forms Les Ballets 1933. Meets Lincoln Kirstein, who invites him to come to America to establish a school and a company.
October 17, 1933	Balanchine arrives in the United States.
January 2, 1934	School of American Ballet opens.
March 1, 1935	American Ballet Company opens a short season at the Adelphi Theatre in New York with *Serenade,* the first work Balanchine made for American dancers.
Fall 1935	American Ballet engaged as the resident ballet company at the Metropolitan Opera.
April 1936	Balanchine choreographs ballets for *On Your Toes* on Broadway.
April 1937	First Stravinsky Festival, at the Metropolitan Opera.
Christmas 1938	Marries Vera Zorina.
1939	Balanchine becomes a United States citizen.
1940	Stages *Cabin in the Sky,* with the Katherine Dunham dancers.
Summer 1941	American Ballet Caravan tour of South America.

Summer 1942	Balanchine is guest director of ballet at the Teatro Colón in Buenos Aires, Argentina.
1944–46	Resident choreographer of Denham's Ballet Russe de Monte Carlo.
January 1946	Balanchine and Vera Zorina are divorced.
August 16, 1946	Balanchine and Maria Tallchief are married.
November 20, 1946	First Ballet Society program.
March to September 1947	Balanchine is guest ballet master of Paris Opéra.
October 11, 1948	First New York City Ballet performance.
July to August 1950	NYCB's first London season.
1951	Balanchine's marriage to Maria Tallchief is annulled.
April to September 1952	NYCB's first European tour.
December 31, 1952	Balanchine marries Tanaquil Le Clercq.
February 1954	Balanchine stages *The Nutcracker*, NYCB's first full-length ballet.
October 1962	Balanchine returns to Russia for the first time, on a tour with the New York City Ballet.
1963	Ford Foundation grant of $2 million to the New York City Ballet.
April 1964	NYCB moves to the New York State Theater at Lincoln Center.
Spring 1969	Balanchine is divorced from Tanaquil Le Clercq.
June 1972	Stravinsky Festival, in commemoration of Stravinsky's ninetieth birthday.
September 1972	NYCB's second tour of Russia.
May 1975	Ravel Festival. Balanchine receives the Légion d'Honneur.
1978	Made Knight of the Order of Dannebrog, First Class. Receives first annual Kennedy Center Honor.
1980	Receives first National Gold Medal Award of the National Society of Arts and Letters.
June 1981	Tchaikovsky Festival.
June 1982	Stravinsky Festival, for centenary of Stravinsky's birth.
February 1983	Receives the Presidential Medal of Freedom.
March 1983	Balanchine is made Ballet Master Emeritus of NYCB.
April 30, 1983	Balanchine dies in New York.

SELECTED SOURCES

Anderson, Jack, *The One and Only: The Ballet Russe de Monte Carlo.* Dance Horizons, 1981.

Balanchine, George, "The Dance Element in Stravinsky's Music," *Dance Index,* 1947, reprinted in *Ballet Review,* Vol. 10, No. 2 (Summer 1982).

———, "Notes on Choreography," *Dance Index,* Vol. 4, Nos. 2 and 3 (February/March 1945).

———, and Francis Mason, *Balanchine's Complete Stories of the Great Ballets.* Doubleday and Company, revised edition, 1977.

Blackmur, R. P., "The Swan in Zurich," *The Yale Review,* Spring 1958, reprinted in *Ballet Review,* Vol. 1, No. 2.

Buckle, Richard, *Buckle at the Ballet: Selected Criticism.* Atheneum Publishers, 1980.

———, *Diaghilev.* Atheneum Publishers, 1979.

Choreography by George Balanchine: A Catalogue of Works. The Eakins Press, 1983.

Chujoy, Anatole, *The New York City Ballet.* Alfred A. Knopf, Inc., 1953.

———, and P. W. Manchester, eds., *The Dance Encyclopedia.* Simon and Schuster, revised edition, 1967.

Clarke, Mary, and David Vaughan, *The Encyclopedia of Dance and Ballet.* Pitman Publishing Limited, London, 1977.

Croce, Arlene, *Afterimages.* Alfred A. Knopf, Inc., 1977.

———, *Going to the Dance.* Alfred A. Knopf, Inc., 1982.

Denby, Edwin, *Dancers, Buildings and People in the Streets.* Horizon Press, 1965.

———, *Looking at the Dance.* Pellegrini and Cudahy, 1949.

Geva, Tamara, *Split Seconds: A Remembrance.* Harper & Row Publishers, Inc., 1972.

Goldner, Nancy, *The Stravinsky Festival of The New York City Ballet.* The Eakins Press, 1973.

Grigoriev, S. L., translated by Vera Bowen, *The Diaghilev Ballet, 1909–1929.* Penguin Books, 1960.

Hurok, S., *S. Hurok Presents: A Memoir of the Dance World.* Hermitage House, 1953.

Kirstein, Lincoln, "Balanchine and the Classic Revival," *Theatre Arts,* December 1947.

———, "Balanchine Musagète," *Theatre Arts,* November 1947.

———, *Thirty Years: Lincoln Kirstein's The New York City Ballet.* Alfred A. Knopf, Inc., 1978.

Koegler, Horst, *The Concise Oxford Dictionary of Ballet.* Oxford University Press, 1977.

Martins, Peter, with Robert Cornfield, *Far from Denmark.* Little, Brown and Company, 1982.

Nabokov, Ivan, and Elizabeth Carmichael, "Balanchine, an Interview," *Horizon,* January 1961.

Nabokov, Nicolas, *Old Friends and New Music.* Little, Brown and Company, 1951.

Reynolds, Nancy, *Repertory in Review: Forty Years of The New York City Ballet.* The Dial Press, 1977.

Slonimsky, Yuri, translated by John Andrews, "Balanchine: The Early Years," *Ballet Review,* Vol. 5, No. 3 (1975–1976).

Stokes, Adrian, *Russian Ballets.* Dutton, 1936.

Stravinsky, Vera, and Robert Craft, *Stravinsky in Pictures and Documents.* Simon and Schuster, 1978.

Taper, Bernard, *Balanchine: A Biography.* Macmillan Publishing Company, revised edition, 1974.

Terry, Walter, *I Was There: Selected Dance Reviews and Articles, 1936–1976.* Marcel Dekker, 1978.

Twysden, A. E., *Alexandra Danilova.* Kamin Dance Publishers, 1947.

ABOUT THE AUTHORS

Robert Tracy completed the interviews for this book while on scholarship at George Balanchine's School of American Ballet. He appeared in Balanchine's recreation of *Le Bourgeois Gentilhomme* with Patricia McBride and Rudolf Nureyev and later in the same production with Suzanne Farrell and Peter Martins. He has danced twice on Broadway with Nureyev and the Boston Ballet. This is his first book.

Sharon DeLano is Managing Editor of *The Movies,* and the coauthor of *Texas Boots.*